SMART
PLANTS

SMART PLANTS

Power Foods & Natural Nootropics for Optimized Thinking, Focus & Memory

INCLUDES 65 RECIPES

JULIE MORRIS

STERLING EPICURE
New York

STERLING EPICURE
New York

An Imprint of Sterling Publishing Co., Inc.
1166 Avenue of the Americas
New York, NY 10036

Text and photography © 2019 Julie Morris
Cover and illustrations © 2019 Sterling Publishing Co., Inc.

ISBN 978-1-4549-3342-7

Library of Congress Cataloging-in-Publication Data

Names: Morris, Julie (Chef), author.
Title: Smart plants : power foods & natural nootropics for optimized thinking, focus & memory / Julie Morris.
Description: New York, NY : Sterling Publishing Co., Inc., 2019. | Includes bibliographical references and index. | Summary: "Smart Plants offers a practical strategy for optimizing brain health through plant-based foods containing a unique array of nutrients and natural compounds-including nootropics, cognition-enhancing substances that can improve memory, learning, and problem solving. Bestselling author Julie Morris shares 65 easy, inviting recipes that are unbelievably delicious. Feed your brain with such palate-pleasing dishes as Berry-Almond Amaranth Porridge, Fig & Hazelnut Wild Rice Salad, Garlicky Butter Bean Soup with Greens, and Matcha Custard with Berries"-- Provided by publisher.
Identifiers: LCCN 2019029163 (print) | LCCN 2019029164 (ebook) | ISBN 9781454933427 (hardcover) | ISBN 9781454933434 (ebook)
Subjects: LCSH: Vegan cooking. | Cooking (Natural foods) | Food allergy--Diet therapy--Recipes. | Nutrition. | LCGFT: Cookbooks.
Classification: LCC TX837 .M687 2019 (print) | LCC TX837 (ebook) | DDC 641.5/6362--dc23
LC record available at https://lccn.loc.gov/2019029163
LC ebook record available at https://lccn.loc.gov/2019029164

Distributed in Canada by Sterling Publishing Co., Inc.
c/o Canadian Manda Group, 664 Annette Street
Toronto, Ontario M6S 2C8, Canada
Distributed in the United Kingdom by GMC Distribution Services
Castle Place, 166 High Street, Lewes, East Sussex BN7 1XU, England
Distributed in Australia by NewSouth Books
University of New South Wales, Sydney, NSW 2052, Australia

For information about custom editions, special sales, and premium and corporate purchases, please contact Sterling Special Sales at 800-805-5489 or specialsales@sterlingpublishing.com.

Manufactured in China

2 4 6 8 10 9 7 5 3 1

sterlingpublishing.com

Cover design by David Ter-Avanesyan
Interior design by Shannon Nicole Plunkett
Photography by Oliver Barth
Illustrations by Samara Hardy

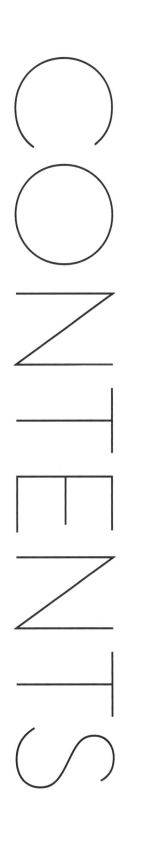

CONTENTS

INTRODUCTION

"I'm sorry to tell you this, detective, but the forensic lab called and they won't have any answers until Friday. We need to find another way."

No.

"I'm sorry to tell you this, detective, but the forensic lab called and they won't have any *of the results* until Friday. We need to find another way."

Was that it?

As I parked my car on a side street off Santa Monica Boulevard, I picked up the crumpled script on the passenger seat and read the highlighted section:

> JOCELYN: I'm sorry to tell you this, detective, but the forensic lab called and they won't have any of the results until Friday. *It's not looking good.* We need to find another way.

It's not looking good. It's not looking good. Got it now?

"It's not looking good is right," I said out loud to myself as I readjusted my dress, which had become awkwardly pasted to my body after sitting in traffic for more than an hour.

———

Even from a very young age, I had always enjoyed acting. In fact, you may recognize me from my incredible first-grade school performance (as I am told . . . by my mom) as Snoopy in *You're a Good Man, Charlie Brown*. Or perhaps you know me from some of my finer work: as a background actor in an antialcohol video shown at driving schools in the late 1990s. Yes, unfortunately my commercial success never seemed to match my enthusiasm for the craft, but when you appreciate acting as much as I do and also happen to have grown up in Los Angeles, you get to a point where you decide to at least dip your toe into the water of what's simply known in LA as *The Industry*.

And that's where I was in 2003. At 22 years old, I had scraped the top ceiling of my credit card limit to take twice-a-week acting classes downtown, procure a whole set of headshots to include all my different "looks," and sign with a zealous manager who could just as easily fight off a bear as charm a snake, whichever was required at the time. To put the ramen on the table while I went to college, I had a part-time job at an upscale toy store at The Grove, a celebrity-studded Los Angeles shopping enclave, working as a costumed character. The store had cast me as "Princess Pretty," a mortifying title that made me feel almost as itchy as the costume itself, and it was my job to walk around the two-story environment with my trellised pink cone hat and Febreze-scented gown and interact with children in the store as they planned new outfits for their dolls or begged their parents for the mini electric "child" Ferrari in the front window, which cost more than most real cars on the freeway.

I considered this job a slow path to actual insanity. Nevertheless, it was perfect for my fledging career as an actor, because it just so happened that most of the other costumed characters who walked the floor with me were actual (and would-be) thespians as well, and if you had a sudden midday audition during your shift, it wasn't a big deal to just take off.

The thing is, when I wasn't commiserating with my buddy the Toy Soldier about the unexpected perils of costumed character work, I was actually getting some auditions. Most of them were for fairly small gigs, like the counter girl handing a family their order in a fast-food restaurant commercial, or having a quick one-liner guest spot on a TV show. These opportunities were a bit like playing the casting lottery, because, basically, if you had a freckle in the wrong spot, you weren't getting the part.

But my audition that warm day in Santa Monica was different. I was up for the role of the main character in a TV show pilot, which can be a bit of acting gold, because if you get cast and the pilot gets picked up by a network, you've got yourself a show—and a steady paycheck. As I clacked down the street in my favorite merlot-colored platforms, I tried to ready myself. *Chill out, Julie, just chill.* I had rehearsed the scene ad nauseam ever since getting the script a few days earlier. I knew I would be good for the part: a tall, brunette junior detective determined to claw her way up the professional ladder, but with a secret past on the wrong side of the law that could compromise everything—juicy stuff. The tailored pinstripe dress I was wearing clearly screamed young business-professional, and it was even a good hair day. There was only one small problem: I was having trouble remembering the lines.

Memorizing had never been my strong suit. Though I was a good student in school, I found test-taking extremely difficult, as the load of random facts and figures I was expected to remember never seemed to stay in my head for very long. And my memory issues trickled into the rest of my life, too: I'd often forget the names of places where I'd vacationed, people I'd met, movies I'd seen, and heaven help me if I needed to remember a phone number or an address, even if only for a minute. I never gave it much thought, as my mom is similarly "absent-minded," as she calls it, but my penchant for acting really brought this handicap to the forefront. To be an actor, you absolutely have to memorize your lines.

By the time I got called into the little office for my audition, I was, without question, 100 percent totally nervous. *I'm sorry to tell you this, detective . . . I'm sorry to tell you this, detective . . .* I chanted the lines over and over in my head like a personal mantra, trying to keep a close grip on my starting point. The casting director, a short woman with a friendly smile, ushered me into a private room, while an assistant fidgeted with a small video camera pointed toward me.

"Okay! Julie Morris. It's nice to meet you." The casting director grinned at me warmly with what looked like genuine hospitality.

"So great to meet you, too!" I said, trying to mirror her friendliness. *What did she say her name was? Did she say? I'm sorry to tell you this, detective . . .*

"Jason, are we all set?" she asked the assistant.

"All set," Jason replied, having clearly done this routine a dozen times already that day. He pushed RECORD.

I'm sorry to tell you this, detective . . .

The casting director tilted her chin upward and set her gaze squarely on me. The comforting smile was gone, and she looked much more focused as she leaned back in her chair. "Okay, Julie. Whenever you're ready."

I'm sorry to . . .

Now the room was silent except for the low hum of the air conditioner. I took a deep breath. I cleared my throat. I looked straight at the casting director. And then . . .

I asked for a copy of the script.

I had forgotten the lines.

———

More than anywhere else in our bodies, we identify the inner environment between our ears with who we truly are. A tattoo may ensure that the world can see your love of cats, flat abs may make you feel "strong" or "sexy," and the sudden appearance of a pimple on your chin may knock your self-confidence down one notch for the day. But your mental microclimate feels like the real "you." It makes sense: We live in our heads all the time! So, to be perfectly honest, I didn't give my cognitive shortcomings a whole lot of thought for an embarrassingly long time, because I thought they were just part of me. My short-term memory was very poor, and that was that. For the most part, I learned to work around it in my professional life, practicing talks and presentations I needed to make weeks ahead of time to create a routine, rather than a memory; developing a few skills like image or word associations to memorize quick facts ("His name is Chad . . . like my cousin"); and, above all else, writing *everything* down, before it slipped away forever. It didn't seem like that big of a deal.

Also on my list of "not a big deal" were ongoing bouts of brain fog, the frequent occurrence of noncircumstantial depression (relatively minor in its severity, but no laughing matter, either), and, worst of all, the gripping anxiety that took over my thoughts from time to time—a double-edged, paralyzing, fear-filled combination of "not being able to get it all done" and "it's not good enough" that would roll over my chest with the weight of an army tank. But, since these conditions weren't severe enough to impede my career or social life, I just considered them an annoying, hidden part of who I was—just "me," *right*?

Then, in the summer of 2014, something happened to change all that. It had been about 10 years since I'd come to the realization that the acting thing wasn't exactly going to "work out" for me and found my *real* creative passion as a healthy chef and recipe developer. I was working on a specialized food project for a restaurateur seeking a new superfood energy drink to add to the menu. While messing around with ingredients, I pulled out an old bag of rhodiola powder, which had somehow ended up in my pile of oddball superfood testing ingredients. I vaguely remembered that rhodiola is energizing and good for athletes, so I decided to try it out in the recipe. Although the resulting drink tasted like dish soap and the addition of rhodiola was promptly rejected, I was curious to know why a rhodiola stash had found its way into my kitchen in the first place and began to do research on what made it a superfood. My search yielded an array of fascinating results, but what I found most intriguing was that beyond just being a great energy food, rhodiola is also known as a "nootropic." "A *what*?" I asked at the time. I'll save the details about incredible nootropic ingredients like rhodiola for chapter 6 (page 77), where you can discover all their secrets, too. But at the time I was so intrigued, I decided to do a little self-test. I began taking rhodiola every day, along with bacopa, another Ayurvedic herb. There is only one distinctly nonscientific word that could adequately sum up the results: WOW.

Within days I felt an increase in sustained energy. Within weeks I found it much easier to "stay in the creative flow." And after about a month and a half, I experienced my own personal Holy Grail of brain optimization: an improvement in short-term memory. It wasn't a huge change, mind you, but it was *tangible*. A brief presentation I had put off memorizing rolled off my tongue after just 24 hours of marinating, instead of the usual one-week minimum. I met a new neighbor and *actually remembered her name*. A friend told me about an interesting brand of protein powder and my brain neatly filed it in the "things I know" category, as if that was just how I had been doing business all along. It was exhilarating.

And the benefits kept coming. Over the course of a year, with many more plant food and herbal experimentations underway, I noticed that I was able to focus better and easily ward off distractions while I worked. I was considerably less anxious, too, and, oddly, I felt like I had a little more time in the day (probably from not spending so much time worrying). Even after a six-month period marked by several major personal and family-related challenges, the process of bouncing back to center seemed just a little more fluid. I couldn't believe it: Here

I'd been obsessed with the powerful effects that plants can have on health for well over a decade, with a full-time career based on pursuing functional foods that help to optimize the body. I'd done research on foods and created recipes that balance energy, promote heart health, improve strength, enhance beauty, and increase bone density, to name just a few of the many benefits of consuming superfoods. But I had never realized the extent to which the *brain* could be so malleable, not to mention so powerfully affected by something as simple as food. In fact, I had always assumed that focusing on "brain health" was reserved for individuals who suffer from severe neurodegenerative diseases or psychological imbalances (both of which I can deeply sympathize with, having witnessed their fatal effects firsthand in my own family). Now I was beginning to realize that, in addition to helping prevent and fight disease, even a relatively healthy brain could enjoy significant improvements, too, with just a few simple optimization strategies. It quickly became abundantly clear to me that so many of the challenges I had experienced in the past weren't "me" at all—they were just signals that my brain needed some extra TLC!

If I sound exuberant, please know that you're just picking up on my excitement about finally having the opportunity to share with you the best nuggets of what I've learned and experienced in the past few years. I wish I had this information and the "food tools" I now have when I was in school, struggling over tests. Or when I was hitting my head against the steering wheel of my car on the way home from yet another failed attempt at a memorized audition. Or even just a few years ago, when I found myself hyperventilating, in tears, because of work-related anxiety. But I'm glad I know what I know now.

I'm not a neuroscientist or a physician, and the subtle changes I've made in my diet have most definitely not turned me into a genius or a Zen master, or anything close to them. I'm not able to access the (fully mythical) "extra 90 percent of the brain" any better than anyone else, and I still "lose" the glasses on my head at least once every few days. But a tangible improvement has taken place: There's a little more light at the top of the stairs these days, so to speak. The brain is an insurmountably complicated environment, and we are all so very different. Yet I, along with thousands of researchers and natural medicine practitioners around the world, can confirm that if you feed your body well, not only will you protect your brain, but, in the process, you just might be able to enhance your experience of life as well.

Wouldn't you like to know how much your amazing mind is truly capable of? That's what this book can help you to find out.

In health,
Julie

Part One

CHANGE YOUR MIND

CHAPTER 1

Shift Happens

"When you're finished changing, you're finished."

—BENJAMIN FRANKLIN, founding father of the United States

In 2014, a group of Stanford bioengineers had a big announcement. For the past few years, they had been trying to create a computer that could function like a human brain, an advance that could hold great promise in the world of robotic prosthetic limbs. Now they had successfully developed a $40,000 circuit board that could mimic the way brain cells communicate with one another, albeit on a much less complex scale. Most exciting, the microchips they had created demonstrated a new level of energy efficiency: They could process data 9,000 times faster than an everyday personal computer, while using significantly less power.

But even with all their sophistication, the models the scientists created still paled in comparison to an actual human brain. The biggest issue was not speed; it was efficiency. In an article published in *Stanford Engineering*, the project's lead bioengineer,

Kwabena Boahen, admitted, "The human brain, with 80,000 times more neurons than [our computer board model], consumes only three times as much power." Had the engineers just used the wrong materials? Or is the brain capable of such a superior level of power that researchers couldn't even come close to matching it?

In 2007, several years before completing his brain-like circuit board, Boahen shared just how efficient a human brain really is during a powerful TED Talk. At the time, the fastest supercomputer in the world was nicknamed "Blue Gene." Blue Gene, an IBM project using 120,000 processors to process 10,000,000,000,000,000 (10 to the 16th power) calculations a second, was viewed as an absolute beast. But even though Blue Gene was also considered one of the most power-efficient supercomputers in the world, it required 1.5 megawatts of power, or the energy needed to power around 1,200 homes in the United States, to achieve this great processing feat. Incredibly, Boahen estimated that the human brain has a very similar processing speed—around 10 to the 16th power calculations a second. Yet, unlike Blue Gene, our brains only use about 10 watts of energy to achieve all this—about as much as it takes to run a laptop computer.

Although faster supercomputers are now emerging, we still haven't come close to matching the kind of energy efficiency used every day in a human brain. Indeed, our brain is still vastly better engineered than the best design attempts of our most brilliant scientists—and even the uppermost echelon of researchers aren't afraid to admit that we still have much to understand and discover about how the brain functions. So, given how powerful, essential, and seemingly automatic this function may be, why are so many of us running around with what might still be considered suboptimal cognition? What does optimized cognition even feel like? And is it even achievable? Can we really change our brains for the better?

These were the nagging questions that led me to track down Dr. Andrew Hill, a cognitive neuroscientist and creator of the Peak Brain Institute, a family of neurofeedback centers located throughout the United States. I had listened to many podcast interviews with Dr. Hill during my initial forays into learning more about what it takes to build a healthier brain and had become increasingly fascinated by his valuable insights into brain performance. Unfortunately, the night before our meeting, my ability to fall asleep took a random and unexpected turn for the worse and, much to my chagrin, it clearly showed the next morning. There were no telltale bags under my eyes, thanks to an effective swoosh of concealer, but even my best attempt at camouflage was no match for the neuroscientist. After one look at a file on his computer (essentially a map of my brain), Dr. Hill politely observed, "It looks like you may be a little under-rested." I'm not sure what's worse: Someone telling you that you look tired or someone telling you your brain looks tired.

Since I was meeting Dr. Hill at Peak Brain's Los Angeles location, I had made the most of my trip by partaking in one of the institute's quick quantitative electroencephalogram sessions, otherwise known as QEEG or "brain mapping." QEEG records your brain waves—the patterns of neural activity made up of the same kind of biological electrical pulses the Stanford engineers were trying to replicate in their computer board model—to gain a visual map of brain activity. After sitting perfectly still in a chair for a bit with a cap on my head, the "that was easier than I thought" procedure was over, and my brain was officially on the map—ready to be scrutinized. Which is where, of course, my long night of tossing and turning, along with a decade-old concussion and a few other pesky traits and habits, stood out like flies on a wedding cake to Dr. Hill's trained eye.

But Dr. Hill's work with Peak Brain doesn't simply entail pointing out how your brain differs from what's considered to be in the "normal" range. He's interested in helping you *improve* it. Described as a kind of "gym for your brain," Peak Brain Institute uses neurofeedback programs to train your mind and upgrade cognitive performance, helping you to enjoy the incredible experience of an optimized brain. Still, I wanted to know what this seemingly elusive "optimized brain" feels like, so I prodded Dr. Hill for more details. "It's like the windshield wiper fairy paying you a visit and squeegeeing your world," he said, clearly excited. I was getting excited, too, as he went on to describe how getting your brain into a healthy state means that you'll find your ideas crisper, your thoughts clearer, and colors seeming brighter. Optimization might also mean that you find it easier to focus or get to sleep, and you may simply experience life more vividly, more intensely, while also feeling more relaxed. You may gain a certain resiliency, too, in the way you think and feel—things that might have bothered you or stressed you out previously may now

seem less important and easier to dismiss. In short, you should feel more like *yourself.*

Even after your brain stops growing—a phase that doesn't end until you're in your late 20s or possibly even your early 30s—it is constantly changing, truly from one minute to the next. As I came to the end of my conversation with Dr. Hill, his parting words expressed the intense passion that he feels about his work: "Your brain is going to change to respond to the pressures, the privations of life, the motivations, the access to yummy things, the avoidance of pain—you're built like this. The system's job is to adapt the whole time you are alive to minimize pain and maximize gain. So if it's doing this already, why not get in the driver's seat and decide what resources you want to adjust. You're in control of your brain health. Don't be satisfied with anything in terms of cognition, mood, sleep, or stress that isn't doing what you want, because the resources are actually tractable to change. Shift happens. So you might as well be in charge of it."

As I drove home, I ruminated on Dr. Hill's words. We have drastically more control over our experience of reality than most of us have ever realized, and, without a doubt, neurofeedback is an incredible way to effectively guide cognitive transformation. But, as it turns out, there's certainly more than one way to literally change your mind.

It's no accident that your brain is one of the very first organs that begins to develop when you are still just an embryo, beginning around week six of gestation, right when your neural cord has closed. It's highly likely that your brain (and, theoretically, your consciousness) will also be the last organ to power off, not when but *after* you take your last breath. Scientific evidence repeatedly shows that brain cells die independently and at their own rate, which can take days—and potentially even longer—to degrade to a point where they are no longer viable, outliving the very body in which they once resided.

Of course, sandwiched between those extremes is the ineffable adventure of life, for which your body may be the vehicle but your brain is ultimately the driver. Your brain controls every single aspect of your experience, from enabling you to understand the words on this page, to processing the emotion you feel when hugging a friend, to making sure you take a breath without even consciously thinking about it. Your brain controls the colors you see, the way a rock feels in your hand, how you process the smell of a neighbor's barbecue—and the fond memories of previous summertime dinners that come with it. It controls how you make judgments and decisions, allows you to ponder the future, determines what you perceive as reality, and lies at the core of what makes you feel like *you*. In essence: The brain defines human experience.

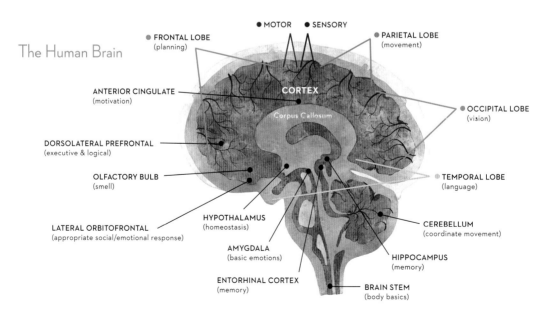

The Human Brain

● MOTOR   ● SENSORY

● FRONTAL LOBE
(planning)

● PARIETAL LOBE
(movement)

ANTERIOR CINGULATE
(motivation)

CORTEX

Corpus Callosum

● OCCIPITAL LOBE
(vision)

DORSOLATERAL PREFRONTAL
(executive & logical)

OLFACTORY BULB
(smell)

● TEMPORAL LOBE
(language)

HYPOTHALAMUS
(homeostasis)

CEREBELLUM
(coordinate movement)

LATERAL ORBITOFRONTAL
(appropriate social/emotional response)

AMYGDALA
(basic emotions)

HIPPOCAMPUS
(memory)

ENTORHINAL CORTEX
(memory)

BRAIN STEM
(body basics)

Looking at this illustration, the important thing to note is that, while we tend to think of the brain as a single organ or unit, it is actually composed of multiple areas, each of which performs a unique set of vital functions. Although all aspects of the brain are important—and interconnected—the ones that are most affected by the information coming up in the chapters ahead are the hippocampus, which controls memory and learning; the amygdala, which is responsible for brokering emotional balance; and the prefrontal cortex (frontal lobe), which is both the most complex and the most recent expansion in human brain biology. The prefrontal cortex is also generally thought of as the "CEO" of the brain, determining what you pay attention to and how you respond to it. Bordering the brain is a semipermeable layer of cells called the "blood-brain barrier," which, when it functions correctly, helps to maintain a constant and stable environment for the brain, allowing only certain nutrients to enter, while keeping out whatever the brain deems to be a "foreign substance."

Of course, this is a massive oversimplification of brain function, and since this is essentially a book about food, there's no reason to plunge into the abyss of neural anatomy here. But the only way to understand how to best nourish your brain is to zoom in just a bit more, because when you do, you'll realize that your brain is not just a jelly-like organ; it is a profoundly systemized *network*. It is, in fact, the most complex system in the universe—*there are more cells inside your skull than there are stars in our galaxy.* The average human adult brain contains approximately 100 billion nerve cells, or neurons, and it's the incredible way that all these neurons communicate with one another that dictate how you act, think, and feel.

YOUR MENTAL MICROCLIMATE

What did one neuron say to the other neuron so they could connect?

"Call me on my cell."

Forgive me for telling you the world's worst joke, but while neurons may not reach for an iPhone anytime soon, they are constantly trading messages nevertheless. Neurons come in all shapes and sizes, but most have a similar composition.

Do You Have a Big Head?

Even though the size and weight of the brain may vary by several ounces from one person to another, these differences have nothing to do with intelligence. What *does* impact how well you think is the health of the cells in the brain and how effectively they are able to function and communicate with one another.

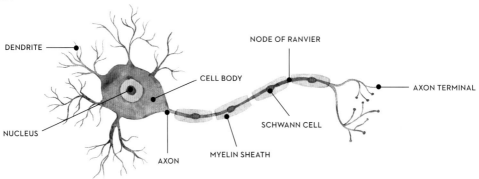

Like other cells, neurons contain a nucleus with genes, mitochondria, cytoplasm, and other organelles and are surrounded by a cell membrane. But among the things that make a neuron unique are the branch-like structures called dendrites and axons, which are located on opposite ends of the cell. Dendrites are responsible for bringing information into the cell body, while axons are responsible for taking information away from the cell body. Where's all this information coming from and going to? Other neurons! Through an electrochemical process, each and every neuron is capable of sending thousands of messages to other neurons, and these special messages say everything there is to know about who you are and what your "mental microclimate" looks like. You've likely heard of these message carriers before: They're called *neurotransmitters*.

The role of neurotransmitters is to facilitate the communication between neurons throughout the brain, via synapses, the small gaps that separate these cells. Neurotransmitters are actually a group of brain chemicals that act as a catalyst for all kinds of mental and physical tasks that affect everything from your current mood to how well you'll sleep tonight, to whether you're motivated to go to the gym today or remember the name of the person you sat next to last night at a dinner party.

More than 100 distinct neurotransmitters have been discovered so far, each playing a slightly different role. Gaining even a baseline understanding of how neurotransmitters function can give you tremendous insights into your behavior, feelings, and cognitive performance . . . and how you can begin to improve that performance.

To begin with, all neurotransmitters are continually made by your body—just like your hormones and blood cells. Understanding this gives you a much deeper appreciation of how the kinds of foods you eat can affect how well your neurotransmitters are produced and perform. And that's a valuable insight, as in so many ways, it's these brain chemicals that really run the show.

HOME ON THE NEUROTRANSMITTER RANGE

Professional fighters are just as tough as you might imagine. The months and years of constant physical and mental battering they endure to prepare for the public ring (only to undergo more of the same) is truly relentless. And while we tend to associate fighters primarily with their bravado—a hyped-up mix of aggression, intimidation, and, in some cases, charisma—their demeanor in the hours directly leading up to a fight may come as a surprise. What you won't see is the blatant expression of adrenaline that is so obvious during a fight (adrenaline is a neurotransmitter, by the way). A growing number of outlier fighters are now doing the opposite of what you might expect during the pre-fight prep: They're meditating, listening to classical music, and practicing cutting-edge, structured breathwork.

So why all the calm before the storm? "There's a sweet spot between arousal and calm," Alex Jamora tells me as we sit down after a workout. Alex is a good friend and a performance coach who works with professional fighters and athletes, specializing in mobility and breathing techniques as well as the usual strength and conditioning training. Instead of firing up his clients in the hours before a fight, Alex guides them through specialized breathing protocols. Remarkably, these techniques can help enhance focus and emotional control while decreasing anxiety. The longer fighters can maintain a lower level of excitement, the more control and the greater the energy reserves they will have for the fight itself. Even though we tend to think of breathing as an unconscious function, regulatory breathing protocols, like the ones Alex prescribes, are quite purposeful. "The brain controls the body, but the breath can control the brain," he explains.

As it turns out, neuroscientists fully agree. Studies show that some volitional breathing exercises can trigger the "rest and digest" component of your autonomic nervous system, also called the parasympathetic nervous system. This, in turn, stimulates the body's longest nerve, the vagus nerve, which connects the brain to the rest of the body. With this prompt, the vagus nerve releases a neurotransmitter called *acetylcholine*, a catalyst for increased focus, enhanced calm, and decreased symptoms of anxiety. Breath training is an incredible tool for athletes, as well as for the rest of us, for that matter, but having a well-functioning system of neurotransmitters at work behind the scenes can literally help make you a champion . . . or at least feel like one.

While there are a number of ways to classify them, from a functional standpoint neurotransmitters work in systems that can be divided into two categories: inhibitory and excitatory. Inhibitory neurotransmitters slow actions down, while excitatory neurotransmitters turn actions on and/or speed them up. Of course, you don't need to be a prizefighter to understand that inhibitory and excitatory neurotransmitters are equally important in regulating your body—your overall well-being depends on *all* your neurotransmitters functioning together as a happy family.

Three of the most common types of excitatory neurotransmitters are glutamate, norepinephrine, and epinephrine. GABA and serotonin are two of the main types of inhibitory neurotransmitters. Acetylcholine, which was mentioned previously, and dopamine, which may already be familiar to you, are two examples of critical chemicals that can actually be *both* inhibitory and excitatory, depending on where they're found in the brain. And when all neurotransmitter systems are firing properly, the result is a balanced mental state with a high level of cognitive productivity.

Unfortunately, many of us suffer from a bit of neurotransmitter malfunctioning from time to time. You might experience this in any number of ways, including depression (from minor to severe), brain fog, loss of motivation, overaggression, and an inability to fall asleep, to name just a few. But your personal menu of neurotransmitter malfunction does not have to be a life sentence. Brain chemistry can change by the second, either positively or negatively. And while it sure may feel like it at times, "you" are not the sum of your neurotransmitters. Furthermore, you can drastically improve your body's ability to manage your neurotransmitters—and influence how you feel and perform—for the better. The key is to encourage a healthy neurotransmitter *range,* between low and high zones of activity.

Arguably, the biggest misunderstanding about neurotransmitters is that they need to be "balanced." But the fact is, a "neurochemical imbalance" is no more than a theory because, neurologically speaking, your neurotransmitters function as a *regulatory* type of system—they are always in flux. That's why there are no optimal "levels" of neurotransmitters that need to be maintained, as in, say, the case of a nutrient like calcium. Instead, it is the ability to flow up and down the neurotransmitter range, as circumstances dictate, that is an indicator of healthy brain function. Getting "stuck" in either the low or high zones of neurotransmitter activity is often what can lead to problems.

To get a better perspective on how these incredibly influential neurotransmitters work, let's take a closer look at the most common neurotransmitter systems and how they function inside your central nervous system—and how they impact your life.

Serotonin

Even though serotonin is among the most widely studied neurotransmitters, it's also one of the most complicated to understand. Although it's best known for its influence on mood and emotion—and often called "the happy molecule"—serotonin is important for integrating many aspects of brain function, like sleep and appetite. But serotonin has many other roles in the body as well, including regulating the digestive process. In fact, recent studies have shown that up to 95 percent of the serotonin in your body is found in your gastrointestinal tract!

Moreover, serotonin only produces the "happy" results we long for when it is working as a balanced, optimized system. Conversely, when a serotonin system is out of whack, it can produce many ill effects, ranging from severe depression (too little serotonin), to irregular heartbeat and seizures (too much serotonin). Outside of cases that warrant medical attention, arguably the best ways to steady your body's ability to produce and process serotonin is to regularly partake in relaxing activities that bring you joy; to use supplements or superfoods that naturally offer all the building blocks to create adequate serotonin as your body requires it; and to eat a brain-healthy and gut-healthy diet overall.

SEROTONIN PLAYS A ROLE IN:

- Mood and social behavior
- Feelings of contentment and calm
- Appetite and food cravings
- Sleep quality
- Sexual desire and function
- Memory and learning

Serotonin and Depression

Depression is surprisingly common. The American Psychiatric Association estimates that one in fifteen people suffer from depression each year, while one in six of us will experience depression during our lifetime. Additionally, depression is multifaceted. No one, including the experts, fully understands its cause—although biochemical, genetic, personality, and environmental factors, among many others, have been cited as likely contributing factors. The good news is that depression is among the most treatable of all mental disorders: Between 80 percent and 90 percent of people who experience depression respond to treatment. But while many people assume that serotonin is the antidote to depression, that assumption is vastly flawed, as not all depression is caused by serotonergic problems. Nevertheless, working to naturally strengthen your serotonin system (and all your neurotransmitter activity, for that matter) can at least be a very good place to start when tackling depression.

Dopamine

Ahh . . . the pleasure chemical. Dopamine is an extremely malleable neurotransmitter, and when you can tie it into a beneficial activity, you'll gain extra motivation and drive, along with a major boost in cognitive performance. As I briefly mentioned earlier, dopamine can either be inhibitory or excitatory, and it plays a significant role in many parts of the body, including your cardiovascular system and kidneys. In the brain, however, it's best known for manipulating our behavior, due to its strong "pleasure-reward" influence; and its numerous effects on overall cognitive function are well studied. But for all the good it does, dopamine also has a bit of a bad-boy reputation in the medical world because of the many problems that can develop from overstimulating its production.

In a way, you can think of your dopaminergic system of neurotransmitters as the key that turns on the bratty little kid who lives inside all of us. Your brain loves the feel-good "rush" that comes with a dopamine surge—a

surge that might be initiated, for example, when you buy something that you really want; but at that point, rather than being satisfied, your brain greedily cries, "More!" And do you know what ignites a dopamine response more than anything else? Surprises! In fact, if I were to pack this book with occasional random images—maybe a cluster of yellow balloons on one page, followed by a photo of a cute sloth on another—these images would increase your motivation to keep turning the pages, thanks to a sneaky, mild surge of surprise-induced dopamine.

While you may think this idea is ridiculous, chances are you're already proving its validity every day by indulging in a little habit called social media. The endless scrolling of photos, news updates, videos, and other "surprises" spurs the release of one tiny microdose of dopamine after another, and it is truly addicting on a biochemical level, as your brain screams, "*More, more, more!*" The creators of social media sites know this power well and they use it—even hiring so-called "attention engineers," so they can capture more of your time and information for their advertisers' benefit.

And it's not just social media. The developers of many apps use the same psychological tactics, too. For example, some fitness apps give you "points" for the number of hours you've worked out or the number of steps you've taken. Or you may find that, in addition to learning a new language on an app, you can also earn "gemstones," complete with sparkly animation and an audible "bling!" as a reward. Even my favorite meditation app keeps a running count of how many days in a row I've meditated and how many hours I've meditated in total. I get a little surge of dopamine at the end of each session when I watch the number grow . . . and it keeps me coming back.

So is dopamine good or bad? Like most things in life, it's both. While dopamine motivates us into action and feels good when we get a rush, it's also at the root of addiction. The dopamine "rush" is one of the reasons why it's so hard to stop using many drugs, such as cocaine or nicotine, and users constantly require larger and larger quantities to supply the desired high; or why gamblers become hooked, unable to cut themselves off from the thrill of just one more chance to win. What's more, to further understand the pleasure-reward dichotomy, disappointment causes a *decrease* in dopamine, a phenomenon called "reward prediction error." For example, if you open a birthday present, expecting the awesome new shoes you asked for, only to discover a pair of itchy wool socks, you'll experience a *drop* in dopamine, instead of a surge.

Yet dopamine can be of great benefit, too. For example, in prehistoric days, dopamine motivated us to seek food, build shelter, and create tools, making the dangerous or unknown tasks that were necessary to our survival intuitively pleasurable—"addicting," even—in a good way.

But you don't have to forage for berries in the woods to experience a dopamine rush. If you've ever spent a good part of a weekend mowing the lawn or cleaning out your car and have experienced a strong feeling of satisfaction and personal gratification from a job well done, that's dopamine at work. Setting and achieving goals, regardless of how big or small they may be, is one of the best ways to naturally increase your dopamine levels. Not surprisingly, since such a large part of your brain is dedicated specifically to hand control and touch, the more tangible a goal is, the better you'll feel when you've accomplished it. (And good news: The act of cooking—especially whipping up new recipes like the ones in this book—serves as an excellent hands-on, goal-oriented way to naturally experience a healthy rise in dopamine!)

DOPAMINE PLAYS A ROLE IN:

- Mood and behavior
- Motor control
- Motivation and drive
- Concentration and memory

Norepinephrine (and Epinephrine)

If you're wondering what the purpose of this pair of neurotransmitters is, here's a hint: They're also known as noradrenaline and adrenaline. These "excitatory" neurotransmitters have similar arousal qualities, which is why they're often paired. Both have dual roles as neurotransmitters and stress hormones, with these differences: Norepinephrine is primarily released by and activated in your brain, while epinephrine is mainly secreted by the adrenal glands (and some select neurons) and distributed throughout your body.

Epinephrine/adrenaline is released as a reaction to acute stress and pushes you into immediate action, a phenomenon commonly known as the "fight-or-flight" response. The release of these stress hormones also plays an essential role in metabolism, mental focus, arousal, and overall cognition—and it most certainly helped our ancient ancestors fend off and survive attacks from wild boars.

Norepinephrine is a bit different. As a kind of mental "jump-start" neurotransmitter, norepinephrine plays an important role in creating a cognitive environment that promotes focused attention. It also enables us to respond to stress. Its release also impacts mood (when your brain feels energized, you're often in a better mood). Norepinephrine is very closely related to dopamine—both are synthesized using the same amino acid, tyrosine—and a norepinephrine release is much more impactful and beneficial when it is combined with dopamine, or any other neurotransmitter for that matter. A norepinephrine and dopamine surge brings on the kind of euphoric feeling you'd experience while playing competitive sports, performing music onstage to a cheering audience, or even just finishing the arduous process of doing your taxes for the year. Your brain loves being put to work with ambitious challenges, and norepinephrine is a key component in ensuring that you have the mental "juice" and attention for whatever task you're tackling. Incorporating exciting or industrious activities into your life that push you out of your comfort zone—as well as including natural sources of tyrosine (such as lentils and soy) in your diet—are two great ways to ensure that your norepinephrine system is performing well, enabling you to effectively execute actions and benefitting how you think and feel.

NOREPINEPHRINE (NORADRENALINE) PLAYS A ROLE IN:

- Mental energy
- Motivation
- Focus and attention
- Balanced mood
- Healthy sleep

- Quick decision-making in times of extreme stress (fight-or-flight response)

Can You Balance All the "Mood" Neurotransmitters at Once?

In a way, yes. But it's not with a pill, or even a bar of chocolate. The answer is through exercise! Physical activity is one of the best things you can do to keep your brain chemistry balanced, by increasing natural levels of serotonin, dopamine, norepinephrine, and other feel-good brain chemicals called endorphins. And as if that weren't enough, a habit of regular movement also markedly increases the synthesis of brain-derived neurotrophic factor (BDNF), a substance that can protect your brain cells, promote healthy new neuron growth, and enhance memory.

Acetylcholine

While serotonin, dopamine, and norepinephrine steal the show when it comes to balancing mood and overall outlook on life, acetylcholine is one of the most talked-about neurotransmitters when it comes to overall intelligence. As the first molecule to be named a neurotransmitter, acetylcholine is best known for its all-important role in helping the brain to process information. Part of what makes acetylcholine such a fascinating subject for neuroscientists and neuro-enthusiasts alike is that it acts as a powerful neuromodulator; that is, it helps you regulate other neurochemicals and keeps them in check.

As you age, the amount of acetylcholine decreases in your body, making it a significant factor in cognitive impairment. Having a "senior moment" is one of the most common complaints of its deficiency. Additionally, many people who suffer from degenerative neurological diseases have low acetylcholine levels, leading researchers to believe that a healthy range of acetylcholine can help prevent cognitive decline. A brain-friendly diet can be immensely beneficial in that regard—and may even have the potential to help rebuild what is lost.

ACETYLCHOLINE PLAYS A ROLE IN:

- Memory
- Learning new information
- Focus and alertness
- Mental flexibility
- Homeostasis after times of stress

Glutamate

Glutamate is a major excitatory neurotransmitter that plays a pivotal role in sending signals between nerve cells and is strongly connected to learning and memory. But glutamate isn't just found in abundance in the central nervous system; it's in other parts of the body as well. As a matter of fact, you have a total of about four pounds of glutamate in your own body right now! Considered a nonessential amino acid (meaning you don't need to consume it as part of your diet and can biologically produce it on your own), glutamate is absolutely crucial to health on many levels. But, like so many things, too much of it can be very damaging to your brain. High concentrations of this neurotransmitter may overexcite your nerve cells, even eventually causing neuron damage and death, a condition known as "excitotoxicity." Overly high quantities of the stuff can also contribute to depression, obsessive-compulsive disorder, and autism; and glutamate disfunction is often cited for its roll in neurodegenerative diseases such as Alzheimer's, Parkinson's, and Huntington's diseases. Nevertheless, maintaining healthy glutamate function remains a vital aspect of a well-functioning brain, where it also serves as the precursor to yet another all-important neurotransmitter: GABA.

GLUTAMATE PLAYS A ROLE IN:

- Learning and memory
- Nerve growth and mental flexibility
- GABA production

GABA

GABA (gamma-aminobutyric acid), which functions as the brain's foremost inhibitory neurotransmitter, is so essential that almost all parts of the brain rely on it to function properly. In essence, GABA helps you relax (and is sometimes even called "nature's Valium"). A healthy level of GABA is always needed to ensure that the excitatory system does not become overactive, and it also helps you feel calm and ready to handle stressful situations. Meanwhile, low levels of GABA can leave you feeling anxious, overwhelmed, and unable to "turn off."

As noted earlier, GABA is synthesized from glutamate (and, interestingly, can convert back into glutamate, if needed). But since GABA generally cannot cross the blood-brain barrier, while glutamate can, the conversion from glutamate to GABA occurs within the brain itself. Research indicates that GABA may be involved in the production of the hormone melatonin. As a result, it's thought to influence sleep quality as well.

Many of the tranquilizing drugs on the market are designed to target your body's GABA levels. However, in most cases, eating healthful foods like the ones recommended in this book will encourage your body's natural production of GABA more effectively (and more gently) over the long run, while also reducing feelings of tension and stress.

Neurotransmitters: Myth Versus Fact

Myth: Neurotransmitters are found in foods.

Fact: With the exception of a couple of amino acids (glutamate and aspartate), you can't "eat" more neurotransmitters. However, in most cases, you can eat foods that contain the nutrients that act as direct building blocks for the production of specific neurotransmitters.

Myth: Neurotransmitters are the sole key to brain optimization.

Fact: Many brain-boosting supplements, both chemically derived and of natural origin, would have you believe that neurotransmitters are the "key" to brain health. In reality, neurotransmitters tell only part of the story. Nevertheless, they can certainly have a remarkable effect—particularly on mood and perception—when they are functioning well.

Myth: More neurotransmitters are always better than fewer.

Fact: Your brain, like the rest of your body, seeks balance, not excess. For every powerful benefit of a neurotransmitter, there is an equally undesirable range of nonbeneficial effects when that neurotransmitter is released in excess. (To grasp this point, just think of the side effects of many misused pharmaceutical and street drugs.) Consuming brain-healthy foods and leading a neuroprotective lifestyle overall will not prompt unhealthy "highs" (although these strategies certainly can feel uplifting). Rather, these natural methods will keep you in tune with your actual biological needs.

Myth: The goal is to balance your brain chemistry.

Fact: As mentioned earlier, this statement falls under the "sort of" category. A more accurate way to phrase it might be, "A well-functioning brain has a healthy brain chemistry *range.*" Like the ocean's tides, certain neurotransmitters and hormones need to continually rise and fall within your body. When you become angry, your adrenaline and cortisol levels swell to help you respond appropriately. Then, when what prompted your anger is no longer a threat, these chemicals are excreted or recycled by your body. Most neurotransmitter problems boil down to an intake/outtake malfunction: When the brain struggles to release and dispose of neurotransmitters, they collect in your brain, leaving you with an oversaturation, which can have nasty side effects. Alternatively, when your brain has trouble producing neurotransmitters in the first place, you won't have an adequate supply for situational responses, a deficit that you may experience as brain fog or feeling "off" emotionally. That's why focusing on a healthy, well-functioning brain *as a whole* is more effective in the long run than trying to give specific neurotransmitters a "boost."

- Promoting calmness and
  the ability to relax

- Stress relief

- Enhancing sleep quality

———

While it may be tempting to try to raise the levels of certain neurotransmitters in your brain, the key to improving brain health is not to try and dominate your brain chemistry. Outside of clinical care, of course, you certainly don't want to force a dramatic release of any neurotransmitters or attempt to "stockpile" them in your system. Rather, the most "feel-good," impactful results are gained by supporting your body's ability to produce and release neurotransmitters *naturally* through the nutrients you consume and the lifestyle you maintain.

The moral here is this: Take it upon yourself to create the conditions for the outcomes you desire. The long-term positive cognitive changes you crave will come from optimizing the health of your brain as a whole, not just certain parts of it. This is why the "smart plants" in this book truly live up to their name, as they work in tune with your body to generate homeostasis—the tendency for organisms to self-regulate or maintain their internal environment in a stable condition—safely and effectively. And it just so happens that homeostasis in your brain may bring on more of an enjoyable state than you ever realized.

But general anatomy, brain waves, and neurotransmitters aside, there's still one more area of neurological health that's all too often forgotten. Why? Because it's not in your brain at all.

YOUR OTHER BRAIN

When I spoke with Dr. Barbara Shukitt-Hale, a USDA staff scientist at the Laboratory of Neuroscience and Aging at Tufts University in Boston, I asked her to highlight an area of brain study, within the next five to ten years, that she was especially excited to see continue to develop. Much to my surprise, it was not brain waves, neuron health, or the blood-brain barrier that was on her mind. Instead, Dr. Shukitt-Hale replied, "The microbiome." So

what's so important about this vast ecosystem of microorganisms (bacteria, fungi, viruses and more) that live in and on your body?

Cognitive function is impacted by all parts of the body, but one system in particular has a very direct effect on it: your gastrointestinal tract, otherwise known as your gut. Often referred to as the "second brain," your gut is made from the same kind of tissue as your brain (when you develop as a fetus) and is connected to it via the vagus nerve, the long, acetylcholine-activating nerve we talked about earlier, which runs from your brain stem to your abdomen. The vagus nerve acts like a two-way street—a conduit between your gut and your brain. As a result, the two systems influence each other constantly. For example, you may suffer from tension in your stomach when you're feeling nervous or experience mental "fogginess" after an unhealthy, hard-to-digest meal. What's more, the gut is partially responsible for many of your body's neurotransmitter tasks as well—particularly the production of serotonin.

And this is where the microbiome comes into play. Although it's true that microbes live everywhere in your body, they are most concentrated and have the greatest diversity in your gut (specifically your large intestine). The health of the microbial ecosystem in your gut plays an important role in many of your body's functions, including its critical influence on various autoimmune disorders. About one in five Americans currently suffers from these kinds of disorders, which include multiple sclerosis and Parkinson's disease (both of which cause devastating neurological problems). But believe it or not, around 70 percent of your body's immune system is located in your gut microbiome alone. Consequently, an imbalance in this microbiome, which may be affected by anything from stress to illness to medication, can drastically increase the level of inflammatory chemicals that your body is exposed to, causing you to develop chronic inflammation and potentially serious illness over time. Two preliminary studies have shown that mice injected with compromised gut bacteria were significantly more prone to developing brain inflammation and MS-like symptoms than mice that had a healthy microbiome. It's safe to say that whether or not you develop an illness, your cognitive function will most certainly suffer if your gut is inflamed.

Not surprisingly, the most important factor in keeping your gut healthy comes down to what you put in it. Foods high in sugar, such as whole milk and sugary soda drinks, can attract unwanted bacteria that have a negative impact on the microbial balance of the gut. A 2013 study found that diets rich in animal protein, like meat and cheese, have a dramatically negative effect on gastrointestinal health as well, by promoting the growth of harmful bacteria and causing inflammation. For anyone who is allergic to gluten, glutinous grains like wheat can create a similar problem. Apart from foods, some drugs like antibiotics can have devastating effects on your microbiome balance; these drugs are like little bombs exploding in the healthy world of your gut, and it can take months for your body to recover and replenish the good bacteria it has lost. Consequently, these types of pharmaceuticals, and even antacids, should be taken only when they are truly necessary.

So how can you improve the health of your gut microbiome? Once again, with food! Nourishing your gut flora is extremely important for the health of your body as well as your brain. We'll get into all kinds of delicious fun for your microbiome in the upcoming chapters. But, for now, just remember: Happy gut = happy brain.

———

By now we've delved into how your brain works, as well as just how wondrous your mental universe—a flurry of various chemicals, electrical impulses, and biological components—really is. I have no doubt that you're already aware of many factors that are considered essential to brain health (and whole body health), including quality sleep, adequate hydration, and regular exercise. But, ironically, it's easy to forget one of the most important components of all: diet. After all, the things you put *into* your body are precisely what *become* your body, and that applies to your brain too. In short, your ability to learn, focus, conceptualize, remember, and even shrug off stress is directly related to the food you put on your plate, which can make all the difference in how you think and feel.

Chapter Cheat Sheet:
SHIFT HAPPENS

Although there are many layers of complexity in your brain, ultimately they work together as a network to dictate how you act, think, and feel. Furthermore, your brain is designed to constantly adapt to the decisions you make, including what you choose to eat. Making effective dietary choices puts you in control of your own cognitive performance.

- Identify your specific cognitive goals, including behaviors and emotions.

- Create the conditions for the outcomes you desire: Don't try to forcefully manipulate individual neurotransmitters (unless you're under the supervision of a medical professional); instead, follow a cognition-friendly diet and lifestyle to optimize neurotransmitter activity (and thus, brain function) as a whole.

- Make nourishing your gut flora a priority to support the health of your brain.

CHAPTER 2

Why Plants?

"To ask the right question is already half the solution of a problem."
—CARL G. JUNG, psychologist, psychiatrist, and founder
of analytic psychology

If you're eager to learn more about how to enhance your brain health, I'm excited to tell you that you are living in a truly wonderful time for research. Scientists have only recently moved beyond simply trying to prevent or manage neural disease and are currently looking for ways to better optimize and enhance healthy brains, too. Now, as we learn more about the very organ that allows us to learn in the first place, recent studies have reversed the generally accepted position that as we age, our brain inevitably atrophies. Instead, we are beginning to find ways to rebuild the brain, propelling human potential in the process, which explains why this book takes a multifaceted approach to improving your brain. I call it the **"Three Ps of Brain Building"**:

1. **PRIMING:** The everyday maintenance of your brain

2. **PROTECTION:** Defending your brain from the factors that cause cognitive impairment and disease

3. **PLASTICITY:** Promoting your brain's ability to be flexible, adaptable, and capable of repair and continued growth

By understanding the power of each of these concepts, you'll be able to better reach your personal cognitive objectives, simply through the foods you eat. (No wonder brain health is fast becoming one of the most alluring aspects of personal optimization!) But before we get into what's for lunch, let's take a closer look at the purpose behind each of the Three Ps and how they can serve you.

PRIMING

Even the most casual cyclist has a regular routine to keep their bike in good condition.

They'll check the chains, apply a little grease, and maybe give the tires a fresh pump of air. They know that even a small amount of regular maintenance goes a long way toward ensuring a smooth ride, while extending the life of the bike, too. Theoretically, your brain is not much different. You may be surprised to learn that while the brain is inexplicably complicated, its most basic needs are not (or, I should say, they don't have to be). Think of priming your brain as the most basic form of cognitive maintenance, a daily routine that allows you to put a check in the box next to a few key nutritional needs in your diet—and, ideally, a few healthy lifestyle habits, too. If it sounds easy, that's because it is. Most people are walking around with dietary deficiencies every day (it's estimated that nine out of ten Americans have subpar micronutrient levels) without even realizing what they're missing in the bandwidth of their own potential. That's one of the reasons why, over time, you'll likely feel more cognizant, clearheaded, and just all-around "better" simply by priming your brain with the right nutrition.

PROTECTION

Most of the scientific research on brain health focuses on ways to prevent, or at least manage, the symptoms and progression of cognitive diseases or to stave off neurological decline. While truly bulletproof prevention is probably impossible—given such uncontrollable factors as genetics and environmental hazards—there has been great progress in discovering new ways to *protect* your brain, such as significantly lowering risks, easing disease symptoms, and curtailing mental aging. What's more, an impressive number of protective advances are centered around foods and food-based nutrients. It turns out that a brain housed in a well-fed body tends to stay sharper over the long term. And the beautiful thing about actively making prevention of cognitive decline a priority is that it will not only enhance your life expectancy; it will promote a better *quality* of life as well.

PLASTICITY

In the early 1970s, Michael Merzenich, a professor emeritus in neuroscience at the University of California, San Francisco, conducted experiments to demonstrate the hypothesis that if damage were done to a part of the brain, any lost skills could not be relearned, proving the theory that the brain is both compartmentalized and fixed in its function. What he found, however, was exactly the opposite: Lost skills were actually relearned by different parts of the brain!

This accidental discovery became not only the focal point of a long and lauded career for Merzenich; it also propelled one of the most exhilarating new areas of research in neuroscience: neuroplasticity.

Neuroplasticity is defined as the brain's ability to adapt to change. You are not the hardwired creature you may think you are; your brain was designed to modify itself. Of course, change may be either positive or negative. Change is considered "positive" plasticity when you learn how to walk after a stroke or take a Spanish class to broaden your language skills. On the other hand, drug addiction or obsessive-compulsive behavior falls under the heading of "negative" plasticity. Interestingly, we've learned that plasticity can occur quite rapidly and can also be measured. For example, a 2005 study found that a group of medical students studying for exams not only had a significant increase in "gray matter" in the brain, but that the growth had occurred in just a matter of *months*. (Gray matter—brain tissue that is the richest in cellular bodies and synapses—is associated with so many cognitive functions that it steals 94 percent of the oxygen in the brain to operate.) No wonder the brain is often likened to a muscle—it definitely can be strengthened and improved to work better.

And speaking of the brain's ability to change in positive ways, we need to mention neurogenesis. Up until the 1990s, most neuroscientists supported the theory that the life span of the brain follows a bell curve of growth and decay; that is, once a human brain stops growing a couple decades into life, it follows a slow descent of degeneration. Super depressing, right? But recent developments in our understanding of the brain show a more hopeful vision: It is possible that the brain never stops regenerating new cells.

Now, before you get too excited, there are only two parts of your brain that are thought to be capable of regeneration in adulthood: the hippocampus, which serves as your long-term and spatial memory hub and which is arguably the most plastic part of your brain; and the cerebellum, which controls coordination and muscle memory. Nonetheless, neuroplasticity and neurogenesis remain two very promising means of rewiring your brain, giving you the power to potentially improve your brain as you age.

————

Taking action to prime, protect, and promote plasticity in your brain brings us directly to the core thesis of this book: **Enhancing your diet is one of the easiest ways to beneficially change your brain.**

YOUR MOTHER WAS RIGHT

Years ago, I had the good fortune to meet Dr. Paula C. Bickford at a conference in Hawaii, where we bonded enthusiastically over our mutual love of spirulina, one of our favorite green superfoods (because isn't that how all people connect?). Dr. Bickford is a real-deal legend in the world of nutrient-rich foods and the scientific exploration of their capacity to enhance cognitive function and memory. She currently serves as the senior research career scientist at James A. Haley VA Hospital in Tampa, Florida, and is a distinguished health professor in the Department of Neurosurgery and Brain Repair at the University of South Florida Morsani College of Medicine (also in Tampa). Additionally, Dr. Bickford is the cofounder of Natura Therapeutics. If you've heard that blueberries are good for your brain, you can thank Dr. Bickford, along with her fellow pioneers, who arrived at that conclusion through their groundbreaking research. When I interviewed Dr. Bickford for this book over the phone, we covered a wide range of topics, from healthy fats to the convenience of using an Instant Pot® (the handy gadget that recently sparked the renaissance of the pressure cooker). Yet one thing that really struck me was her reply at the end of our conversation, when I asked, "Is there a particularly important message that you'd really like to drive home to all of us in our quest to enhance cognitive function?" Dr. Bickford took a deep breath, and I could almost hear decades of research and experience churning away in her brain—and the smile in her voice—when she answered: "Your mother was right: Eat your vegetables."

Hey, you heard it from the neuroscientist.

PLANTS FOR LIFE

In the health community, the question "What is the best diet?" has long been the subject of debate, fluctuating trends, studies, and individual doctrines, all of which continue to be as volatile as the stock market. The field of brain optimization is no different. There are myriad opposing theories and polarizing recommendations about which diet is ideal. The confusion is compounded when some brain-oriented dietary information appears to contradict dietary guidelines supporting the health of the body as a whole. For example, it doesn't make much sense to eat a diet that is rich in butter, bacon, and other saturated fats simply because the brain has a high lipid content and demands fat, when, at the same time, saturated fats have been scientifically proven to increase the risk of heart disease, cancer, and accelerated aging. Conversely, in some cases, a very low-fat diet that is beneficial for the cardiovascular system might be severely disadvantageous for the brain. Outside of supervised medical treatment or disease protocols, I, for one, don't see much point in promoting a diet that supports the health of one organ to the potential detriment of another. Ultimately, our organs work together as a team. In other words, no matter what your health objectives may be, it only makes sense to pursue choices that are good for your *entire body*—not just one part of it—otherwise, those choices might not be so "good" after all.

When I first began my quest for the best brain-healthy foods, I naively assumed that I'd find a simple answer just by reading prominent health journals and speaking with respected brain and nutrition experts. Instead, I uncovered a slew of wide-ranging data that had shockingly different and often radically opposing interpretations. The research frequently made my head spin, and even after 15 years of pursuing a heavily studied culinary wellness path in my own career, I found myself utterly deflated, quite early on, in my pursuit of a cognitive-friendly diet. "I seriously don't even know what to eat anymore,"

I moaned to my husband in frustration one day, after being sucked into the logic of a particularly divisive book on the subject. "Well, probably not that," he replied, bemused by the empty box of animal crackers sitting next to me, which I had robotically demolished in my stress-induced state. While I cracked a bashful grin in response to my binge-eating bust, I also knew he was right. But with the "probably not that" food list seeming to grow by the day, I still didn't know where to turn for answers. Suddenly, like a lightning strike, the seed of an idea—a simple question, really—occurred to me: What would Dan Buettner do?

To say Dan Buettner is a well-respected journalist and researcher is an understatement. You may have heard of *Blue Zones*, a term that was initially coined by Buettner in his revolutionary investigative article published in *National Geographic* magazine in 2005. That article was the prequel to several best-selling books. Blue Zones refer to the five areas in the world that boast the longest-living populations (on average). The zones include Sardinia, Italy; the islands of Okinawa, Japan; Loma Linda, California; the Nicoya Peninsula, in Costa Rica; and the island of Icaria, Greece. Utilizing his award-winning journalistic skills, Buettner took a thorough and wide-ranging approach to his study of the lifestyle and dietary habits of these regions.

He assessed everything from overarching cultural factors to the people themselves—their daily physical activity, engagement with spirituality and community, and, of course, what was on their plates every day.

It's understandable to want to pluck individual gems of dietary wisdom and healthy lifestyle secrets from each of these regions, such as the high consumption of nuts in the diet of Loma Linda's centenarian Seventh-Day Adventists or the lack of "time urgency" among Okinawans. Undoubtedly, those are contributing factors to a long and vigorous life. However, the most fascinating and potentially meaningful aspect of the investigation, Buettner realized, did not lie in details that were often specific to a particular region but, rather, in patterns—lifestyle habits that were common in most, if not all, of the five longest-living cultures in the world. The following traits were recognized, by Buettner, as "nine lessons" that can teach us a great deal about longevity:

1. Regular moderate physical activity

2. A sense of life purpose

3. Emphasis on stress reduction

4. Engagement in spirituality or religion

5. Priority on family life

6. Active participation in social life

7. Moderate alcohol intake

8. Moderate caloric intake

9. **A plant-based diet**

To be clear, the phrase *plant-based diet* can have several meanings. In many places in the world, it is merely another way of saying "vegan," a more familiar and widely used term in the United States (and most certainly in my home state of California). Here, however, Buettner uses the expression *plant-based* to refer to a "semi-vegetarian" diet. His research shows that, with the exception of the citizens of Loma Linda (whose diet is exclusively vegetarian and who also enjoy the longest life expectancy of any population we know), the remaining four cultures in the Blue Zones study all fall into the "semi-vegetarian" category. In other words, while they may consume small amounts of animal products from time to time, meat is used quite sparingly, if at all, and only to add flavor to dishes; to provide the centerpiece of a special meal; or to serve as an infrequent side dish. More importantly, the bulk of their diet is composed of what Buettner calls the "plant slant," an approximately 95 percent plant-heavy (and whole-food) base, which generally includes lots of vegetables, legumes, whole grains, nuts, fruits, and plant-based oils (primarily olive oil). Most often, Blue Zone residents have access to fresh, seasonal produce that is locally sourced and pesticide-free.

Furthermore, dietary choices that do *not* play a role in the Blue Zone lifestyle are just as important as the ones that confer such a wealth of health benefits. In other words, there's no heavy consumption of animal products, saturated fat, sugar, or processed foods. In addition, people living in these Blue Zones do not engage in excessive drinking or use substantial quantities of prescription medicine or supplements. So, while we can clearly see from the list of Buettner's nine lessons that diet is not the *only* factor in living a long and healthy life, it's undoubtedly an essential component.

Invigorated by Buettner's longevity findings, I reanalyzed the information I'd gathered about the components of a brain-healthy diet. But this time, instead of focusing on the differences that I came across in my research, I began to look for common threads, gold-starring the strategies that elevated brain function *and* benefited the rest of the body, too. And in what really shouldn't have come as much of a surprise, I found that my independent conclusions about foods that help keep a human brain healthy were remarkably similar to Buettner's dietary findings on living a long life. In so many ways, the answer had been right in front of me the whole time: plants.

Chapter Cheat Sheet:
WHY PLANTS?

Enhancing your diet is one of the easiest ways to beneficially change your brain.

- Build better cognition through the Three Ps, by Priming your brain cells' capacity to function, Protecting your brain from atrophying, and promoting brain Plasticity (the brain's ability to adapt to change).

- Focus on a diet that will enhance the health of your *whole* body, which will result in better brain performance.

- Say yes to a more plant-based, whole-foods diet (your brain certainly will!).

CHAPTER 3

Fueling Your Brain

Having good health is very different from simply not being sick.
—SENECA THE YOUNGER, Roman stoic philosopher

Although the study of how nutrition affects your brain and behavior is still relatively new (and most data in this field stems from animal, not human, studies), the quality of the foods you choose to eat and the dietary patterns you follow overall will always outweigh any subjective "optimization" of a single nutrient or group of nutrients. That's why, with this "qualitarian" food approach in mind, the key to boosting your brainpower really comes down to one simple guideline:

A diet that supports a healthy brain includes some fat, some protein, less sugar, and more plants.

While there's a world of wiggle room in that general protocol, its four dietary "smart tools" are what will have the biggest impact on the health of your brain and help you build greater cognitive power in the process.

Smart Tool #1:
EAT SOME FAT

The next time someone tells you you're getting a fat head, take that as a compliment—it could actually mean you're growing a healthier brain! To put it bluntly, your brain really, really loves fat. After you take away the 75 percent water content in your brain, the brain mass itself is 60 percent fat. Therefore, it's absolutely imperative to incorporate both a healthy amount and a variety of lipids (fats) in your diet to enable new brain cells to form properly, maintain the ones you have, and deter aging. Fat is also needed as fuel for basic brain metabolism to perform its various functions. (Although your brain is used to running on glucose, fueling your brain with fat is important for ketosis, a process that operates like a "backup energy generator" for your body and your brain, and is a key secondary component of metabolism after glucose stores have been used up.) Lipids are crucial fats that can encourage specific neurotransmitter activity, which, in turn, can boost learning and memory, facilitate better blood flow for enhanced cognitive activity, and even improve your mood. Fats are also vital to helping your brain synthesize important fat-soluble vitamins, like vitamin A, D, E, and K—all of which are essential for your neurological function and mental health.

But "some fat" definitely doesn't mean it's time to dust off the deep fryer. The benefits of various fats differ widely. The worst fats for your brain—no huge shocker here—are trans fats (more often known as partially hydrogenated vegetable oils). Trans fats are extremely harmful to cognitive function, causing cellular destruction and inflammation, potentially reducing serotonin, and even sabotaging memory.

Saturated fat and cholesterol, on the other hand, which were once high on the "avoid and reduce" list, have been redeemed in some nutritional circles, after nutritionists shunned them for decades because of their adverse effects on heart health. And, upon first glance, they might indeed appear to be valuable for enhancing brain function, as 25 percent of the body's cholesterol is found in the brain and saturated fat is involved in building brain cells. But the cholesterol in your brain is different from the cholesterol in the rest of your body, and you can biologically make as much cholesterol and saturated fat as your brain needs—and likely as much as your entire body needs, too—without consuming it through diet. (This explains why you'll often find normal levels of brain cholesterol in long-time vegans, whose fully plant-based food choices contain no dietary cholesterol at all.) Indeed, elevated levels of dietary saturated fat would seem to be outright detrimental to the brain: In a 2012 Harvard study exploring fat's effect on the brain, more than 6,000 older women had their cognition tested over a period of four years. Dr. Olivia Okereke, assistant professor of psychiatry at Harvard Medical School and lead author of the study published in the *Harvard Health Letter*, found that "Women who had the highest consumption of saturated fat had the worst memory and cognition over time." And while the amount of total fat intake didn't seem to affect women's brain function, the *type* of fat did. Okereke's conclusion was this: "Women with the most monounsaturated fat in their diets—from foods such as olive oil, nuts, or avocado—performed best."

Martha Clare Morris, PhD, a Rush University nutritional epidemiologist, has built her career on similar dietary findings.

But Morris isn't just worried about our ability to ace cognitive tests; rather, her focus is on preventing neurological disease. I was first introduced to Morris's work after reading about her research contributions to the MIND diet—a popular brain-protective dietary approach, created as a cognition-oriented hybrid of the Mediterranean diet and the DASH diet (Dietary Approaches to Stop Hypertension). I became instantly engaged in her work, and not just because we share an excellent surname. Morris has spent decades researching the relationship between food and brain protection, especially in terms of staving off Alzheimer's disease, while prioritizing a whole-body view of the subject. She knows just how big an impact diet can have on brain protection, citing a 53 percent reduction in the risk of developing Alzheimer's disease for people who follow the MIND diet. In a 2015 podcast interview, Morris talked about the importance of fats for a healthy brain, but emphasized that type and quality of those fats are the key factors. "Having a fat composition [in the brain] that is higher in the monounsaturated and poly-unsaturated fats and lower in the saturated fats is the driving force. So, based on that, we listed five food groups to limit: red meat, fast foods, pastries and sweets, butter, and cheese." Many other leading researchers concur: The same detrimental effect saturated fat has on the heart—namely, inflammation—is also responsible for causing problems over the long run for the brain.

Even within the delicious realm of good, plant-based fats, eating a fat-inclusive diet still relies on balance. For example, most neurological experts agree that, outside of a specific treatment protocol, practicing something like a ketogenic diet, which encourages 70 percent caloric fat consumption or more, is far too extreme—and we certainly don't have any kind of broad, long-term studies to confirm its effects on a normal human brain. The concept of eating "some fat," however, gives you permission to be a bit more flexible than you may have been in the past. You'll want to adapt your fat consumption to your own needs and lifestyle, of course, but many experts have found that it is advantageous for your brain to take in about a third of the calories you consume daily from good fats. If you use moderate amounts of desirable oils, such as olive oil, in whole-food cooking, incorporate nuts and seeds frequently into your dishes and snacks, and throw some avocados into your weekly menu, you're probably getting enough fat. (You'll find plenty of food sources for good fats in the chart of Everyday Smart Plants on pages 64–68, as well as in the recipes, starting on page 127.) Overall, you can look at these fats as friends that should be part of most of the meals and snacks you eat, not dietary foes that should be avoided at all costs.

Key Nutrients in Your Quest for Healthy Fats

Omega 3 Fats

Let's just cut to the chase: If we're going to talk about healthy brain nutrients, omega 3 fats, or "omega 3s," as the group is often called, should be at the top of the list. Omega 3s are polyunsaturated fats that are part of a collection of "essential fatty acids." These fats are deemed "essential" because your body can't produce them—they must be acquired from your diet. From a biological standpoint, this leaves us in a rather vulnerable position, because omega 3s have an enormously important role in the function of the brain; they are a crucial component of neurogenesis (the growth of new brain cells) and are needed to protect the neurons and brain tissue you already have. Moreover, all that important fat in your brain is made up of a full third of omega-3 fatty acids alone (of which more than 90 percent is a variety called DHA). Did you catch that? *A third.* That means your total brain tissue is made up of about 20 percent omega 3s (or a third of the 60 percent fat that composes your neural mass)! So it's not a huge stretch to understand why so many studies have shown the benefits of consuming plenty of healthy omega-3 fats to promote brain growth and mental stability.

Reaching for your bag of walnuts yet? Alas, not all omega 3s are created equal. Without drilling too far down into the intricacies of nutrition, there are many different kinds of omegas, and while they're all beneficial to our health in general, only some can be used by our brain. Yes, as it turns out, that mind of yours is pretty picky! Your two main "brain omega-3" varieties are eicosapentaenoic acid (EPA) and docosahexaenoic acid (DHA). Although the USDA has not established an official recommended daily allowance for omega-3 fats, most health professionals recommend that the average person consume between 1 and 2 grams daily, including 250–500 mg of DHA and EPA combined, with a larger ratio of DHA. Surprisingly, despite the crucial nature of this nutrient, the average American only consumes an estimated 100 mg of DHA daily—not even half of what the brain needs.

I'll admit, when I first embarked on my own quest for wellness, in my early 20s, I was strongly convinced that I had omega 3s well covered in the plant-based diet I was following. Nuts, seeds, and even some vegetables are great sources of omega 3s, and in quite high concentrations, too. That's a fact. But plant-based sources—even favorites like hemp seeds and flaxseeds—are composed of a variety of omega 3 called alpha linolenic acid (ALA), about which there is both good and bad news. The good news is that your body can often convert ALA into DHA and EPA. But here's the bad news: Your body's ability to make this conversion effectively is extremely limited. Human trials have shown that, in all likelihood, you'll only be able to convert 9 percent (or even far less, all the way down to 0 percent) of the amount of ALA you ingest through food into EPA and DHA, based on your personal biochemistry. Now, ALA has many other positive functions in the body (it, too, is "essential"), including its contribution to increased cardiovascular health and protection from inflammation. But unless you eat absolutely massive amounts of nuts and seeds daily (an excess which I'm certainly not recommending), just consuming ALA-rich foods alone is probably not enough to protect your brain.

Now for a moment of truth: Although this book centers on plant-based brain foods, it would be truly irresponsible not to talk about fish. While doing interviews for this book, every—and I do mean every—neurological and dietary expert I spoke with (except for the vegans among the group), suggested eating fish for brain health. Fish and other seafood are the most common, concentrated food sources of DHA and EPA, while meats from land-based animals are very distant secondary sources. Nutrition facts don't lie. But they also don't tell the whole story.

Although the experts are right to point out the potent good-fat concentration in fish and other seafood, the sad fact remains that our waters today are not the same waters our ancestors fished from. This means that eating fish on a regular basis comes with its own set of undeniable problems. First, there's the well-documented potential for toxic heavy-metal contamination (such as methyl mercury, which can cause severe neurological disorders). Second, we also need to acknowledge the grave environmental impact that fishing to feed a planet of some 8 billion people has had on the ocean ecosystem. This volume of consumption is in no way sustainable. And speaking of harming the ecosystem, there's a third, even newer, threat: plastics. A 2013 study published by the National Cancer Institute linked large doses of fish oil (more than 3 grams daily) with a marked increase risk of prostate cancer in men. My hunch is that this finding might be just the tip of the iceberg: A 2017 report published in *Scientific Reports* describes how plastic microparticles are often found in the flesh of fish eaten by humans: "Microplastics were suggested to exert their harmful effects by providing a medium to facilitate the transport of other toxic compounds such as heavy metals and persistent organic pollutants to the body of organisms. Upon ingestion, these chemicals may be released and cause toxicity." And it's not just large fish that can cause harm—ingestion of smaller fish can be dangerous to your health as well: "A team of scientists from Malaysia and France discovered a total of 36 tiny pieces of plastic in the bodies of 120 mackerel, anchovies, mullets, and croakers," according to an article by Ian Johnson, who covered the story for *The Independent*, a London-based newspaper. With that information in mind, the safest animal source of DHA/EPA is likely plankton (krill), which are very low on the food chain and usually don't build up large levels of toxicity, like larger fish or land animals.

But wait! There's still one more DHA option on the table, and it appears to be the safest, healthiest, and most sustainable one yet: eating what krill eat—an ever-renewing supply of omega-3-packed algae. Whether you prefer to abstain from eating animals or just want to avoid as many toxins as possible, you can easily take DHA/EPA supplements made from algae (there's a list of brand recommendations on page 265), which have been shown to be just as bioavailable as cooked salmon and will keep the levels of all your brain's favorite omega 3s well-balanced. It's important to note that eating just any kind of algae (like chlorella, for example) won't offer the specific omega benefits you're looking for in this case, however. DHA supplements contain concentrated oil derived from a special type of algae that is grown for its high omega-3 content. Recently, this DHA-rich algal oil has also been infused into some delicious plant-based products, including nondairy milks and juices, and these fortified foods can certainly count toward your daily quota as well! Regardless of its source, getting DHA and EPA into your diet should be a top nutritional priority for the health of your brain.

PLANT FOOD SOURCES OF OMEGA-3 FATS

DHA/EPA: Algal oil (consumed via supplements and fortified foods). (Seaweeds, like nori, kelp, and dulse, also contain extremely small concentrations.) ALA: Hemp seeds/hemp seed oil, chia seeds/chia seed oil, flaxseeds/flaxseed oil, walnuts, pecans, leafy greens (in small concentrations).

Pregnancy Brain

You may have experienced or heard about "pregnancy brain," the bouts of confusion and forgetfulness that can take hold of an expectant mother. Truth be told, a pregnant woman's brain shrinks slightly in volume while a baby is in the womb. Although researchers have not yet determined the exact reason for this phenomenon, some theorize that shrinkage is due to a partial DHA redistribution from the mother's brain to the baby's—for the baby's own brain development. But don't worry about mama—her brain returns to normal size after she gives birth!

Monounsaturated Fats

There are few things that diet gurus can agree upon, but one of them is the importance of consuming monounsaturated fats, which are found in many nuts, seeds, a few fatty fruits (like avocados), and some algae. These fats are famously good for heart health. But they're also quite healthy for your brain, too! Because of their anti-inflammatory properties, monounsaturated fats can help maintain robust neurotransmitter activity (which is why they've been linked to reducing depression), and they strongly support overall neural health. As far as your fat priorities go, monounsaturated fats may be edged out a bit by the importance of omega-3-rich polyunsaturated fats, but the health-giving properties of monounsaturated fats still make them an important part of any brain-boosting diet.

PLANT FOOD SOURCES OF MONOUNSATURATED FATS

Nuts like almonds and macadamia nuts; seeds like sesame seeds and pumpkin seeds; fatty fruits like avocados and olives; and any oil produced from these foods.

Medium-Chain Triglycerides (MCTs)

While you don't "need" medium-chain triglycerides (or MCTs, as they're frequently called), studies indicate they may be very helpful in your quest for a better-functioning brain. Nevertheless, I often think a more suitable meaning for the acronym MCT is *Moderately Choose These*. Here's why.

Although research warns of the negative ramifications of consuming excess saturated fat, it appears that there is one type of saturated fat that has a better reputation: plant-based saturated fat. This subcategory is naturally found in foods like coconut, macadamia nuts, palm kernels, and cacao (chocolate). Unlike animal-based forms of saturated fat, plant-based saturated fats do not appear to cause inflammation, do not contain cholesterol, and, in some cases, may even *improve* overall health. In the case of coconuts, the story deepens even more. "We really should not ever be lumping animal fats and coconut oil together and saying they're both high in saturated fat—they're not the same," Dr. Mary Newport explained to me over the phone on a rainy evening. Dr. Newport is a physician, author, and sought-after speaker on the subject of ketones. Having witnessed firsthand the devastating effects of Alzheimer's in my own family many years ago, I felt a particular kinship with Dr. Newport's books, particularly *Alzheimer's Disease: What If There Was a Cure? The Story of Ketones*, which chronicles her husband's journey with the disease and his positive experiences with using coconut oil as an alternative fuel for the brain.

The saturated fats in coconut are quite complex, as they contain a significant concentration (about 60 percent, Dr. Newport tells me) of MCTs, which is a very rare find in nature. This medium-chain carbon structure of fats makes them quick to digest and easily absorbed by your brain. Indeed, MCTs are digested very differently than most fats: They go directly from the intestines straight to the liver, where they are used as energy or converted into ketones (fat-derived fuel), making them less likely to be stored as fat. Although your brain uses glucose as its main source of fuel, it also uses ketones, when they're available, to ensure that the fuel-hungry engine keeps running.

What's more, one of the MCTs found in coconuts is a special variety known as lauric acid, which appears to be a particularly good provider of ketones for the brain—and you don't even have to be in a state of ketosis (a condition naturally produced by fasting, or through strict carbohydrate restriction and increased fat consumption) to create them. Dr. Newport explains that lauric acid "directly stimulates the production of ketones in the astrocytes, which are brain cells that nourish other brain cells," and adds that "it's possible ketones are being made directly in the brain, stimulated by lauric acid." Aside from weight management, this long-lasting, consistent energy source is one of the biggest benefits

of a ketone-producing, MCT-inclusive diet, helping to provide greater mental stamina and endurance.

These benefits of medium-chain triglycerides are certainly no secret. If you were to cruise through a health food store, judging by the number of product displays alone, you might think that coconut oil (and its MCTs) was here to save the world. Nevertheless, despite all its advantages, coconut oil is not our savior. While the MCTs in coconut oil are certainly beneficial, the oil also contains a large quantity of long-chain triglycerides— the rigid, "heavier" fats that make coconut oil solid at room temperature—and potentially problematic for the body if regularly consumed in large quantities. That's because, while coconut oil does not contain cholesterol itself, it does appear to slightly raise your body's cholesterol levels (mostly the good kind—HDL—but also the bad kind—LDL), prompting some cardiovascular experts to wave yellow caution flags. However, if you are consuming a mostly plant-based diet (with little to no cholesterol), utilizing moderate to small amounts of coconut oil from time to time in cooking should be enough to offer you the ketone-producing MCT benefits your brain appreciates, without negatively impacting your health.

And speaking of cooking, coconut oil is exceptionally useful in the kitchen, too: It's a great oven- and pan-friendly oil, thanks to its high smoke point—meaning that it doesn't easily oxidize from heat and can withstand higher temperatures. If you want to avoid the cholesterol issue even further, consider using MCT oil, a coconut-derived oil that is processed to include an even higher concentration of MCTs than standard coconut oil (and therefore contains considerably fewer "bad" long-chain fatty acids than the regular variety). While there's not much research at this time to support its tremendous popularity as an intelligence "booster," the MCT fats in coconut oil do appear to help with brain energy. Unless you are using it for a particular treatment or under a doctor's care, there's no need to take this type of fat as a supplement, but you should feel free to use it in small quantities as a "best of" in the category of saturated fats and as a useful addition to your cognition-focused kitchen.

PLANT FOOD SOURCES OF MCTS

Coconuts and coconut oil, MCT oil. (Palm oil is another MCT source but is associated with severe environmental impacts, like the deforestation of rainforests.)

Smart Tool #2:
EAT SOME PROTEIN

Protein plays an essential role in keeping your brain functioning at its best, boosting neurological activity as a whole, and helping the chemical messengers in your brain work smoothly so you can enjoy focused attention, balanced mood, reliable memory, and sharp cognition.

But, believe it or not, if you're like most North Americans, it's very likely you are already eating enough protein—and possibly even far more than you need. The USDA recommends that the average person should consume only about 12 percent of daily calories from protein (an amount still higher than what most of the world consumes), which amounts to approximately 56 grams for men and 46 grams for women. While you may need to slide this number up or down a bit, based on your individual lifestyle and health needs, the important thing to remember is that, to your brain, the quantity of protein is less important than the *quality* and the *source*. Your brain's main concerns are which amino acids you're consuming and how easily it can access them. Now, I don't know about you, but as a child of the "protein boost" era, I am prone to nagging concerns about "getting enough protein." So I turned to several experts on the subject to get further clarification. After all, if some amino acids are good for neurotransmitter activity, wouldn't more be better? (Spoiler alert: Not even close.)

Even over a tinny-sounding speakerphone, Ray Cronise is loquacious and convincing. A former NASA scientist, Ray is well-known for his groundbreaking weight-loss techniques. These days, he has turned his attention to the fascinating study of longevity and its relationship to nutrition and metabolism. After speaking to me about his 2014 published medical paper, "The Metabolic Winter Hypothesis," which explores how human beings are designed to eat—and how not to eat—Ray drives the point home: "Starting at the cellular level, there is a particular coincidence of when we are exposed to mild cold stress versus what happens during dietary restriction. The only science we have in health span and longevity increasingly suggests less is more. Every biological system that you can think of follows this pattern."

Ray's partner, Julieanna Hever, agrees. A renowned dietitian and the author of several peer-reviewed articles and books, including *Plant-Based Nutrition,* second edition (Idiots Guide, 2018), Julieanna has helped thousands of clients and readers become healthier by switching to a plant-based diet. Together with Ray, she has even created a helpful system called the "Food Triangle" to simplify the concept of consuming nutrient-dense, plant-based foods. In a separate conversation, Julieanna mirrored Ray's conclusion: "If you're talking about living longer, you're talking about eating less—eating fewer amino acids and fewer calories."

Although it may seem initially counterintuitive, it turns out that the "less is more" approach doesn't just help you live longer—it can help you live smarter, too. Fasting has been shown to boost the production of brain-derived neurotropic factor (BDNF)—a compound that's basically like fertilizer for your brain cells—which increases neuroplasticity. Even short periods of caloric restriction or intermittent fasting (a type of fasting that limits the number of hours during the day in which you consume food) has been shown to have profound effects on neurogenesis, with one study on fasting reporting an increase of neuron growth in the brain between 50 percent and 400 percent.

Without question, these scientific findings have exciting implications for proactively building the brain and boosting its function. Nevertheless, the truth remains that, for most of us, dietary restriction is extremely difficult to implement—so much so that many of the individuals who study caloric restriction rarely practice it in their own lives. So if a future of swapping out meals with nothing but water, from time to time, doesn't sound particularly attractive, it may interest you to know there *is* something else that mimics the helpful effects of fasting surprisingly well: protein—or more specifically, *eating less of it.*

Remarkably, scientists have recently discovered that many of the benefits of fasting may not come from the restriction of calories but, rather, from the restriction of protein. In 2012, a comprehensive meta-analysis of dietary restriction, published in the peer-reviewed scientific journal *Aging Cell*, statistically analyzed the combined results of multiple scientific studies on many species. "Surprisingly," the authors wrote, "the proportion of protein intake was more important for life extension via [dietary restriction] than the degree of caloric restriction."

In 2013, another scientific report in *Biochemical Journal* expanded on the findings reported in *Aging Cell*, stating, "In mammals, reduced dietary protein and essential amino acid intake can extend longevity, improve metabolic fitness, and increase stress resistance." (Note: Researchers do not recommend that people who are 65 and older reduce protein intake because they are more prone to muscle wasting.)

We know that protein is absolutely essential to life and to the brain—so why would we want to eat less of it? Dr. Michael Greger, author of *How Not to Die* and the founder of Nutritionfacts.org, explains that much of the "protein-longevity" phenomenon boils down to reducing certain amino acids more than others—leucine, in particular. Leucine is an amino acid that is most concentrated in animal-based protein, and some research has shown that there is a connection between a diet that is low in leucine and a reduction of two biological processes that lead to aging and cancer. Based on these findings, it's quite plausible to connect a low leucine level with factors that contribute to the high life expectancy of the vegetarian-leaning, lower-protein consuming Blue Zones populations. (The diet of the long-living Okinawans, for example, includes only a 10 percent protein intake.) One might also conclude that lower levels of certain amino acids may actually promote an anti-aging environment in the brain, too.

In short, when it comes to protein, more is not better—"some" is just enough. And by leaning on various plant-based proteins to enjoy a full spectrum of essential amino acids, you can confidently set the stage to live long and think well.

Key Amino Acids for Your Brain-Boosting Diet

There are more than 50 kinds of amino acids we are aware of, but only 20 are used to make the proteins in your body. Of these 20, just

9 are considered "essential," meaning that your body cannot produce them on its own and you must consume them through your diet. While many amino acids are involved in specific functions of the brain, here are three of the most common amino acids used for cognitive enhancement.

Tryptophan

Although tryptophan is commonly thought to cause sleepiness after a big Thanksgiving meal (which turns out to be highly unlikely; eating too much of your favorite pie is probably the reason for any sluggishness), it is a major essential amino acid that plays a very important role in our day-to-day lives: It's the precursor to serotonin. (When tryptophan is consumed, your body turns it into 5-Hydroxytryptophan [5-Htp] and then into serotonin.) Consistent with the effects of serotonin on your well-being, adequate levels of tryptophan can positively alter your mood and alertness, as well as lower aggression, pain sensitivity, and depression. And, yes, tryptophan can even help you sleep better. Of course, just consuming "more" of this amino acid alone won't instantly turn up the volume on bliss, and you'll likely only feel a difference if you were previously deficient in it. Nevertheless, ensuring that your body has a good supply of tryptophan means that when a positive situation in life does arise, you'll have all the tools you need to experience a "feel-good" response.

PLANT FOOD SOURCES OF TRYPTOPHAN

Seeds and nuts (especially walnuts), beans and legumes (particularly soy-based foods and white beans), mushrooms, asparagus, and cauliflower.

Tyrosine

Tyrosine is a behavior-influencing champ— the precursor of three major neurotransmitters: norepinephrine, epinephrine, and dopamine. Although it is not considered an essential amino acid (your body can synthesize it from another amino acid, phenylalanine), some research has indicated that consuming some tyrosine via diet is likely needed, as your brain can't harvest quite enough of it just from your own synthesized version. And since norepinephrine is such an important neurotransmitter in times of stress, science suggests that adequate levels of tyrosine can also help you respond to excitatory conditions more effectively and perform tasks that require attention and learning with greater ease.

PLANT FOOD SOURCES OF TYROSINE

Seeds and nuts (especially pumpkin seeds), beans and legumes (particularly soybeans and lentils), pseudo-grains and whole grains (especially oats).

Theanine

Think of theanine as a "calming amino acid." Theanine counteracts anxiety and promotes relaxation by boosting the levels of GABA and other relaxant chemicals in the brain. In fact, theanine is so effective at calming the nervous system, it's sometimes used in clinical practices to treat behavioral disorders, including anxiety, panic, obsessive-compulsive disorder (OCD), bipolar disorder, and schizophrenia.

But as relaxing as it may be, theanine can simultaneously increase your attention span and reaction time, too, rather than make you feel sleepy. If you consume a lot of coffee or caffeine, you may want to consider upping your theanine game, as well, because the two compounds are very synergistic: Theanine can help balance out some of the less than desirable effects of caffeine, such as jitteriness, while caffeine can add a focused edge to the calming aspects of theanine. And if you'd like to experience the caffeine-theanine combination naturally, just drink tea, which offers a small boost of caffeine along with nature's richest source of theanine. (We'll dig a little deeper into this special tea-based relationship in chapter 6.) Although theanine is a nonessential amino acid, it may be worth seeking it out on occasion to gain the additional brain-friendly benefits it confers.

PLANT FOOD SOURCES OF THEANINE

Tea leaves (black, green, and white varieties).

Smart Tool #3:
EAT LESS SUGAR

From a survival standpoint we—along with most animals—are impelled to seek sugary foods as a quick source of calories. It makes sense: Sugar and carbohydrates are easily digested into glucose, which is used by every cell in the body, with our brains claiming about half the bounty.

In an *On the Brain* article, published by Harvard Medical School; Vera Novak, MD, PhD, and an HMS associate professor of medicine at Beth Israel Deaconess Medical Center, wrote, "The brain is dependent on sugar as its main fuel. It cannot be without it." In other words, it's not weird to crave cookies. . . . You're *wired* to crave them.

Of course, thanks to effective sugar refinement processes and the ubiquitous inclusion of sugar in the foods we eat, we've drifted far away from nature's original sweet offerings, such as apples, berries, and carrots. I'm sure I don't need to tell you how high our sugar consumption has risen over the years, but it may not be apparent by just how much: At the time of the American Revolution, sugar consumption was about 4 pounds per person, per year. These days, it's closer to *160 pounds per person, per year*, and that number is still rising (according to Michael Greger, MD, FACLM, in an article published by NutritionFacts.org in 2016). This means that, every year, each of us is eating the equivalent of the average person's body weight—*in sugar*!

To quote Dr. Obvious, what was once a survival tool is now a full-blown addiction. Research suggests that overconsumption of sugar looks very similar to the effects of drug addiction on a brain scan, and the compromised dopaminergic system in obese individuals may appear similar to that found in cocaine addicts and alcoholics. The medical community now loudly warns that sugar is destroying us, rather than helping us survive, as it once did, and our overconsumption of the sweet stuff can lead to deterioration of the brain in a shocking number of ways. High quantities of various forms of sugar have been shown to speed up the aging of cells, negatively impact neurotransmitter activity, change gene expression (a process that ultimately dictates how a cell responds to its environment), and cause a multitude of cognitive deficiencies and memory problems. Simply put, a sugar-saturated diet will mess with your capacity to concentrate and learn, screw with your mood, and get in the way of your ability

to maintain healthy brain cells and make new ones. If you've ever experienced a bout of brain fog after a sweet meal or snack, now you know which s-word to use.

Excess sugar intake is also a well-known cause of diabetes, a disease that can have myriad harmful consequences for the brain. High blood glucose can affect the functional connectivity of neurons, spur brain atrophy (shrinkage), and lead to restricted blood flow to the brain, causing cognitive difficulties and even potentially triggering the onset of dementia. Additionally, sugar is a direct cause of inflammation in the body, as well as on the blood-brain barrier and in the brain itself. High amounts of inflammation disrupt the normal production of neurotransmitters, like serotonin and glutamine, and leave the brain and body exposed to infection and autoimmune diseases.

So how could something so important—something that your brain unequivocally "needs"—also be so harmful? Just as it is with fat and protein, the answer can be summed up like this: source and quantity.

Saying "all sugar is equal" is a bit like saying there's no difference between a wallet and a wallet filled with money. That's why the rich dietary "wallets" we seek should be whole, plant-based foods, which are the best sources of naturally-occurring sugar for your brain— the ones with the greatest "spending power" per calorie. Excellent options include fruits, roots, starchy vegetables, and whole grains, all of which are less saturated forms of sugar that offer a wealth of benefits at the same time. In addition to valuable micronutrients, like vitamins and minerals, the dietary sugar in whole foods also comes packed with fiber, which improves the health of your gut, slows down the release of sugar into the bloodstream, and actually uses up much of the sugar found in food simply for metabolism! This is the kind of sugar your brain was designed to consume and thrive on.

Condensed forms of sugar, like cane sugar, as well as various types of syrups, including honey, are examples of a sad, nutritionally empty "wallet" (the equivalent of mere pennies in the nutritional change jar), and should be consciously limited. In addition to obvious high-sugar foods, like pastries and sugary sodas, it's also important to be wary of packaged consumer goods, such as salad dressing, sauces, and other processed foods, which are sometimes sources of added sugar that sneakily bump up your daily quota.

When you're cooking foods that absolutely demand something sweet (or when you're just craving a treat!), try to use less processed, more natural sources like coconut sugar or maple syrup—which, at least, contain a few trace nutrients. This way you get a little nutritional bang for your buck, even if that bang is admittedly small. To help reduce your sugar intake overall, I suggest using naturally sourced, sugar-free sweeteners like stevia and monk fruit as replacements whenever you can.

As for the total quantity of sugar you should consume, the American Heart Association currently recommends no more than 9 teaspoons (36 grams) a day for men and 6 teaspoons (25 grams) a day for women—of *added* sugars. Seeing these numbers, many people become alarmed, thinking that a "binge" of two bananas will topple them over their daily sugar budget. But fear not: By specifying "added" sugars, the AHA isn't demonizing fruit. Instead, the AHA is referring to *sugar concentrates only*. So eat the banana but keep the consumption of pancake syrup to a minimum.

Any diet will benefit from a reduction in refined carbohydrates. But make no mistake: Your brain does need some natural sugars for fuel, along with other nutrients found in carbohydrate-rich whole foods, for the repair and maintenance of brain cells. The trick is to choose whole foods—whole grains, whole fruits, whole vegetables, and the like—and pair them with healthy fats and proteins for balance. If you're craving sweets, choose lower-sugar foods and enjoy them as a treat, keeping the AHA recommendations in mind. Moderation always wins, but in the case of sugar, when in doubt, err on the side of a little "less."

PLANT FOOD SOURCES OF SUGARS

GOOD SUGAR SOURCES: Fresh fruits, roots, starchy vegetables and tubers, and whole grains. (Pure, fresh fruit juice and no-sugar-added dried fruit are certainly much healthier options than juices and dried fruit that contain added sugars, but their sugar content is still relatively high; use them in small amounts.).

HELPFUL SUGAR-FREE NATURAL SWEETENERS: Stevia, monk fruit, and erythritol.

SUGARS TO LIMIT: Fruit juice concentrates, agave syrup, maple syrup/maple sugar, coconut syrup/coconut sugar, raw sugar, honey, and molasses.

SUGARS TO AVOID: High-fructose corn syrup, cane sugar, cane juice, and corn sweetener.

ALSO AVOID: All artificial sugar-free sweeteners, such as aspartame and sucralose, which can cause a variety of health problems, including an increased risk of cancer.

Smart Tool #4:
EAT MORE PLANTS

As a superfood chef, I've spent the majority of my career speaking about the virtues of "functional foods"—foods that offer your body a plethora of health advantages in every bite—and developing recipes that maximize both the flavor *and* the benefits. It's a simple concept, and yet every part of this food methodology applies directly to building a healthier, fitter brain, too.

We know the human brain is hungry and utilizes more energy than any other organ in the body. But it's not just calories that your brain craves—it's micronutrients. Take away all the water and fat in your brain, and what's left is a cellular mass that is either composed of, or wholly dependent on, micronutrients

to function. While your body can make some micronutrients on its own, many of them must be regularly supplied by your diet to help your neurons function and communicate properly, maintain the health of your existing neural cells and prevent decay, and build and strengthen new cells and inner-brain connections. In other words, these micronutrients play a critical role in helping to Prime, Protect, and promote Plasticity in your brain—the Three Ps of brain optimization discussed in chapter 2, page 21. In addition, micronutrients support keeping the rest of your body in good condition and enhance overall longevity, too—undoubtedly a secondary means of supporting brain health. The very reason that plants are so valuable to your health boils down to their impressive micronutrient saturation: a concept known as nutrient density.

The Value of Nutrient Density

While I've spoken at length about nutrient density in *Superfood Kitchen* and other books I've written on superfoods, this concise indicator of food quality is so vital that it bears repeating here. Nutrient density is the ratio of micronutrients per calorie in food. Vitamins, minerals, antioxidants, and phytochemicals (beneficial plant-based chemicals) all fit into the category of micronutrients, and while these elements are only needed in small quantities, every cell in your body is in constant need of them to function optimally.

A sufficient amount of macronutrients—the fat, protein, and carbohydrates you need to feed your brain—is easily obtained if you eat enough calories every day. And as important as this "macro" category of nutrition is for the brain, it only supplies a rudimentary level of nutrition, one that can be maintained relatively easily if you eat enough calories, and with little effort.

On the other hand, it's not so simple to get adequate amounts of micronutrients. Their world is vastly more complex—mainly because there are so many of them—and they are each responsible for hundreds of different body functions. Although micronutrients are often lacking in the standard North American diet, ideally they can and should come primarily from the food you eat. (While dietary supplements are helpful in addressing particular health concerns, they should not be used as a replacement for the layered benefits of good food choices overall.) I know of no better models of natural nutrient density than plants—vegetables, fruits, mushrooms, herbs, spices, nuts, seeds, legumes, and even some whole grains. Animal-derived foods provide micronutrients as well, but they are typically less nutrient dense than most plants, due to their higher calorie content. And while there is no such thing as a perfect food, most edible plants offer tremendously generous net benefits to every cell in your body. In other words, your brain absolutely loves the saturated nutrients found in plant-based whole foods, so it is smart, on every level, to incorporate them in your diet whenever and wherever you can.

The truth is, if you're looking for just one dietary tip that can exponentially improve your wellness, energy, longevity, and most certainly your brain function, it is simply this: *Eat more plants*. There is no higher priority than this! A diet rich in a variety of "more plants"—and particularly vegetables—offers diverse, protective micronutrients that can build a healthy brain like no other type of food. So while there are countless tweaks and nuances to creating a perfect diet just for you and your personal set of needs and circumstances, simply getting more plants onto your plate is one of the very best things you can do to feel and truly be more vital, from your head to your toes.

Nutrition is a profoundly complex science, but the process of keeping your body healthy and your brain happy doesn't have to be, especially when you discover how easy it is to source the most available brain-boosting micronutrients—just from the food on your plate.

Key Food Rules in Your Quest for Nutrient-Dense Foods

1. **Eat green as much as possible.** Leafy greens are the king of the vegetable world when it comes to nutrient density, and they're lauded the most for their positive effects on brain health and protection. Try to get in at least 1–2 servings a day (or more): Kale, spinach, broccoli, and dark lettuces are all superb sources of the nutrient density your brain loves.

2. **Variety is important.** The mix of nutrients in every plant is unique and nuanced, and your job is to incorporate as many of them as possible into your diet. This doesn't mean that you have to make a salad with 20 ingredients. But it does imply that eating several different types of plants a day, and rotating your choices from meal to meal, is beneficial. So give a big yes to lots of vegetables, some fruits, good grains, healthy mushrooms, satiating nuts and seeds, hearty legumes, and more. There are three simple ways to incorporate variety: Include at least two to three colors on every plate, eat seasonally, and aim to "try something new" at least once a month.

3. **Keep it whole.** Whole foods naturally offer the diversity of nutrition on which your body is designed to thrive. Avoid processed foods, which are filled with ingredients that can create or exacerbate health imbalances. Making your own meals is one of the best ways to ensure that every bit of food that goes onto your plate and into your body has a purpose; the simple recipes in this book can certainly be a useful step to help you achieve that goal.

FUELING YOUR BRAIN

When it comes to brain health, the quality of the food you consume and your eating patterns overall will outweigh any single dietary hack. That's why the "smart tools" in this chapter are merely guidelines: A diet that supports a healthy brain includes some fat, some protein, not much sugar, and lots of plants.

- Regularly consume moderate amounts of monounsaturated fats, omega-3 fats (especially DHA and EPA), and even small amounts of plant-based saturated fats to nourish and energize neurons.

- Keep your dietary protein plant-based as much as possible. Consuming moderate—but not large—amounts of protein overall (around 10–12 percent of calories) will provide your brain with important amino acids, while also promoting longevity.

- To ensure greater cognitive productivity, minimize your consumption of refined sugar and rely on whole fruits or natural sugar-free sweeteners like stevia whenever you crave something sweet.

- Focus on eating more plants—especially vegetables—to glean their vast and varied micronutrients.

CHAPTER 4

The Power of Micronutrients

*"Every day of our lives, we are on the verge of making
those slight changes that would make all the difference."*

—MIGNON MCLAUGHLIN, American journalist and author

Buzzwords. That's what the natural food industry uses to call attention to the nutrients they slap on their packaging to entice you to buy their products. These buzzwords change almost as quickly as trends in fashion: Products that were once labeled "gluten-free" and "with vitamin C" a couple years ago may now be emblazoned with "protein-infused," "with 10 million probiotics," and "a good source of omega 3s." For the most part, the nutritional features brands love to brag about are favorable: They promote the health-giving advantages of their products. And, as consumers, we're apt to feel positive about a company that has taken extra steps to create a product that will benefit our health, even if the motive for taking those steps may have more to do with increasing profits than any real concern about our well-being. But this kind of marketing can also prompt distorted thinking about nutrition, leading consumers to believe that taking in only certain kinds of nutrients is the end game of a healthy diet or that consuming one "good" nutrient will compensate for a poor diet overall.

On the contrary, we are very complex organisms, and there is no single nutrient or group of nutrients in any given product or food that will give us everything we need to be healthy from the top down. So when we talk about a few of the micronutrients that are important for brain health, it's good to file the information under "valuable guidelines for optimizing cognition." But you should also take that information with a figurative grain of salt, as there's certainly more to your health as a whole than consuming a bunch of nutrients that might be particularly good for your brain.

Even so, current research into the brain's nutritional demands indicates that there *are* specific micronutrients that truly offer broad benefits to brain health. Gaining an understanding of those micronutrients—and how best to access them—can have a direct impact on the dietary choices you make, too. If you buy micronutrients as supplements, you will certainly be taking a favorable stride toward supporting the health of your brain. However, if you consume the same micronutrients through a whole food diet, you'll not only gain the health advantages of those specific micronutrients, you'll also benefit from *all the other* nutrients in foods that can make your health gains even greater. Either way, optimizing your micronutrient intake will significantly upgrade the quality of your life and benefit both your mind and body. Or, to put it in completely unscientific terms, you'll simply *feel really good*.

Let's take a look at some brain-healthy micronutrients that can help make your food choices all the wiser.

MAGNESIUM

Your entire body loves magnesium. This ubiquitous mineral is involved in more than 300 of your body's reactions and functions, and your brain's reliance on magnesium is high on that list. Magnesium is considered neuroprotective on several levels, particularly for its role in helping to prevent excitotoxicity—a condition where neurons are damaged and killed by overactive excitatory neurotransmitters. The impact of magnesium on diminishing excitotoxicity is also believed to be the reason that it appears to reduce brain damage sustained during a stroke, and, in cases of hypertension (high blood pressure), it may even help prevent the stroke from occurring in the first place.

Magnesium also slows down the body's stress response by reducing the secretion of stress hormones like cortisol and diminishing the extent to which they can negatively impact the brain. One of the most tangible benefits of magnesium is the affect it has on helping us to simply relax. This is why taking a bath with Epsom salts is so helpful in unwinding both your muscles *and* your mind, as the high magnesium levels in the salts become absorbed through your body's biggest organ—your skin. Magnesium also acts as an excellent sleep aid and antianxiety mineral, and there is even a strong correlation between magnesium levels and serotonin levels (low magnesium is very clearly linked with low serotonin). Consequently,

Magnesium, Meet Stress. Stress, Meet Magnesium.

Because magnesium is a "cofactor nutrient" (a nutrient that functions like a key that can open a "door" to certain kinds of biochemical reactions), magnesium deficiencies can cause a host of neurological problems, such as anxiety and sleep disorders. Deficiencies of this nutrient are surprisingly common and mostly due to poor diet. But now there's another culprit: stress. Stress triggers your internal fight-or-flight response and this reaction consumes lots of magnesium. So, *chronic* bouts of stress can seriously deplete your magnesium stores over time. These days, even if it's not a grizzly bear popping out of a bush that provokes a fight-or-flight response but instead the dread of an overscheduled week on a Sunday night, the biological result is the same: The magnesium in your body is used, excreted, and lost.

The relationship between stress and low levels of magnesium can form a vicious cycle over time and lead to chronic problems with anxiety, which causes more stress. Therefore, regularly incorporating magnesium-rich foods into your diet (or taking a supplement for an immediate boost) can be a very helpful way to get out of a stress-induced rut . . . and stay out of it.

---

magnesium therapy has now joined the ranks of antidepressant treatments.

Although magnesium supplements and topical applications are helpful, you should try to get as much magnesium as possible from your diet, because in food the magnesium is often naturally bound with synergistic vitamins and minerals that are essential to its proper absorption and vice versa. And the good news is that nature has you well covered: Plant-based foods are absolutely brimming with this important mineral.

PLANT FOOD SOURCES OF MAGNESIUM

Tofu and soy products, leafy green vegetables, nuts and seeds, dark chocolate/cacao, legumes, whole grains, and seaweeds.

Note: Phytates, naturally occurring compounds in legumes and grains, can partially inhibit the process of magnesium absorption, so if you need to maximize your magnesium gains, aim to reduce phytates by soaking beans very well before cooking them and enjoy sprouted grains, more than regular grains, whenever possible.

More Minerals for Your Brain

While it's easy to get caught up in the importance of magnesium to the health of your brain, the truth is it takes a wide range of minerals to keep it functioning well, and too little of any essential mineral will compromise your mental performance. This is yet another reason to eat whole foods that contain a broad array of micronutrients, rather than relying on isolated supplements. (And it's a mental challenge in itself to imagine just how to balance all those pills!) Here are a few other minerals that, together with magnesium, can also help make your brain happy:

- Calcium
- Copper
- Iron
- Iodine
- Manganese
- Potassium
- Selenium
- Zinc

You can find these minerals in many different kinds of plant foods—like nuts and seeds, legumes, vegetables and fruits, and even in some grains. For a great mineral-oriented "multivitamin" food, try seaweeds, such as nori or dulse, which offer a vast array of minerals that your brain will gladly soak up.

VITAMIN D

Vitamin D plays many roles, but in terms of brain health, it acts as an anti-inflammatory agent that helps the brain heal and regenerate. There are two main varieties of D used by the body: vitamin D_2 and vitamin D_3. Dietitians disagree on whether or not D_2 can be digested properly by your body, which is why D_3 is considered the "preferred" variety. Because vitamin D is actually more closely related to a steroid hormone than a vitamin, your body prefers to fill its vitamin D needs through an unusual source: the sun. Sunlight causes a biochemical reaction with your skin, synthesizing the light and producing vitamin D_3

in your body—a biological marker that certainly indicates the importance of regular sun exposure for human health. Consequently, it shouldn't be much of a surprise that vitamin D_3 and moderate sun exposure have long been linked, both scientifically and anecdotally, to a balanced mood.

Of course, in the conversation about vitamin D and exposure to the sun, skin cancer is an understandable concern, but it needn't be: A mere twenty-minute dose of sunshine on a small area of "unprotected" skin a day should be enough to maintain healthy levels of vitamin D_3 without increasing the risk of cancer. And if you're worried about getting enough sun in the winter for an adequate vitamin D_3 dose, you may feel better knowing that if you attain adequate sun exposure during warmer, sunnier months, you should be able to store enough vitamin D in your body fat to make it through a winter sunshine "fast." Your body is very smart!

As important as it is, vitamin D_3 appears to be a common deficiency for many people these days, regardless of their dietary preferences. Very few food sources contain vitamin D_3, and traditionally it has been thought that these foods are limited to animal sources (particularly fish). Today, we are just beginning to understand that there are plant-based sources of vitamin D_3, such as certain algae (which is where fish get their vitamin D_3 from) and possibly in the Solanaceae plant family, which includes nightshades like tomatoes, potatoes, and peppers (although significantly more research is needed on this topic—so don't brag about your D-infused baked potato just yet). You can also use a plant-based D_3 supplement, if you're concerned about not getting enough sun and want to avoid animal products. If you do go the supplement route, consider pairing it with vitamin K_2, a synergistic nutrient.

PLANT FOOD SOURCES OF VITAMIN D

We don't have solid confirmation that plants contain vitamin D_3, except for some types of algae. Vitamin D_2 is naturally present in mushrooms, and you'll also find it in plant-based foods that are intentionally fortified with vitamin D_2 (such as orange juice). Some plant-based foods are also fortified with vitamin D_3, such as protein powders and nondairy milks.

CHOLINE

Most drug companies can only dream of making claims for their products like "boosts overall brain function," "helps retain memory," "optimizes motor control," and "eases anxiety." But these claims *can* be made by choline, a naturally-occurring micronutrient. Needless to say, choline is crucial for brain function.

Choline is not a drug, or even a vitamin or a mineral, for that matter; it is simply considered a "vitamin-like" essential nutrient. Since choline is water-soluble (your body can't store it well) and essential (your body can't produce it on its own), regular amounts of choline are required from your diet.

Part of what makes choline so brain protective has to do with its relationship to fat. As mentioned previously, your brain is largely made up of lipids (fats). Choline plays a critical part in helping to build as well as maintain healthy lipid levels in your brain. Choline is also vital for the production of acetylcholine, the neurotransmitter that ensures smooth communication between neurons and acts as an antiaging agent for the brain. The choline-acetylcholine connection also explains why choline is directly linked to enhanced memory, an increased ability to learn, and overall neurotransmitter maintenance. Choline plays a key role in methylation, too, a process that is used to create DNA, activate nerve signaling, and carry out overall detoxification. I know

what you're likely thinking, and I fully agree: That's a lot of roles for one micronutrient to play in the health of your brain.

Before you run off on a choline-seeking journey, here's a quick tip: Folate, a B vitamin, helps control how much choline your body can absorb from the foods you eat. So now you have yet another reason to load up on folate-packed leafy green vegetables while you enjoy choline-infused meals.

PLANT FOOD SOURCES OF CHOLINE

Cruciferous vegetables, such as cauliflower, broccoli, and Brussels sprouts; beans, such as garbanzo beans and navy beans; legumes, such as split peas and lentils; and nuts and seeds, like pistachios, cashews, and flaxseeds. (Organic soy lecithin and sunflower lecithin, an easy-to-add supplement for smoothies and sauces—is a highly saturated source of naturally-occurring choline.)

B VITAMINS

In 2010, the results of a game-changing, two-year-long study in England were revealed. The study involved a group of elderly individuals suffering from "mild cognitive impairment"—a condition considered to be a major risk factor for degenerative neurological diseases, like dementia and Alzheimer's. The study's findings were astounding: The

patients who supplemented their diets with large quantities of B vitamins were able to cut their initial rate of brain shrinkage *by half*. (Yes, the same kind of B vitamins that are so abundantly found in all kinds of vegetables, nuts, and fruits!) And in 2015, a second two-year-long study took place in Oxford, again supplementing the patients' diet with extra

B vitamins, while also boosting it with additional omega 3s. With this new combination, the study found that brain atrophy slowed by *70 percent* in patients suffering from memory decline. In the exuberant words of David Smith, the Oxford professor who led the study, "This is a very exciting and important result. It is the first treatment to show Alzheimer's-related brain shrinkage can be prevented. It means that something so simple as keeping your omega-3 levels high and supplementing B vitamins if you are at risk could dramatically reduce a person's risk."

While researchers stop short of claiming that B vitamins are a "cure" for neurological diseases, I'll be a little more bullish about both the ramifications of including too few B vitamins in your diet and the advantages of consuming them on a regular basis: If you have an ongoing B vitamin deficiency, you will not enjoy optimal neurological function, plain and simple. A long-term deficiency of any of the Bs can even cause debilitating neurological disorders, ranging from dementia to Wernicke-Korsakoff syndrome (severe memory loss and confusion). I'm not citing this as a scare tactic, as early-stage deficiencies of B vitamins are easily remedied and even some damage can be reversed. Still, I do hope you'll be motivated to take stock of your current B vitamin intake, because getting an adequate amount of these vitamins is not "just" about

managing potential health hazards. Quite simply, balancing your Bs can help you obtain a more powerful brain on a number of levels.

The term *B vitamins* actually refers to a large number of vitamins, all of which are on the brain's "required" nutrient checklist for day-to-day functioning. B vitamins are water-soluble, which, for the most part, means that they are not stored in your body (unlike fat-soluble vitamins like vitamin D, for example) and are constantly flushed away, as your body has nowhere to store them for later use. As a result, you need to consistently replenish your stores of these vitamins, through diet or supplementation, to ensure that your body is regularly on what you might call a "nutrient drip" of B vitamins.

Here is a snapshot of the B vitamin family and a look at the many important roles it plays in supporting and maintaining the health of your brain.

THIAMINE (VITAMIN B_1): Thiamine is critical for brain metabolism as well as the production of acetylcholine (the neurotransmitter that helps promote motivation, focus, memory, and more). The bad news about thiamine is that it's only stored in your body for about 14 days—and deficiencies can result in irritability, confusion, and memory problems—so you need to be sure to get a regular supply into your system.

Plant Food Sources of Thiamine

Thiamine is fairly abundant in many whole foods and can be found in legumes, like lentils and peas; seeds, including sunflower seeds; many vegetables, like cauliflower and spinach; and nutritional yeast.

RIBOFLAVIN (VITAMIN B$_2$): Riboflavin is an absolutely vital component of glutathione synthesis—your brain's main excitatory neurotransmitter. You need to consume riboflavin regularly, as your body doesn't store it well.

Plant Food Sources of Riboflavin

Riboflavin deficiency is quite rare, probably because it's so plentiful in plant-based sources, including leafy green vegetables, mushrooms, quinoa, and almonds.

NIACIN (VITAMIN B$_3$): This vitamin is a potent antioxidant that maintains healthy brain cells and protects them from age-related cognitive decline. Along with choline, niacin is a key component in the production of acetylcholine transmitters and contributes to overall brain "energy," enhancing mental agility and cognition, memory, and neuroplasticity. Your body can synthesize its own niacin from the amino acid tryptophan, but additional niacin in the diet is needed to maintain optimum levels.

Plant Food Sources of Niacin

Many plants contain niacin, such as mushrooms, sweet potatoes, sunflower seeds, avocados, peas, peanuts, peaches, and citrus fruits.

PANTOTHENIC ACID (VITAMIN B$_5$): A critical cofactor in the production of acetylcholine, pantothenic acid is a well-known aid for boosting cognition, as it can enhance memory and recall, concentration, learning, and overall mental clarity. Additionally, vitamin B$_5$ supports the synthesis of fatty acids, is a key part of overall cellular energy and metabolism, and is often referred to as an "anti-stress" vitamin.

Plant Food Sources of Pantothenic Acid

Good plant sources of pantothenic acid are easy to find. They include broccoli, sunflower seeds, avocados, mushrooms, and potatoes.

PYRIDOXINE (VITAMIN B$_6$): Pyridoxine is essential for the production of many neurotransmitters, including serotonin, dopamine, and norepinephrine. A strong tool in fighting depression and anxiety, it also helps your body make melatonin, a key hormone required for quality sleep.

Plant Food Sources of Pyridoxine

You can find an abundance of pyridoxine in foods like garbanzo beans, bananas, potatoes, squash, nuts, and tofu.

BIOTIN (VITAMIN B₇): Biotin may be one of the less important Bs for brain function, but it does play a crucial role in your ability to metabolize the fatty acids that are so vital to your brain.

Plant Food Sources of Biotin

Seeds, nuts, sweet potatoes, and spinach are all good sources of biotin.

INOSITOL (VITAMIN B₈): We don't hear much about inositol, but perhaps we should: This B vitamin can help boost serotonin levels (if needed) by improving serotonin's ability to move between neurons. Known to ease anxiety and promote calm, inositol supports overall neurotransmission (the signals between your neurons) and can also heighten mental stamina and make thoughts flow more easily. Fortunately, your body can produce its own inositol, which disqualifies B₈ as a "true" vitamin (even though it's included in the B family). However, consuming inositol through your diet may offer an enhanced experience of the vitamin's benefits.

Plant Food Sources of Inositol

Inositol is plentiful in leafy green vegetables, citrus fruits, brown rice, and cereal grains.

FOLATE (VITAMIN B₉): Folate (or "folic acid," as it is called in its synthetic form) is well known as the "pregnancy vitamin" because it is needed in large quantities by expectant mothers to support the formation of the fetus's all-important spine and neurological system. That should give you a clear indication of the fundamental importance of folate, and your need for it does not stop in the womb! Folate has a number of functions in your brain, including the manufacture of dopamine, epinephrine, norepinephrine, and serotonin. It also functions as a coenzyme in DNA and RNA synthesis, helps metabolize amino acids, and creates and repairs the important myelin sheath, which protects individual neurons from damage.

Plant Food Sources of Folate

You can easily remember what foods to eat to get enough folate because it is often found in *fol*iage, and green leafy plants, like kale and spinach, are among the densest sources of this B vitamin. You can also obtain folate from legumes, like lentils, and citrus fruits, like oranges.

COBALAMIN (VITAMIN B₁₂): B₁₂ is a little different from the other Bs, as it's not directly related to neurotransmitter production or neurogenesis. However, deficiencies of this vitamin are the most commonly occurring in the B group and can also have a serious cognitive impact, such as brain fog, mental lethargy, poor sleep, lack of motivation, or depression. That's because B₁₂ plays a key role in processing carbohydrates into glucose, your body's main source of fuel, as well as turning fatty acids into energy. Without this crucial vitamin, your brain can't get energy from sugar or fat and literally starves. Needless to say, severe damage can occur.

If you're eating lots of vegetables, legumes, nuts, seeds, and a few grains (such as the ones used in the recipes in this book), you probably don't have to worry too much about getting more dietary support via supplements from B vitamins—*with the exception of vitamin B_{12}*. While a type of B_{12} can be found in a few plant-based foods, like seaweed and fermented foods (such as kimchi), it is delivered in an inactive form; in other words, the B_{12} is in a form that your body is not able to use. That's why, if you are following a fully plant-based diet, dietitians, nutritionists, and brain specialists across the board strongly suggest that you take a supplement of this vitamin, preferably in the form of methylcobalamin, for maximum absorption. And even if you do consume some animal products, like fish or eggs, you may still want to consider supplementing: Your body significantly loses its ability to metabolize B_{12} as you get older, and you will inevitably need to consume increasingly larger amounts of B_{12} to maintain a healthy balance (see page 57 for daily recommended intakes).

The good news is that B_{12} is usually stored in your body much longer than other B vitamins, so a deficiency will not occur overnight, or potentially even for a couple of years. My advice: Don't gamble—take the supplement.

Plant Food Sources of Cobalamin

None confirmed. (Supplement recommended.)

Balancing Versus Boosting

Remember: Consuming B vitamins won't "boost" your neurotransmitters, but it will ensure that your brain's nutritional stockpile is balanced to produce optimal levels of neurotransmitters as you need them. If you currently have a nutritional imbalance, you may experience a positive effect on cognition *just* from consuming more B vitamins. If your Bs are already balanced, continuing to consume them will help you avoid deficiencies and maintain healthy neurological biochemistry.

More Vitamins for Your Brain

In addition to the vitamins we just discussed, there are many other vitamins that play a role in the way your neurotransmitters behave and that influence the health of your brain overall. If you're eating a variety of plant foods, you should have little trouble meeting your daily needs of these:

- Vitamin A
- Vitamin C
- Vitamin E
- Vitamin K

DAILY RECOMMENDED INTAKE FOR BRAIN-FRIENDLY MICRONUTRIENTS

Listed here are the major micronutrients needed for brain health and their daily minimum intake requirements (to avoid deficiencies), as set by the Institute of Medicine. The Linus Pauling Institute's (LPI) recommendations are noted when different. All recommendations are for adults 19 years of age and older and expressed in micrograms (µg), milligrams (mg), or International Units (IU).

Micronutrient	Daily Intake Recommendations	Micronutrient	Daily Intake Recommendations
Vitamin A	Men: 900 µg RAE* Women: 700 µg RAE Pregnancy: 770 µg RAE Breastfeeding: 1,300 µg RAE *Retinol Activity Equivalents	Biotin (Vitamin B_7)	Adults: 30 µg Pregnancy: 30 µg Breastfeeding: 35 µg
		Inositol (Vitamin B_8)	No USDA guidelines currently set
Thiamine (Vitamin B_1)	Men: 1.2 mg Women: 1.1 mg Pregnancy: 1.4 mg Breastfeeding: 1.4 mg	Folate (Vitamin B_9)	Adults: 400 µg DFE* Pregnancy: 600 µg DFE Breastfeeding: 500 µg DFE *Dietary Folate Equivalents
Riboflavin (Vitamin B_2)	Men: 1.3 mg Women: 1.1 mg Pregnancy: 1.4 mg Breastfeeding: 1.6 mg	Cobalamin (Vitamin B_{12})	Adults: 2.4 µg Pregnancy: 2.6 µg Breastfeeding: 2.8 µg **LPI: 100–400 µg from supplements for adults over 50**
Niacin (Vitamin B_3)	Men: 16 mg Women: 14 mg Pregnancy: 18 mg Breastfeeding: 17 mg	Vitamin C	Men: 90 mg (125 mg*) Women: 75 mg (110 mg*) Pregnancy: 85 mg Breastfeeding: 120 mg **LPI: At least 400 mg for all adults** *Smokers
Pantothenic Acid (Vitamin B_5)	Adults: 5 mg Pregnancy: 6 mg Breastfeeding: 7 mg		
Pyridoxine (Vitamin B_6)	Adults: 1.3 mg Pregnancy: 1.9 mg Breastfeeding: 2.0 mg Men over 50: 1.7 mg Women over 50: 1.5 mg	Choline	Men: 550 mg Women: 425 mg Pregnancy: 450 mg Breastfeeding: 550 mg

Micronutrient	Daily Intake Recommendations
Vitamin D	Adults: 600 IU Pregnancy: 600 IU Breastfeeding: 600 IU Adults over 70: 800 IU **LPI: 2,000 IU from supplements for all adults**
Vitamin E	Adults: 22.5 IU Pregnancy: 22.5 IU Breastfeeding: 28.5 IU
Vitamin K	Men: 120 µg Women: 90 µg Pregnancy: 90 µg Breastfeeding: 90 µg
Calcium	Adults: 1,000 mg Pregnancy: 1,000 mg Breastfeeding: 1,000 mg Men over 70: 1,200 mg Women over 50: 1,200 mg
Copper	Adults: 900 µg Pregnancy: 1,000 µg Breastfeeding: 1,300 µg
Iodine	Adults: 150 µg Pregnancy: 220 µg Breastfeeding: 290 µg

Adapted from and reprinted with permission from the Linus Pauling Institute of Oregon State University, accessed in 2019. For more information, visit: lpi.oregonstate.edu/publications/micronutrients-health

Micronutrient	Daily Intake Recommendations
Iron	Men: 8 mg* Women: 18 mg Pregnancy: 27 mg Breastfeeding: 9 mg Adults over 50: 8 mg* *Men and postmenopausal women should avoid taking iron-containing supplements.
Magnesium	Men: 400 mg Men over 30: 420 mg Women: 310 mg Women over 30: 320 mg Pregnancy: 350–360 mg Breastfeeding: 310–320 mg
Manganese	Men: 2.3 mg Women: 1.8 mg Pregnancy: 2.0 mg Breastfeeding: 2.6 mg
Potassium	Adults: 4,700 mg Pregnancy: 4,700 mg Breastfeeding: 5,100 mg
Selenium	Adults: 55 µg Pregnancy: 60 µg Breastfeeding: 70 µg
Zinc	Men: 11 mg Women: 8 mg Pregnancy: 11 mg Breastfeeding: 12 mg

When we analyze our diet as a whole, it's helpful to look at how our eating habits have evolved as a species. I still remember squirming in my high school Latin class when I heard about the affinity ancient Romans had for a substance called "fish paste"—a "recipe" consisting of rotting fish parts that a Roman might leave outside their front door to ferment for a week or two and then enjoy as a spread for bread and vegetables. But the Romans weren't just weird (well, okay, they were a little weird—google *vomitorium* sometime, preferably on an empty stomach). Rather, fermented foods have been a part of the culinary traditions of almost every culture in the world, whether in the form of Indian chutneys, Korean kimchi, German sauerkraut, Chinese soybean curd, or *chicha de jora*, a beer made from corn in Peru. Even ketchup, deeply beloved in the United States, was originally a condiment made from fermented tomatoes. These common recipes may have served as a means of preserving food initially, but they also helped to keep many ancient cultures healthy.

The reason fermented foods have such a strong impact on health is simple: They're a stellar source of naturally-occurring probiotics, the "good" bacteria that help keep your microbiome and your gut (aka your "second brain") balanced. What's more, probiotics aid every aspect of brain vitality by supporting better digestion and absorption of cognition-friendly nutrients in your diet. Probiotics also reduce inflammation by bolstering your immune system, and they support the ability of neurons to communicate efficiently with one another.

In a 2013 study, researchers at UCLA Geffen School of Medicine found that participants in a small test group of 36 women who regularly consumed a probiotic-infused beverage enjoyed a marked improvement in brain activity in just four weeks. By testing their responses to emotion-recognition tasks, the researchers found that the group of women who consumed probiotics, compared to the probiotic-free control group, showed lower activity in areas of the brain linked to emotion and sensation. However, this interesting decrease appeared to have some positive (and productive) ramifications for the women, including a more steady state of emotional homeostasis (serving as an antianxiety and antidepression mechanism), as well as greater connectivity in areas of the brain associated with cognition (linked to sharper thought), such as the prefrontal cortex. This change in brain activity led the researchers to conclude that the processing of both emotion and cognition was improved simply through the use of probiotics.

Powerful? Absolutely. But you don't need to take probiotic supplements to enjoy their benefits. Probiotics abound in many fermented foods, like yogurt and tempeh, which you may already enjoy eating. The probiotics in your gut also thrive on high-fiber foods, like apples, lentils, and spinach—another reason your microbiome is so content with a plant-centered diet.

And although *pre*biotics don't enter the gut-health conversation as often as probiotics do, they're another important player in keeping your digestive tract happy. Many fermented foods (and some nonfermented vegetables and fruits, like onions, yams, and apples) contain prebiotics, which are like the "food" that probiotics need to develop, grow, and flourish. Essentially, prebiotics

are probiotic magnets that set the stage for a healthy gut. If you want to rebuild and maintain your gut's microbiome for the benefit of your brain and your body overall, both prebiotics and probiotics should be regular fixtures in your wellness plan.

PLANT FOOD SOURCES OF PROBIOTICS AND PREBIOTICS

Probiotic foods include fermented vegetables, such as sauerkraut and kimchi. They also include cultured products, like tempeh, miso, yogurt, and kefir with active cultures (for best results, use plant-based yogurt and kefir to avoid the counterproductive and brain-detrimental inflammatory effects of dairy). Prebiotic foods include onions, garlic, yams, apples, and yacón root. All high-fiber foods are helpful for gut health (and therefore brain health) in general.

ANTIOXIDANTS

Sure, *free radicals* may sound like a cool new indie band, but, in reality, free radicals are pretty worrisome; they're the unruly, malignant cells that are the result of an unpaired "free" electron, which makes them highly reactive and prone to disease. Worse still, free radicals have a damaging effect on other cells, too, causing this dangerous

condition to spread. The formation of free radicals in your body or brain is the precursor to many kinds of degenerative diseases, including cancer. But when antioxidants are introduced, these oxidation-fighting micronutrients can counter the destructive activity of free radicals, as well as help to offset the premature aging of cells. It's easy to see why antioxidants are considered such tremendously valuable micronutrients! However, you must consume them through your diet, since your body can't make them.

Although there are thousands of different kinds of antioxidants, each with its own protective "specialty," you could easily make the case that most antioxidants are brain-friendly. Vitamin C, for example, is one of the most effective and versatile antioxidant vitamins in our diet; it helps with nerve cell development and the production of myelin, the insulating sheath that guards nerve cells. Beta-carotene (the precursor to vitamin A) is a known inflammation fighter and may slow cognitive decline. Vitamin E is an antioxidant that not only protects your cells overall; it also increases brain tissue and helps with dopamine release. And carotenoids like lutein and zeaxanthin (antioxidants found in produce like leafy green vegetables and carrots) are thought to improve overall cognitive function, particularly in older adults. Antioxidants are a big part of the backstory that explains why so many vegetables, roots, fruits, and plant-based foods are such useful tools in helping to create a healthy environment for a sharp brain.

Researchers have focused on a few antioxidants that are known to be particularly effective in both the delay of neurological decline and the improvement of cognitive function. Astaxanthin is a compound sourced from algae and is such a powerful anti-inflammatory agent that it is commonly referred to as a "super-antioxidant." Curcumin, an antioxidant found in turmeric, has gained tremendous attention for its ability to improve memory, enhance mood, delay aging, and much more. (We'll bite into the subject of curcumin in much more juicy detail starting on page 110.) But the most famous group of brain-friendly antioxidants are known as flavonoids (also called bioflavonoids). This subgroup of polyphenol antioxidants has shown great promise in improving memory, learning, decision-making, and reasoning. Luckily, these plant-based chemicals are quite easy to identify—they're the colorful pigments plants use for flowering and fruiting—and, when they're consumed, polyphenols supply a highly protective shield for the brain, keeping neurons in peak condition by preventing inflammation and oxidation and even improving the way neurons communicate and grow. Many studies have also shown that flavonoids offer strong protection from cognitive decline, including staving off major neurological diseases, like Alzheimer's and Parkinson's. You can find flavonoid antioxidants in dark-colored natural foods, like blueberries, grapes, black rice, dark chocolate, and coffee, as well as some red and orange foods. (Interestingly, some of the most-studied flavonoids, those known for promoting the growth of neurons, are found in a variety of polyphenols concentrated in the flesh of coffee fruit.)

To get the most variety and benefits from antioxidants, your best bet is to eat the rainbow—that is, beets, broccoli, bell peppers in every color, tomatoes, avocados, blackberries, strawberries, leafy greens, dark chocolate, carrots, and more.

Chapter Cheat Sheet:
THE POWER OF MICRONUTRIENTS

Compromised brain function due to micronutrient malnutrition is quite common. While there's no such thing as a "best" nutrient or food that can wholly address impaired cognition, eating a variety of nutrient-dense natural foods will go a long way toward fueling your brain with the most important micronutrients it needs to function at its best.

- Assess your diet: Make sure it is rich in the vitamins and minerals your brain needs to function optimally.

- Use supplements only as required by a special diet or your personal biochemistry. (Vegans in particular—but even nonvegans, too—should strongly consider a vitamin B_{12} supplement.)

- Help your body help your brain by fueling your microbiome with prebiotics and probiotics and lowering excess inflammation with antioxidants.

CHAPTER 5

Shaping Your Diet to Sharpen Your Mind

"Nothing will work unless you do."

—MAYA ANGELOU, American poet, memoirist, and actress

Now that you are familiar with the nutrients your brain craves, you're so much better equipped to enjoy the fun part: food. Unless you love taking handfuls of pills every day, there's very little need to rely too deeply on the world of supplements (outside of seeking extra nutrients that can help balance your personal biochemistry and lifestyle). That's because the majority of foods found in nature are inherently designed to keep your whole body functioning well, and that certainly includes your brain. As a matter of fact, just by maintaining a healthy diet, you are effectively protecting your brain from disease and premature aging, as well as setting the stage for a more flexible and adaptable mind that's primed to take on new challenges and learn new skills.

If you've skipped ahead to the grocery list in this chapter, I understand (admittedly, I've done the same thing in other books). But I do encourage you to work your way back, at some point, through the previous chapters in *Smart Plants* so you'll have a better appreciation of what makes the foods in this list so advantageous. All whole, plant-based foods are beneficial to your health in general, but some have substantially more benefits for your brain than others—and these are what compose our list of Everyday Smart Plants (see chart on page 64–68).

Everyday Smart Plants

Good Fats: Good source of healthy fat. Contains 3 grams or more per serving.

Quality Protein: Good source of plant-based protein. Contains 3 grams or more per serving.

Low Sugar: A low sugar (or even sugar-free) food with 10 grams or less of naturally occurring sugars per serving. (*Note:* Fruits not marked as low sugar may contain higher amounts of natural sugars but do not count toward your daily *added sugar* [or refined sugar] quota.)

Micronutrients: Provides a wide-reaching supply of beneficial vitamins, minerals, antioxidants, and phytochemicals.

Food	Source of Good Fats	Source of Quality Protein	Low Sugar Food	Source of Important Micronutrients
VEGETABLES				
Asparagus		√	√	√
Artichokes		√	√	√
Arugula		√	√	√
Beets			√	√
Broccoli		√	√	√
Brussels sprouts		√	√	√
Cabbage			√	√
Carrots			√	√
Cauliflower		√	√	√
Celery			√	√
Collard greens			√	√
Eggplant			√	√
Fennel			√	√
Garlic			√	√
Ginger			√	√
Kale		√	√	√
Lettuce (all varieties)			√	√

Food	Source of Good Fats	Source of Quality Protein	Low Sugar Food	Source of Important Micronutrients
Mushrooms, especially wild			√	√
Parsnips			√	√
Peppers, bell			√	√
Peppers, spicy			√	√
Radishes			√	√
Seaweeds		√	√	√
Spinach			√	√
Squash, summer			√	√
Squash, winter			√	√
Sweet potatoes		√	√	√
Swiss chard			√	√
Watercress			√	√
FRUITS				
Avocados	√		√	√
Bananas				√
Blackberries		√	√	√
Blueberries			√	√
Cherries				√
Cranberries			√	√
Grapes				√
Kiwis			√	√
Mangos				√
Olives	√		√	√
Raspberries			√	√
Strawberries			√	√

Food	Source of Good Fats	Source of Quality Protein	Low Sugar Food	Source of Important Micronutrients
Tomatoes			√	√
Watermelon				√
LEGUMES				
Adzuki beans		√	√	√
Black beans		√	√	√
Garbanzo beans/chickpeas		√	√	√
Kidney beans		√	√	√
Lentils (all varieties)		√	√	√
Peas and split peas		√	√	√
Pinto beans		√	√	√
Roman (cranberry) beans		√	√	√
Soybeans (and soy products, such as tofu)*		√	√	√
White beans		√	√	√
GRAINS & PSEUDO-GRAINS (SPROUTED WHEN POSSIBLE)				
Amaranth	√	√	√	√
Barley	√	√	√	√
Buckwheat		√	√	√
Bulgur		√	√	√
Freekeh	√	√	√	√
Kamut		√	√	√
Millet	√	√	√	√
Oats	√	√	√	√
Quinoa	√	√	√	√
Rice (all varieties)		√	√	√
Teff	√	√	√	√
Whole wheat (least beneficial)	√	√	√	√

* Always choose organic soy products.

Food	Source of Good Fats	Source of Quality Protein	Low Sugar Food	Source of Important Micronutrients
NUTS & SEEDS				
Almonds	√	√	√	√
Brazil nuts	√	√	√	√
Cashews	√	√	√	√
Coconut	√		√	√
Chia seeds	√	√	√	√
Flaxseeds*	√	√	√	√
Hazelnuts	√	√	√	√
Hemp seeds	√	√	√	√
Macadamia nuts	√	√	√	√
Pecans	√	√	√	√
Pine nuts	√	√	√	√
Pistachios	√	√	√	√
Pumpkin seeds	√	√	√	√
Sesame seeds	√	√	√	√
Sunflower seeds	√	√	√	√
Walnuts	√	√	√	√
FERMENTED FOODS				
Fermented vegetables (all kinds)			√	√
Kefir	√	√**	√	√
Kimchi			√	√

* Your body is not able to break down much of the ALA (alpha lipoic acid, an antioxidant omega-3 fat) in whole flaxseeds. Therefore, it's best to use ground flaxseeds. For best results, grind fresh, whole seeds in a coffee or spice grinder as you need them, as ALA is highly perishable. Or, if you make or buy a large batch, keep it in the refrigerator to help preserve its nutritional value.

** Yogurt-based kefir is a good source of protein, while water-based kefir does not contain protein.

Note: All kinds of "butters" made from nuts and seeds, like almond butter and tahini, are good choices, too, provided they are free of added sugar(s) and/or added polyunsaturated oils.

Food	Source of Good Fats	Source of Quality Protein	Low Sugar Food	Source of Important Micronutrients
Kombucha			√	√
Miso	√	√	√	√
Natto	√	√	√	√
Nondairy yogurt (unsweetened)	√	√	√	√
Sauerkraut			√	√
Tempeh	√	√	√	√
OTHER STAPLES				
Algae oil or avocado oil (for high-heat cooking)	√		√	
Chocolate (with high cocoa content)	√	√	√	√
Coconut oil	√		√	
Fermented sauces and spreads			√	√
Fresh and dried herbs and spices			√	√
Hot sauce (like sriracha)			√	√
Lecithin	√		√	√
Mustard			√	√
Nondairy milks (unsweetened)			√	√*
Nutritional yeast		√	√	√
Olive oil	√		√	
Stevia (liquid)			√	
Tamari			√	√
Teas, all varieties			√	√
Vinegar			√	

* Nondairy milks contain micronutrients when fortified.

You may have heard a famous quote from Paracelsus, a Swiss chemist and physician (1493–1541): "The dose makes the poison." In other words, too much of anything—no matter how "good" it may be for you—can kill you. Almost *everything* you eat or take as a supplement can be convincingly argued as a positive or a negative, as far as your health is concerned. But in the realm of nutritional science, practitioners and pundits often have a troubling tendency to compartmentalize the function of certain foods by categorizing them as "good" or "bad" for a specific aspect of health and developing diet strategies based on this narrow view. Instead, I urge you to keep in mind the bigger picture of whole-body health, even while pursuing a specific goal like brain optimization. While the foods and antinutrients* in the following list may have a diminishing effect on the health of your brain, the bigger purpose for listing them is to give you the informed power to make wise choices based on your personal wellness goals.

1. PROCESSED STARCHES AND SUGARS: Any diet will be improved by avoiding processed foods. Consuming highly processed starches, condensed sugars, and even artificial sugar-

*Antinutrients are compounds in foods that can interfere with the absorption of good nutrients and minerals.

free sweeteners can lead to a long list of health problems over time, including gut imbalances, inflammation, inhibition of neurotransmitter function, and even cellular atrophy, among many other detrimental effects. Look to actively reduce processed foods in your diet, or avoid them altogether.

2. SOME POLYUNSATURATED VEGETABLE OILS: While certain types of polyunsaturated fats are good—and even crucial to good health—balance is always key. Case in point: The ideal ratio of omega 6s to omega 3s (both polyunsaturated fats) is around 4:1 for most people. We've already discussed how important omega 3s are for the health of your brain, but omega 6s are crucial for cognition, too. Yet a diet that's too high in omega-6 fatty acids disrupts this important omega *balance* and can become a major cause of inflammation, which has been shown to impair cognition. Unfortunately, since omega 6 fats are so common in modern diets, a lopsided ratio is quite common. This is why we often hear so much about eating more omega 3 fats (to help rebalance the ratio).

An effective way to avert disorders related to a polyunsaturated fat imbalance is to avoid oils that have poor omega ratios—that is, oils that are especially high in linoleic acid (omega 6) and low in omega 3. These unbalanced oils (some of which are often genetically modified and/or contain residues of toxic pesticides) include corn oil, sunflower oil, canola oil, and soybean oil, as well as certain types of margarine made with these oils. It likely goes without saying that deep-fried foods are also a no-go.

3. MEAT, ESPECIALLY RED MEAT: Large quantities of animal-based saturated fats are like a ticking time bomb ready to go off in your body. The protein in meat may help build a little muscle in the short term, but your gut, heart, and brain simply cannot handle the long-term stress and inflammation that a heavy meat-based diet causes without ultimately succumbing to damage and disease, thereby reducing quality and longevity of life. If meat is something you don't want to give up, aim for a diet that is similar to that of some of the Blue Zone cultures (see page 25), whose populations enjoy peak longevity and where meat is eaten in very small quantities. You can find plentiful plant-based protein sources on pages 64–68, or try replacing meat with the occasional pasture-raised egg.

4. ALCOHOL: For the most part, alcohol and brain health don't mix. That's because alcohol doesn't just make you drunk and act silly—it's a known neurotoxin. Chronic alcohol consumption changes your brain structure and can actually reduce brain weight, due in part to neuron death and a reduction in myelin (the protective sheath surrounding your brain cells). Even moderate drinking can compromise neurotransmitter activity, causing serotonin levels to plummet and diminishing your ability to achieve deep sleep, the essential sleeping stage your brain requires for housekeeping and rebuilding.

On the other hand, a 2018 follow-up of a 23-year study investigating the relationship of alcohol to dementia, published in *BMJ* (the *British Medical Journal*), found that "moderate alcohol consumption has been suggested to lower the risk of dementia." Scientists are still unclear as to why there is a correlation between some "beneficial" drinking and disease prevention, but it is reasonable to assume that it is not the alcohol itself that is helpful but rather other micronutrient components in the drink. So, with those micronutrients in mind, if you choose to have a glass of alcohol from time to time, your best choice is probably wine—particularly red wine—due to the cell-protective antioxidants in the grapes that are used to make the beverage. However, since these antioxidants don't negate the detrimental effects of drinking alcohol, wine and all other alcoholic drinks should be consciously limited—try to stick to a single serving a day (or less).

5. DAIRY: If you find cheese addictive, you're not crazy. Dairy cheeses contain morphine-like compounds—opiate-simulating molecules that attach to the same brain receptors that heroin and other narcotics hook up with. And, like these drugs, dairy is nothing you want to be enslaved to. From our discussion in chapter 2 (page 21) we know how damaging an excess of saturated fat is to cardiovascular and cognitive health. Unfortunately, this same type of fat is often found in very high quantities in cheese and dairy.

But even low-fat dairy products can cause health problems. It's estimated that 75 percent of the world's population is dairy-intolerant (or lacking adequate lactose enzymes to digest dairy products properly). For these individuals, extensive inflammation in the gut's microbiome is the result of consuming dairy, which then leads to inflammation and damage in the brain. (Dairy is one of the most common culprits of "brain fog" as well.) What's more, lactic acid in dairy products has been shown to fully block some of the most important brain-protective antioxidants, such as flavonoids, which are gained from consuming other foods in your diet, like green tea, chocolate, and berries. For example, if you eat a handful of blueberries with a glass of fat-free milk, you won't digest any of the protective ellagic acid (a micronutrient with antioxidant properties) in the berries—meaning you won't enjoy the brain-protective benefits of eating them! Avoid extra inflammation and help protect your brain against disease by keeping dairy at a minimum, if you consume it at all.

Controversy in the Brain Game:
LECTINS

Who doesn't love a free lunch? That's what the administration of a British hospital thought in 1988, when it catered a "healthy eating day" for its employees. But within just a couple hours of serving the midday meal, the problems began. First, the surgical registrar vomited. Then, one after another, the staff members crumpled, falling sick. By the following day, everyone had recovered, but the worse-for-wear employees had their suspicions about the ingredients in the "healthy" meal they'd eaten the day before. An investigation found no pathogens in the food, but it did reveal an abnormally high level of phytohaemagglutinin—a lectin—which pointed directly to the culprit: undercooked red kidney beans.

If you're familiar with gluten, you're aware of at least one type of lectin. Lectins are protein compounds, and are sometimes considered "antinutrients"—substances found in foods that, when consumed, can have negative effects on the body, such as blocking the absorption of vital nutrients. All plants, animals, and microorganisms contain lectins in various amounts. Some scientists theorize that plants use certain lectins to discourage predatory insects from eating their seeds or fruit by making them ill. But you don't have to be gluten-intolerant (or a bug) to get sick from eating lectins. All of us are lectin-intolerant to some extent, although the level of intolerance differs from person to person.

There are certain lectins that no one can digest, like those found in raw kidney beans, as the poor British hospital workers will confirm. Some lectins are deadly, like ricin, a toxin found in caster beans. Other lectins, such as those found in nightshade plants, like tomatoes and peppers, can occasionally cause problems for people with sensitivities. Any amount of intolerance, however, activates your immune system to send antibodies to "fight" the lectin invader, causing a surge of inflammation throughout your body, and ultimately hindering brain function.

In a few cases, the effect that specific lectins can have on your brain is much more direct. For example, wheat germ agglutinin (WGA)—a lectin found in many grains but primarily in wheat—is an inflammatory type of protein that can cross the blood-brain barrier through a process called "adsorptive endocytosis," meaning that it can pull other substances with it, whether they're good or bad. Once WGA is inside the brain, it may attach to the myelin sheath that protects neurons and diminish the production of nerve growth factor (NGF), a fertilizer-like substance for your brain, thereby lowering levels of cell maintenance and proliferation. What's more, studies have found that lectins in grains may increase the risk of depression for some people who are gluten-intolerant, by binding to cells on the gut wall where they can limit serotonin production.

But there is another factor that makes lectins problematic: *They're in just about everything we eat.* And while grains, legumes, seeds, nuts, squashes, nightshades, fruits, dairy, eggs, corn-fed meat, and yeast are the most common sources of lectins, any food you put on your plate will also contain at least some lectins. So, are all lectins, and the foods that contain them, bad for the brain?

Clearly, it's not that simple. There are many different kinds of lectins, and not all are created equal. So while ricin may be downright death-dealing, the lectins found in some mushrooms, on the other hand, have the potential to heal, thanks to their immune-supportive benefits. Certain lectins may promote the growth of good bacteria that live in your gut and positively impact your mood, and some research indicates that specific varieties of lectins may have a future in cancer therapy as well.

Good or bad, lectins tell only a small part of the larger story about a food. Oats may be a source of lectins, but they also improve blood flow to the brain to improve cognition. Or consider this dichotomy: Potatoes contain lectins that negatively affect nerve growth factor. Yet one recent study found that eating certain types of pigmented potatoes actually *reduces* inflammation and oxidation, instead of increasing it (as you might expect from a high-lectin food). And what's more, the impressive amount of naturally occurring chlorogenic acid (an antioxidant) found in the potato skins appears to be neuro*protective*.

So once again, we circle back to "the dose makes the poison" mantra. A certain amount of lectins is normal, or even good, but too many lectins may have harmful effects. Keeping in mind the numerous benefits of lectin-containing foods, the *Smart Plants* approach is to simply reduce the intake of lectin-containing foods that affect *you* adversely (see page 74 for ways to do this), if any, and increase your consumption of anti-inflammatory foods overall.

THE BOTTOM LINE ON LECTINS

- An excess of certain types of lectins can lead to inflammation—and long-term inflammation can lead to serious medical conditions, including brain degeneration. Some individuals, especially those suffering from autoimmune disorders, may benefit from consuming fewer of these lectins.

- There's no such thing as a lectin-free diet. *Scientists have yet to find a single organism that does not contain lectins.* Even overemphasizing a "low-lectin" lifestyle is not easily sustainable and would likely pose health risks of its own, because you would be missing out on so many "high lectin" foods that are abundant sources of valuable micronutrients.

- Not all lectins are created equal. Most do not seem to pose significant danger to humans in clinical trials, and some are actually beneficial!

- Many lectin-containing plants are important sources of vitamins, minerals, and anti-inflammatory antioxidants, some of which may counteract the impact of lectins.

- It is easy to reduce the content of lectins in lectin-saturated foods through proper cooking and preparation, as cultures all around the world have been doing for thousands of years. You, too, can likely enjoy grains, beans, vegetables, and more, while simultaneously gleaning healthy brain benefits from them, just through smart food prep.

Simple Ways to Reduce Lectins in Plant Foods

Grains (highest priority): Whole grains have more lectins than refined grains, but before you pull out the empty-calorie white flour that has been gathering dust in the back of your kitchen cabinet, I recommend that you keep a broad view of the lectin-grain debate. Refined grains are not a healthy alternative to whole grains, since the process of refinement strips them of the bran and germ, along with all their nutrients, fiber, vitamins, and minerals.

Instead, if you wish to enjoy the full benefits of grains, use whole grains or nutrient-dense sprouted forms of whole grains in flours, pastas, and bread products. Rely on ancient grains, like spelt, rather than higher-gluten grains, like modern wheat, and lean on whole grains that you can boil (wet cooking) rather than grain flours used in baking (dry cooking), whenever possible.

Legumes (high priority): Soak beans in baking soda and water (about $1/16$ teaspoon per quart) for 8–12 hours before cooking them to remove antinutrients and reduce lectins. Rinse the beans thoroughly, and then cook them in a pressure cooker until they are well done. (Alternatively, you can boil beans on the stovetop.) For some "extra credit" lectin reduction (although this step is not always possible with some bean recipes), rinse the beans again, *after* cooking them, to remove the lectins that have leached out of the beans while they cooked. If you use canned beans, rinse them thoroughly, as the liquid in the can and on the beans is saturated with lectins.

Seeds (low priority): Use sprouted seeds whenever possible.

High-Lectin Vegetables and Fruits (lowest priority—only for high sensitivity): The highest lectin-containing produce includes nightshades, like tomatoes and eggplants; squashes, like pumpkins and zucchini; and most fruit, especially if it's not in season. To reduce the lectins in these foods, you can remove the peel and seeds, when possible, but keep in mind you will often be discarding valuable micronutrients at the same time, so only take this step if advised by a health practitioner.

BE THE CAT

In the Aesop fable *The Fox & the Cat*, a cat and a fox are traveling together when the fox starts to become quite boastful and ends up picking a fight with his feline acquaintance. He accuses the cat of being overly confident. "You think you are extremely clever, don't you?" he says to the cat, and points out that, as a fox, he is privy to a whole world of fancy trickery and hundreds of ways of escaping his enemies. The cat replies that while it is indeed true that she has only one trick, it has always served her well. As they continue to argue, a hunter's horn suddenly sounds. Immediately, the cat scurries up a tree. The fox, on the other hand, is full of ideas for ingenious escape plans but can't make up his mind about which one to try. He dodges back and forth, jumps into various holes, sprints at top speed . . . but, sadly, with all his indecision, the hounds soon catch up to him. Meanwhile, the cat remains unscathed. Aesop's moral? "Common sense is always worth more than cunning."

The truth is that, when it comes to diet, we simply don't have all the answers. We don't know what the "best" foods and nutrients are or precisely how they work in the body. Nevertheless, we do have a baseline understanding—an instinct, as some might call it—for what we should be eating, and, not surprisingly, that instinct doesn't take us very far from the path of nature and moderation. So while it may be tempting to seek ways to "hack" your system to achieve peak brain health and cognition, my hope is that you can see how much it can really pay off to be the cat: the one who rejects the latest diet fads that instinctively sound "out of balance" or that offer a bag of tricks (like a laundry list of branded supplements and synthetic formulas) in place of real food. Your inherent common sense will always serve you best. Eat as close to nature as possible and you will obtain what you were always intended to have—a healthy, well-functioning, and balanced mental universe.

Yet, innately, there's a bit of the fox in all of us, too. After all, we humans have a deep-seated drive to explore, progress, build, and improve; we have been pursuing purposeful development for thousands of years, if not longer. So, while following the guide to eat "some fat, some protein, less sugar, and more plants" may help you gain considerable ground on your cognitive journey—and get you up the tree, metaphorically speaking—there are other powerful elements in the world of natural foods that can bring you even closer to your goals. These are not tricks or hacks; they are long-term healing strategies that have shown tremendous promise in the realm of true brain optimization. And in the next chapter, you'll discover exactly how a very special group of extraordinary plants can take your brain performance entirely to the next level.

Chapter Cheat Sheet:

SHAPING YOUR DIET
TO SHARPEN YOUR MIND

In terms of cognitive performance and overall brain health, you will derive the most benefits from a diet structured around Everyday Smart Plants (see list on pages 64–68). Always be on the lookout for ways to incorporate these foods into your diet!

- Reduce your consumption of processed starches and sugars; polyunsaturated vegetable oils with high omega 6 fatty acids; meat, especially red meat; alcohol; and dairy products.

- Don't overthink the isolated role that lectins* found in plants can sometimes play in inducing inflammation; focus instead on the abundant brain-friendly micronutrients that a *Smart Plants* diet can offer you.

- When in doubt, lean on a variety of whole, plant-based foods, and enjoy them in moderation. Common sense outweighs any "hack."

* If you are suffering from an autoimmune disease or are sensitive to lectins, consult your physician for dietary advice.

CHAPTER 6

The World of Nootropics

"Man is not going to wait passively for millions of years
before evolution offers him a better brain."

—DR. CORNELIU E. GIURGEA, Romanian psychologist, chemist,
and the "Father of Nootropics"

What does a Mesopotamian barley farmer living 10,000 years ago and a Viking warrior living 1,000 years ago have in common with you and me, right now? We function with basically the same brain.

Our life today may be ferociously fast-paced, but evolutionary biology moves at an extremely slow rate, and the development of our modern brain is no exception. About two million years ago, our first ancestors, *Homo erectus*, had rather small brains, not much larger than an ape's. It took over 1.5 million years for our brain volume to double in size, enabling our ancient *Homo sapiens* family to cognitively handle walking upright, develop language, and come up with some additional problem-solving skills. To be sure, brain size alone doesn't account for intelligence: Our brains have actually shrunk since peak Neanderthal size; yet our smaller modern brains boast far greater cognitive capacity compared to the cave dwellers of yesteryear. (Most scientists attribute our smaller-than-Neanderthal brain to our relatively small body size and more efficient use of energy.) Nevertheless, human anatomy takes an exceptionally long time to change. In fact, in the past 10,000 years, the human brain hasn't changed much at all.

Not that you'd guess by our society today. Even within just a couple of centuries—from around the time of the US Industrial Revolution (beginning in the late 1700s) to today—changes in how we live have been transformative on every level, in part spurred by the development of urban centers and mass production. Or consider the massive shifts that have occurred in just the last century—how differently your grandparents and even your parents describe their life as they were growing up. Can you even relate to it? And forgetting everyone else for a moment: Look at the changes you've experienced in your own life. I don't know about you, but nothing makes me feel older than when I hear myself say, "I remember before we had the Internet . . ."

Think about it: In the last 100 years alone, we've equipped every home in the United States with electricity, we've put cars on every road, we've traveled to the moon . . . and now we can dance to Beyoncé's latest gem any time we want to from the same device we use to chat with friends, keep up with the news, track our heartbeat, sign a client proposal, learn to speak French, buy new sponges, and tell time . . . *instantly.* A gorilla today still performs the same tasks and still has the same needs as a gorilla did 10,000 years ago. Our situation, however, is far different. Our lives have sped up immeasurably—especially in the last century—but

in contrast, our biological evolution hasn't even begun to catch up.

That's not to say that the advances we've made as a species, and the speed with which those advances have been made, are all inherently negative. (I love online shopping with next-day shipping just as much as the next person.) But our brains are simply not used to the volume of daily stress and strain—"continuous partial attention," as it's often called—that we currently experience. So just as we've made quick adaptations to civilization (such as wearing shoes to walk comfortably on the hot concrete paths that crisscross our cities), we desperately need extra support for our brain to help it adjust to the innumerable requirements, interests, and stimulations that are part and parcel of what we know as normal, modern life. It's not just you. Internally, we're *all* crying out for balance; seeking to regain an elusive ideal of mental clarity that seems like it should just be a built-in feature of our brains.

Which is exactly why need the power of nootropics more than ever before.

WHAT'S A NOOTROPIC?

Nootropics, most commonly pronounced "new-TROH-picks," are actually not very new at all, despite what the pronunciation might imply. Derived from the Greek words

noos, meaning "mind," and *tropos,* meaning "turned" or "changed," nootropics are indeed "mind-changing," cognition-enhancing substances that can improve the way you think, feel, and function. Historically, nootropics have been put to use in one form or another by almost every culture around the world for millennia, whether to increase stamina or focus during a hunt or a battle or as a way to elevate consciousness and better connect with the world on a spiritual level. The current view and use of nootropics as cognition-boosting tools is still rather new, however. "Neuro-enhancing drugs" as a research category first emerged in the 1960s. In 1972, Psychologist and chemist Dr. Corneliu Giurgea coined the term *nootropic* several years after he developed a memory-boosting compound called Piracetam. Born in 1923 in Bucharest, Romania, Dr. Giurgea dedicated his life to studying human evolution and ways to enhance personal progress. Not only did he call attention to the idea of optimizing brain function; he is also responsible for bringing the concept of cognitive enhancement into the world of chemistry. Despite his focus on synthetic substances, Giurgea was adamant about the "rules" of nootropics and put together a master list of their characteristics, called the Five Nootropic Principles.

With his "do no harm" credo, Dr. Giurgea had only the noblest vision for neuro-enhancing drugs. But their development in the nootropic movement in the decades that followed didn't always play by the same rules.

Dr. Corneliu Giurgea's Five Nootropic Principles

1. A nootropic should enhance learning and memory.

2. A nootropic should enhance the endurance of learned behaviors and memories, making them more resistant to conditions that would disrupt them (such as lack of oxygen).

3. A nootropic should protect the brain from damage caused by physical or chemical injury.

4. A nootropic should increase the efficacy of the cortical/subcortical control mechanisms, thereby improving conscious and subconscious behaviors.

5. A nootropic should lack the usual pharmacology of psychotropic drugs (meaning it shouldn't impair motor function or possess sedative qualities), and it must have very few (if any) side effects, as well as extremely low toxicity.

By the time Eddie Morra (played by Bradley Cooper in the 2011 movie *Limitless*)—the once disheveled, struggling writer turned magnetic, creative genius—finally meets the celebrated financial icon Carl Van Loon (played by Robert DeNiro), Morra is just beginning to discover that perhaps the miracle drug he's been taking to enhance his mind has an unexpected dark side. But after watching Morra become hooked on the incredible cognitive effects of the drug NZT after the very first dose, the viewer can't help but become a little bewitched by the fantasy, too: the idea that taking a single pill might be able to give you instant access to the full potential of your brain in a way that removes all limits to what you might possibly accomplish in your life.

Unfortunately, nootropics don't work that way. So before you rush off on a Google search, there's no such thing as NZT or a "limitless pill," in either the legal or illegal drug kingdom. Nevertheless, the development and use of so-called "smart drugs" (which, unfortunately, are often grouped under the heading of "nootropics") are most certainly on the rise. We've seen this kind of performance enhancement behavior before. In the arena of sports, for example, some of our greatest professional athletes have turned to steroids or illegal drugs

to gain a physical edge in competition. Now, for anyone looking to get ahead in the "game of life," cognition is the new frontier. Our drive to excel, to accomplish more, and to manipulate the world around us is part of what makes us human, all of which makes the idea of aggressively controlling neurochemistry through drugs an understandable leap. And leap we have.

"Smart drugs" are essentially chemical compounds (or blends of compounds) that are primarily used to treat individuals with certain diseases or imbalances. In many cases, those suffering from neurobiological disorders may find that smart drugs can transform their lives, *if* they are used appropriately. But when they are taken outside the purview of a medical diagnosis, or by a "healthy normal" person (the unsexy term science uses for the "Average Joe"), smart drugs can have a very different effect.

Nonmedical users seek out smart drugs (also referred to as a pharmacological cognitive enhancement, or PCE) to stimulate a measurable uptick in mental performance, such as heightened alertness, enhanced memory, and increased motivation. With effects like those, it's no surprise that we've seen an increase in the "lifestyle use" of prescription drugs like Adderall, Ritalin,

Modafinil, and even illegal substances like cocaine. These drugs have become popularized in both school and workplace culture, not just as a way to party, but increasingly as tools to get ahead . . . or maybe, just to keep up. In a 2017 survey with tens of thousands of participants from 15 countries, an average of 14 percent of the respondents reported using chemical stimulants at least once within the past year, marking a 5 percent increase from just two years earlier. The United States reported the highest rate of use, with 30 percent of those surveyed having taken PCEs, while study participants from Europe reported the largest rise, particularly in the United Kingdom, where usage jumped from 5 percent to 23 percent within the two-year period.

Yet, despite their growing popularity, smart drugs do not offer a free ride. These chemical compounds work in many ways, and sometimes their effectiveness comes at the cost of flushing a healthy brain with too much dopamine. This means that some smart drug users may inadvertently jeopardize their health by potentially developing new behavioral problems, such as increased risk-taking and aggression. With the use of some smart drugs, there's also a danger of overstimulating the nervous system, which can damage and even kill brain cells. It's important to be aware that any substance you put into your body has many other biological effects in addition to the one(s) you expect or immediately feel. In the case of smart drugs, the brain will compensate for synthetically stimulated changes in neurotransmitter activity by adjusting—and often diminishing—the way it naturally produces and processes neurotransmitters (as if your amazing brain was attempting to outsmart your attempts to chemically outsmart it). For example, the reason cigarettes become so irresistible over time is because of the concentration of nicotine in the tobacco, which artificially activates dopamine production, causing you to feel temporarily good and mentally upbeat. The problem is that regular exposure to nicotine—and thus extra dopamine—causes your brain to believe it doesn't need to make as much dopamine on its own, now that there's an outside factor ready to take on that task. And, so as not to overload itself and to maintain neurochemical balance, your brain recalibrates. Suddenly, you're making significantly less dopamine on your own, and the need to reach for a cigarette—and get the resulting dopamine hit from the nicotine—becomes increasingly powerful.

There's a word for this behavior: addiction. Because smart drugs can provide a short-term cognitive boost for some, they are often grouped as a category (in popular culture) with nootropics. But due to the multiple side effects these drugs may induce—including addictive behaviors and possible long-term cellular damage—they clearly do not conform to the parameters that Dr. Giurgea originally envisioned for nootropics.

Some chemical nootropics are much less controversial, although still in the fledgling stage of use. Designed specifically for boosting brain function (and not as a party drug or a medication per se), drugs like racetams and Noopept have been the subjects of many short-term studies that verify their safety and effectiveness. The first nootropic invented by Dr. Giurgea, Piracetam, also falls into the category of cognitive enhancement drugs that work on a cellular level and can improve mitochondrial function, giving users increased "brain energy" and thus offering a feeling of being more mentally "on point." Synthetic nootropics like racetams have legions of fans, and in low doses it appears that the risk of using them is probably minimal. However, personal biochemistry plays a huge role in how you experience them.

Since I am generally wary of putting chemicals into my body, I haven't tried any man-made cognitive enhancement drugs myself, so I can't offer any road-tested advice. That's because I believe that a "healthy normal" person who regularly uses chemicals to stimulate or improve cognitive ability might be taking a needlessly aggressive chance— akin to playing with fire. Some "harmless" synthetic nootropics like Noopept have existed for only about a decade, so long-term studies on their effects are not available. I would love to be proved wrong in years to come, but for now, chemically derived nootropics still feel risky, despite the claims that they increase concentration and enhance verbal fluency.

And yet there is another realm of nootropics that Dr. Giurgea *didn't* include in his original vision of these brain-boosting compounds—one that offers your brain more of a handheld approach, instead of a sledgehammer, to help optimize cognition gently, safely, and effectively. This is the exciting world of *natural* nootropics.

THE POWER OF NATURAL NOOTROPICS

Despite the strides made in modern medicine since the eighteenth century, natural nootropics have actually been effectively used

for a much longer time. Ayurvedic medicine, which originated in India, and traditional Chinese medicine are just two of the more

Is Coffee a Nootropic?

"You can do it!"
—COFFEE

I don't need to tell you that drinking a cup of Joe is probably going to offer you anything from a mild mental boost to the motivation to work your magic on the day. Yes, coffee works. But is it a nootropic? The answer may surprise you.

Coffee has many brain-friendly benefits. The beans are naturally high in polyphenol antioxidants, which are greatly neuroprotective. Coffee also increases circulation and blood flow, which can help ensure that adequate oxygen and nutrients are being delivered to your brain, promoting better cognitive function. And the high caffeine content in coffee has the kind of brain-boosting impact you don't need a proper scientific study to prove: Just drinking the stuff will likely evoke an immediate increase in energy, mood, concentration, and drive.

And yet the main reason that coffee works so well is also the same reason it can be harmful: It's a stimulant. Just like nicotine in cigarettes or large amounts of added sugar in food, the high levels of caffeine in coffee directly impact your brain by precipitating a flush of excitatory neurotransmitters, like dopamine and epinephrine/adrenaline—which make you feel "up," at least for a while. But not only does it bankrupt these neurotransmitter systems once the chemical wears off, it also depletes your inhibitory GABA levels (so you'll have a hard time relaxing later). True nootropics should help build and maintain healthy neurotransmitter levels, not break them down.

Despite its desirable traits, coffee is often linked to anxiety, irritability, general nervous tension, and even panic attacks. Moreover, when it is used in excess, coffee can actually lead to *diminished* cognitive performance: That's why you may feel great while drinking half a cup of coffee, but after two or three cups you may begin to experience brain fog, fatigue, and the feeling that you "need" more coffee. (Be on the lookout for these symptoms, as your brain is very clearly telling you to ease up on caffeine, and the answer is definitely not to have another cup at this point.) Because of these negative side effects—including even mild addiction—most neuroscientists do not consider coffee a nootropic and advise moderation in its consumption.

Small amounts of coffee and caffeine can certainly be useful now and then to temporarily boost energy and productivity, and it's possible that coffee can continue to have a place in your life if you love to drink it. (Occasionally I enjoy a well-made cup myself.) But think of drinking coffee as a treat, rather than making it a regular habit. Ideally, when you wake up, you shouldn't *need* a cup of coffee to get going. The objective is not to "need" anything but, rather, to perform well naturally, without stimulation. That's why the natural nootropics that we'll be looking at in this chapter—with their power to produce lasting, stable, and optimized cognitive performance—are perhaps the best coffee replacements of all.

prominent practices that have expounded the benefits of natural nootropic remedies for thousands of years.

Today, although there is still no standardized definition for the word *nootropic*, most health professionals agree that **a nootropic is simply a substance that can enhance cognitive function without side effects.**

Natural nootropics also offer the benefit of enhanced cognitive function, but with this difference: They are foods (or at least food-derived supplements) rather than chemical substances. Like other true nootropics (as Dr. Giurgea defined them), natural nootropics have no negative side effects. On the contrary, they offer additional *positive* side effects or "bonus benefits," as you'll soon discover.

The biggest argument for eating a wholefoods diet, as opposed to eating processed foods or taking supplements, is gaining all the naturally occurring compound nutrients (that is, two or more nutrients that have synergistic effects) in whole foods. Together, compound nutrients can offer many layers of benefits for both the brain and the body as a whole. Chemical nootropics, at their best, can only mask deficits and may not help build lasting change. Natural nootropics, on the other hand, can improve the entire baseline of your brain health while giving you a cognitive edge that can make

a positive difference in the way you think and feel.

As we've seen, there are many everyday foods that are fantastic for overall brain health, but the difference between these so-called everyday "smart foods" and foods that are considered natural nootropics comes down to the brain "boosting" ability of nootropics—think of them as the superfoods of the cognition world. Natural nootropics not only maintain and protect neurological function, they can also *improve your mental performance*. Futhermore, every natural nootropic works differently: Some will help you down-regulate and keep stress at bay, and some will help you remember things more easily. Others will help you focus and support your ability to smoothly deliver a business presentation or an impromptu wedding speech. All in all, it's exciting to see how the unique biological makeup of natural nootropics can help you realize your own cognitive potential and enhance what you go on to do, achieve, and enjoy.

Although natural nootropics are "just plants," I have to admit that I had some trouble actually finding some of them in a form that could be used in recipes. Are there fresh ginseng roots at some Asian markets? Of course! But my ultimate intention was to create recipes with ingredients that you can easily find. At "worst," a few of the less readily available ingredients in this chapter can be found online, and, like spices, they'll last a long time in your pantry. (The Resources Guide on page 265 can help you find some ingredients that may not be available in your local stores.)

The second challenge I encountered was flavor. The truth is that some nootropic plants taste absolutely awful—or are too hard to find as bulk ingredients—so as a solution, I decided to divide and conquer with nootropic recommendations. That's why you'll find two sections on ingredients in the following pages: Top 10 Natural Nootropic Foods for use in recipes (on page 86), and Mind-Enhancing Supplements (on page 118)—the natural nootropics that can be taken on the side.

What to Expect from Natural Nootropics

NATURAL NOOTROPICS ARE NOT:

- A way to instantly make you the next Albert Einstein

- A heavy stimulant (like coffee, nicotine, or Adderall)

- A way to get around doing real work

- A substitute for a healthy diet

- A replacement for sleep or a balanced lifestyle overall

- A substitute for medications prescribed for serious neurological or psychological conditions

- A "hack" of any kind

NATURAL NOOTROPICS ARE:

- Highly neuroprotective (that is, helpful in protecting nerve cells from damage or degeneration)

- A way to help optimize your cognitive performance by bolstering the health of your brain *and* your body

- A means of boosting memory, motivation, mood, attention, learning ability, and thought flow

- A way to increase intelligence over the long term

Smart Plants Natural Nootropic Principles

It's been many decades since Dr. Giurgea first developed his original Five Nootropic Principles, and it's time we make a clear division between natural nootropics and the synthetic pack.

These are the requirements, in *Smart Plants,* for a substance to be considered a natural nootropic:

- A natural nootropic must be a natural, nutrient-dense food, not a patented or proprietary blend.

- A natural nootropic must have the biological potential (supported by trials and studies) to enhance one or more cognitive functions, such as memory, learning, mood, etc.

- A natural nootropic must enhance the brain function of people who are already healthy, as well as individuals who may have a neurological disease or cognitive impairment.

- A natural nootropic must offer holistic benefits that affect the whole body, as well as the brain.

- A natural nootropic must provide overall neuroprotection (that is, protect neurons from injury or degeneration), in addition to enhancing cognition.

- For the purposes of this book, a natural nootropic food must be readily available in whole food form to be used as an ingredient in recipes. Other natural nootropics may be taken as supplements.

TOP 10 NATURAL NOOTROPIC FOODS

Excited yet? You're about to discover a very special group of nature's most brain-boosting foods. Imagine what they can do for you! And since these foods are so much more powerful than, say, just eating an avocado or a plate of broccoli to help boost cognitive function, I have a couple of final flight instructions—suggestions, really—that you may want to consider before heading off on your own nootropic journey.

First, don't expect to experience massive changes overnight. The time frame is a little different for everyone, but for the most part, natural nootropics take anywhere from several days to a few weeks of consistent use to produce a noticeable effect.

Second, experimentation is paramount to getting the results that you're looking for. A natural nootropic that works well for someone else may not work for you, and vice versa. That's totally normal. Initially, it may take time to find the combination of foods that's perfect for you, but it is definitely worth the effort. And keep the bell curve of using these powerful ingredients in mind: If you use too little or, for that matter, too much of them, you will negate their efficacy. But the right amount can result in truly impressive changes. As a general guide, stick with the recommended daily amounts listed on the packaging of any products you're using.

Last, choose a couple—or several—of the incredible nootropics from the following Top 10 Natural Nootropic Foods list to start with (there's no urgency to pack in every ingredient on this list), and get ready to experience the power of changing your mind for the better.

How Much Is Right for You?

Although natural nootropics are edible ingredients and not synthetic medicines, they are often potent enough to warrant guidelines for dosage that can range from large and loose, such as a "big handful" of fresh blueberries, to small and precise, like 150 grams (or about $\frac{1}{16}$ of a teaspoon) of rhodiola powder. What's more, the effectiveness of every nootropic varies from person to person, and with continued use, the amount taken may need to be adjusted in order to yield the desired results. As mentioned, use the recommended serving size on the package as a general guideline. Start small (more is *not* better), listen to your body, and consult your doctor if you have any questions or concerns about using natural nootropics.

Cacao—"The Happy Bean"

BOTANICAL NAME: *Theobroma cacao*

PART USED: Seed

TASTE: Unsweetened chocolate

COMMONLY SOLD FORMS: Powder, nibs, chocolate bars

WHAT IT IS: Cacao is the unroasted form of cocoa and the raw, unsweetened form of chocolate. Every chocolaty bite you've ever consumed began as cacao, and every health benefit you've ever heard about chocolate is because of cacao (and definitely not the milk or sugar that's often added to turn it into a sweet treat!). While there hasn't been much historical use of it as a nootropic, cacao was first popularized in Central and South America, revered by the Mayans and later the Aztecs, who used it in spiritual ceremonies.

Even the Greek origin of its botanical name suggests there may be more to this ingredient than meets the eye: *Theobroma* is translated as "food of the Gods."

Several different types of products are harvested from cacao trees. Upon maturity, the trees bear large, colorful fruit pods, each of which is packed with 30–40 thumb-size brown seeds called cacao "beans." Once they're harvested, the beans are left to ferment for several days to allow the chocolate flavor to develop. Finally, they're dried, cleaned, and peeled. At this point, the cacao beans easily crack into pieces, and these small bits are what you may know as "cacao nibs." Ground down, the nibs form a fat-rich paste, which is usually made into chocolate. Sometimes the paste is ground down even further until the fat and the cacao mass (the fiber) separate, resulting in two additional products: cacao butter (the fat) and cacao powder (the mass). From a nootropic standpoint, the main cognitive benefits come from the powder and the nibs.

Cacao or Cocoa?

The difference here is simple: Cacao is raw and unroasted. Cocoa is roasted and processed. Both products offer benefits, but cacao has significantly higher levels of the nutrients that make it a nootropic and a neuroprotectant.

WHAT IT DOES: What can cacao do for you? A lot, as it turns out. In some ways, it's almost as if cacao read the preceding chapters of this book and decided to check off the list of brain-boosting nutrients that were discussed, while adding a few bonuses of its own. Cacao is especially high in magnesium—so high that it's one of the top food sources of this mineral. In addition, cacao is full of amino acids (particularly tryptophan and tyrosine); beneficial phytochemicals, like anandamide and phenylethylamine; and a raft of other vitamins, such as several of the Bs, and minerals like iron. It also enhances gut health as a prebiotic, contains a fair amount of plant-based (cholesterol-free) saturated fat, has no sugar, and offers a very small amount of naturally occurring caffeine . . . just enough to get you going. (Cacao beans have about 1/20th the caffeine of coffee beans.) Plus, cacao contains top-of-the-chart levels of antioxidants, particularly polyphenols like flavonoids, and theobromine, which is touted for its ability to increase one's attention span. From the nutrients it contains alone, it's easy to see why the health-giving compounds of cacao have evoked such extensive research on this first-class brain food.

Now let's look at why cacao is such a real-deal "happy food." You may have thought that chocolate just made you feel good because it tastes so wonderful, but it's actually all the valuable micronutrients and plant-based chemicals we just mentioned hard at work behind the scenes that are responsible for the uptick in your state of mind! Studies have shown cacao's nutrients can positively affect your emotions, causing you to feel calmer and more content while lessening depression and decreasing anxiety. These results are likely due to several factors, including the beans' ability to stimulate endorphins in your brain (the "feel-good" chemicals that can override pain and put you in a better mood).

Cacao also provides your brain with a number of tools to make mood-boosting neurotransmitters by supplying an excellent source of tryptophan, the precursor to serotonin, as well as significant quantities of tyrosine, a precursor amino acid to motivation-inducing dopamine. Plus, cacao contains a compound called anandamide, a neurotransmitter that's been called "the bliss molecule"—no explanation needed there! Overall, cacao is a great nootropic to reduce stress, as it helps to suppress excess cortisol, the fight-or-flight hormone that causes inflammation when you're overstimulated.

But when it comes to cacao, the old advertising sales pitch "But wait! There's more!" is definitely not an overstatement. On the contrary, the super-valuable flavonoids in cacao have been linked with improved thinking skills, learning, and memory. Flavonoids also increase blood flow to the brain (thereby increasing oxygen and nutrient accessibility), help protect your nerve cells from free radicals, promote neurogenesis, and even enhance the way your neurons function, connect, and communicate. And because cacao stimulates the release of a lesser-known neurotransmitter called phenylethylamine (PEA), which boosts focus and awareness, it may just help you get into your performance groove a little bit more easily, too. One delicious-sounding study showed that simply eating chocolate before a memory and visual test improved the results of healthy adults, which speaks volumes to the almost immediate difference increased blood flow to your brain can make. One thing is for sure: Cacao doesn't just make your taste buds happy; it makes your mind happy on every level and can even boost mental performance at the same time.

So does cacao really make you smarter? Well, it's been documented that countries with the highest chocolate consumption also appear to produce the most Nobel Prize winners. *Just saying . . .*

HOW TO USE IT: If you like chocolate, you will love using cacao in recipes and enjoy the healthiest, most nutrient-rich form of chocolate on the planet. Both cacao powder and cacao nibs are excellent for smoothies, creamy desserts, and baking; and while the nibs are too bitter to be snacked on by themselves, they can be sprinkled on top of anything sweet, including just plain fruit, as a crunchy component. The biggest challenge with using cacao is to try to get away with using as little sugar and dairy as you can—aim to enjoy the benefits of cacao without causing ancillary damage at the same time. Remember: A little sugar, particularly in natural forms like fruit, is fine. It's large or frequent quantities of refined sugar that can cause problems.

By and large, cacao powder (pure cacao mass) offers the most saturated form of nootropic benefits, while cacao nibs, which contain both fiber and fat, have a lower nutrient density. Lower still on the nutrition totem pole are cocoa and chocolate products, which are more processed and diluted with other ingredients, making them less potent. And although it doesn't contain any of the desirable phytochemicals to be considered a nootropic, cacao butter (the naturally-occurring fat found in cacao nibs) is a cholesterol-free source of plant-based saturated fat for your brain, too.

Note: Chocolate contains two focus-enhancing stimulants—caffeine and theobromine. Neither is found in concentrated amounts, but if you're particularly sensitive to the stimulant effects of cacao, some experts advise against consuming it before going to bed. That being said, theobromine can also promote longer, more restful sleep, so perhaps the best policy is to give yourself a bit more

wiggle room before bedtime if you're craving a cacao-infused treat.

BONUS BENEFITS OF CACAO: Cardioprotective; antioxidant; anti-inflammatory; prevents blood clots; promotes blood-vessel dilation; reduces insulin resistance; and regulates the genes that control body weight. (Yes, you read that last part right, and, yes, we're still talking about chocolate! Sweet deal.)

CACAO TAKEAWAY CHECKLIST:

✓ Elevates mood (and decreases both depression and anxiety)

✓ Boosts learning and memory

✓ Enhances focus

✓ Highly neuroprotective

Percentage Size Matters

If you choose to enjoy cacao in the form of a chocolate bar, choose one that has the highest possible percentage of cacao or cocoa. A 60-percent bar, for example, means you're eating chocolate that contains 60 percent roasted cacao, which sounds good, but when you consider the other 40 percent of ingredients—usually it's mostly sugar—it becomes a lot more motivating to make a better selection. Look for 70-percent, 80-percent, or even 90-percent chocolate bars, all of which offer incredible flavor with far less sugar.

There is one downside to seeking plant-based medicine (that is, medicine consumed through what you eat as opposed to what you "take"). Unlike supplements, the nutrition in food is not standardized. The amount of active compounds in health-giving foods may vary, depending on where and how the plant was grown, environmental fluctuations, and differences in processing methods. Furthermore, some plant-based medicines carry the potential risk of containing unintended compounds (in addition to the beneficial ones), such as heavy metals. This caveat is not meant to alarm you but rather to underscore the fact that not all ingredients are exactly the same and knowing the source and provenance of your nootropics is very important. (This shouldn't come as a surprise, since the quality of *all* foods varies!)

When you're ready to try a natural nootropic, I highly encourage you to look for companies that place a high premium on well-tested and nutritionally effective products. I've put a lot of time over the years into researching and interviewing representatives of companies that sell nootropics before putting their products into my own body or giving them to my family. And while you can certainly use my personal picks in the Resources Guide on page 265, I encourage you to always investigate on your own—a good practice to follow while you're searching for *anything* you want to eat or drink on a regular basis . . . even water.

Matcha—"The Original 'Keep Calm and Carry On' Tea"

BOTANICAL NAME: *Camellia sinesis*

PART USED: Leaves

COMMONLY SOLD FORM: Powder

TASTE: Mildly bitter, astringent, like a slightly nutty green tea (higher-quality matcha can even be faintly sweet)

WHAT IT IS: Chartreuse-green matcha powder is made from specially cultivated green tea leaves. Shade-grown for the last few weeks of their development to amplify their chlorophyll content, the leaves are dried and carefully ground into a fine powder, which is sold as "matcha." The practice of making and consuming matcha is nothing new: Matcha has been used to create consciousness-enhancing drinks for well over a millennium, originating with Buddhist monks, who drank the tea to enjoy a more focused meditation practice.

Ever since, the green beverage has enjoyed a central role in Japanese tea ceremonies. Within the last couple of decades, matcha has also taken the North American culinary scene by storm as a versatile ingredient that offers a multitude of health benefits.

WHAT IT DOES: In the world of synthetic nootropics, a very popular formulated "stack" (a combination of two or more nutrients that are mutually advantageous) consists of caffeine mixed with L-theanine. This yields a feeling of "calm focus," as caffeine and L-theanine have a synergistic relationship and work better as a combination for enhancing cognition than either substance would work on its own. But nature already has its own version of that effective blend: matcha. The naturally occurring caffeine and large amounts of L-theanine in matcha offer the consumer a James Bond–like mindset: cool, calm, and collected. That's because, while caffeine enhances focus, attention, and stamina, L-theanine mitigates the less desirable effects of caffeine—jitters and increased blood pressure—by functioning as a highly effective antianxiety tool. As discussed in chapter 3 (page 28), theanine can cross the blood-brain barrier, fight stress, and reduce depressive symptoms, because it increases the activity of the "calming" neurotransmitter GABA. Scientists have

also found that theanine promotes alpha brain-wave patterns that are associated with concentration and creative thinking. And in an even more fascinating plot twist, also backed by science, another way to increase alpha brain waves is through a mindfulness practice like meditation . . . which brings us back to Buddhist monks and their long-standing affinity for the matcha and meditation combination.

What's the Difference between Theanine and L-theanine?

More often than not, you'll hear both *theanine* and *L-theanine* used interchangeably in the world of supplements and nutrition. Technically, L-theanine is just a particular type of theanine, with a slight difference in molecular structure. Although other forms of theanine are beneficial, too, L-theanine has the advantage of being the most studied for its relaxation benefits and compatibility with caffeine . . . which is why its natural presence in green tea is nothing short of ideal. If you do want to supplement your diet with additional theanine, however, L-theanine is the form to look for.

Matcha is also a highly rich source of well-studied protective antioxidants: polyphenols, tannins, catechins, and epigallocatechin gallate (EGCG). As a result, consuming matcha (and regular green tea as well) has been linked with helping to lessen the risk of brain disorders, like Parkinson's and dementia, by working to prevent neuron damage and death. And the polyphenols in matcha have a further effect on mood, too, by boosting the availability of dopamine when the brain needs it and promoting a positive, motivated state of mind.

Many of the benefits of matcha are similar to those of regular green tea, so if you prefer to savor a cup of green tea instead of using matcha, that's a fine alternative. There is, however, one noticeable difference: Cultivating matcha in the shade causes the leaves to become darker, concentrating more chlorophyll and L-theanine (as well as other amino acids) in the leaves. Therefore, matcha offers you the most bang for your buck in terms of L-theanine and nootropic benefits. You may also find that powdered matcha is fun to enjoy in all kinds of recipes (in blended drinks or a batch of muffins, for example) in addition to using it as a tea.

Because of its caffeine content, some people might not consider matcha a true nootropic (remember, caffeine has side effects). However, most would argue that matcha's powerful and synergistic ingredients make a case for the "whole is greater than the sum of its parts" argument, which would keep this consciousness-elevating superfood squarely on the best-of-nootropics list.

HOW TO USE IT: Matcha may be made from green tea leaves, but unlike tea that you brew (and then discard the leaves), matcha powder can be stirred into recipes and consumed directly. For tea ceremonies, matcha has traditionally been made with nothing more than a cup of mildly hot water in which a small scoop of matcha powder is vigorously whisked. Culinary appropriation of this ingredient has been immense of late, and it has now become popular to use in all kinds of recipes—from creamy drinks and smoothies, to sauces, baked goods, and desserts—where it mostly hangs in the background, adding just a hint of "tea" to the overall flavor. If you'd like to try a simple way to enjoy matcha, whip up the recipe for Perfect Matcha Latte on page 249 (countless cups of which I myself consumed during the time period of writing this book!).

When purchasing the powder, you'll likely come across different grades of matcha, usually "ceremonial" and "culinary." Although the ceremonial grade has the smoothest flavor and is the most gently processed, it comes with a very hefty price tag. If making matcha smoothies and matcha granola is more of your recipe agenda, I suggest using the culinary grade; its much lower cost will make you feel almost as good as the nutrients it offers.

BONUS BENEFITS OF MATCHA: Antioxidant, boosts metabolism, provides full-body energy, improves immune system, anticancer, and heart-protective.

MATCHA TAKEAWAY CHECKLIST:

- ✓ Provides calm energy
- ✓ Diminishes anxiety and improves sense of well-being
- ✓ Boosts motivation and focus
- ✓ Improves memory and cognition
- ✓ Promotes creative thinking and flow
- ✓ Highly neuroprotective

Lion's Mane —"The Smart Mushroom"

BOTANICAL NAME: *Hericium erinaceus*
PARTS USED: Fruiting body and mycelium (the parts of the mushroom that grow above and below the ground, respectively)
COMMONLY SOLD FORM: Powder
TASTE: Very mild earthy flavor (in powder form)

WHAT IT IS: The distinctive appearance of the lion's mane mushroom has inspired more than a few intriguing monikers around the world, such as "monkey's head," "pom-pom," "bear's head," and, my personal favorite, "old man's beard." (So, you see, putting some "lion's mane" in your smoothie isn't so bad when the alternative could be a scoop of "old man's beard!")

Lion's mane has a long history of use in traditional Chinese medicine, but it has also played a role as a popular health food in Japan, Korea, and India. The mushroom gets its fanciful names from its "toothed" appearance. Most likely, though, you'll find it as an innocuous-looking, tan-colored powder at the health food store.

WHAT IT DOES: Can lion's mane actually enhance intelligence? Yes, in a way. This gold-star nootropic contains many compounds that support an impressively wide range of brain-boosting benefits: Lion's mane is brain-protective, brain-healing, cognitively stimulating, and even promotes neural *growth*.

In light of the profound neurological benefits of using lion's mane, I reached out to my friends at Om, Organic Mushrooms (a southern California–based company that specializes in premium-quality medicinal mushrooms) to gain a bit more understanding about what's actually at work under the mushroom's hood, so to speak. As I'd imagined, Om's head mycologist, Steve Farrar, had no shortage of useful information: "Lion's mane produces several nootropic, neurotrophic compounds (including many hericenone and erinacine compounds), which have been reported to support and enhance the overall functioning of the brain," he said, "including improvement of cognition, intelligence, memory, attention, concentration, and mood. These compounds can cross the blood-brain barrier, where they upregulate [increase the cellular response of] the biosynthesis of the nerve growth factor that regulates the growth of neurons and supports the function of the myelin sheath." Assuming you haven't had your lion's mane yet today, allow me to break that down a bit.

From a protective and healing standpoint, lion's mane is extremely anti-inflammatory. As Steve mentioned, its constituents can cross the blood-brain barrier and stimulate the growth of the myelin sheath, the protective covering around your nerve fibers. This helps them become stronger and healthier—a key component in ensuring that proper brain cell communication can occur. Lion's mane can also help regulate your brain's neurotransmitter activity, keeping your mood balanced, combating depression and anxiety, and enhancing sleep quality. In addition, lion's mane has shown early promise in fighting Alzheimer's disease, thanks to its ability to improve the brain's cholinergic systems, and may slow down the progression of Parkinson's disease. And in healthy adults who do not have a neurological disease, cholinergic stimulus can improve learning and memory, as well as optimize attention span.

What's more, as Steve pointed out, lion's mane is well known for its ability to stimulate NGF—nerve growth factor, a neuron-building neurotrophic factor similar to BDNF (brain-derived neurotrophic factor)—which explains why this mushroom has become synonymous with neuroplasticity. Despite the clear advantages of having NGF in your system to help maintain, grow, protect, and proliferate neurons, NGF is also critical for your brain to function properly. Without it, sympathetic and sensory neurons start to undergo programmed cell death! So while we naturally lose brain cells as we age, stimulating the growth of new ones (and protecting the ones we have as best we can) is a key component to maintaining and enhancing brain health overall. This is yet another reason that so many researchers are excited by the mushroom's potential as a treatment for neurodegenerative diseases, as well as the repair of nerve damage induced by trauma. To this point, Steve added, "We have received reports of positive effects from the daily consumption of lion's mane from many [Om] customers suffering from neuropathy conditions and also ADHD [Attention Deficit/Hyperactivity Disorder]."

HOW TO USE IT: The most accessible and versatile way to use lion's mane is in powder form. This offers potent benefits without having much of an effect on flavor, making it an ideal "secret ingredient" that can be used in just about anything, from soups and other savory foods (raw or cooked) to smoothies and sweets. Case in point: A 2010 Japanese study tested the effectiveness of lion's mane on depression by giving a group of middle-aged women *cookies* baked with 2 grams of lion's mane powder. (Happily, the results showed a significant reduction in depression and anxiety.) If you want to re-create the cookie study for yourself, try my recipe on page 235 and use the Brain Boost.

As much as I love the versatility and shelf-stable qualities of powdered lion's mane, it's worth mentioning that, for a limited season, some chefs may be able to find fresh lion's mane, which is usually sold under yet another name mushroom aficionados may recognize: "hedgehog mushroom." Fresh lion's mane/hedgehog mushrooms offer a flavor that comes close to lobster—an obvious reason why the mushrooms are so prized by the gourmet crowd. As a general rule, always cook fresh mushrooms (dried mushroom powders generally do not need to be cooked)—as cooking makes mushrooms easier to digest and removes any potential microbial activity that may have begun during the mushrooms' growth or at harvesting. Some mushrooms, such as morels, for example, contain toxic compounds that are *only* deactivated through cooking.

Good for Your Gut

Lion's mane and reishi mushrooms also support brain and nerve health by supporting a balanced gut! The mushrooms promote the growth of beneficial probiotic microorganisms and limit the development of dysbiotic microorganisms (the microorganisms you don't want) in the gastrointestinal tract. Also, by helping to keep inflammation responses in the body minimal, lion's mane and reishi can stave off chronic inflammation that may occur in both the gut and the brain.

BONUS BENEFITS OF LION'S MANE: Antidiabetic, anticancer, antitumor, antibacterial, anti-HIV, helps with hypertension, antioxidant, helps with gastrointestinal issues, may improve skin quality, reduces scarring, increases collagen, good for cardiovascular health and lowers cholesterol, improves circulation, gut-protective, liver-protective, may increase bone density and strength, decreases inflammation, may lower high blood glucose, and balances the immune system.

LION'S MANE TAKEAWAY CHECKLIST:

- ✓ May help treat neurodegenerative diseases
- ✓ Exceptionally neuroprotective
- ✓ Helps with sleep disorders
- ✓ Contains nerve regeneration capability
- ✓ Decreases depression and anxiety
- ✓ Improves learning, memory, and attention
- ✓ Supports overall cognitive function
- ✓ Increases neuroplasticity and neurogenesis

Reishi —"The Health Insurance Mushroom"

BOTANICAL NAME: *Ganoderma lucidum*
PARTS USED: Fruiting body and mycelium (the parts of the mushroom that grow above and below the ground, respectively)
COMMONLY SOLD FORM: Powder
TASTE: Bitter

WHAT IT IS: Reishi is a species of mushroom that naturally grows in the forests of Asia, Europe, North America, and the Amazon. The Chinese name for reishi, *ling zhi*, translates as "spirit plant" and has been used in traditional Chinese medicine for thousands of years. These days, most types of reishi on the market are cultivated—not sourced from the wild—and there are several: blue/green, red, yellow, white, black, and purple reishi mushrooms. Although each of them is beneficial in its own way, the reishi variety with the most cognitive potential is red reishi, so be sure that *G. lucidum* is on the label of the product you buy.

WHAT IT DOES: The therapeutic benefits of reishi are impressive: As a calming nootropic it can promote deeper and better-quality sleep and improve adrenal function, which makes it a good stress regulator. While its immediate effects may be mild, it has been reported that these effects can increase over time.

Reishi is considered the "premier adaptogen" in all of Chinese medicine. It contains more than 400 bioactive compounds and is most broadly used as an immune system modulator that can both stimulate immune response when the body is weakened (in cases of disease or toxicity) and also calm an overactive immune response (such as an allergic histamine reaction). The mushroom effectively reduces inflammation, detoxifies the liver (thus lowering toxicity throughout the body and brain), and can diminish the accumulation of harmful heavy metals—three conditions that can slow down and ultimately damage healthy brain function if left unchecked. Consequently, reishi may be a particularly beneficial food for anyone who consumes fish frequently, is exposed to environmental toxins on a regular basis, or heavily consumes alcohol.

Consumption of reishi is also often linked to improved learning and memory because the mushroom is highly neuroprotective and can help repair brain cell injury and reduce neuron death. It is particularly protective of the hippocampus, your memory center. I have found that consuming reishi in the evening heightens the beneficial effects—it can help with relaxation before heading off to bed, promotes the health of the hippocampus (which actively rebuilds itself during deep sleep), and refreshes the brain, so that it is ready to focus and learn—without the use of coffee—first thing in the morning. The use of reishi for the well-being of your brain—and your whole body, for that matter—truly is one of the best kinds of natural health insurance you could ask for!

Stack It!

Both vitamin C and ginger support digestive processes and are reported to be particularly effective in increasing the bioavailability of some of the active ingredients in mushrooms, including reishi and lion's mane. And since most mushrooms contain an array of prebiotic compounds, also consider incorporating some probiotic-rich foods, like non-dairy yogurt (or probiotic supplements) with them, to give your brain a threefold benefit!

HOW TO USE IT: Like lion's mane, reishi is an easy-to-use nootropic, although it has a slightly more bitter taste than lion's mane. (The fresh mushroom is very bitter, but the dried reishi powder has a much mellower flavor.) Reishi can be tucked away in blended recipes like smoothies and is surprisingly good with cacao in sweet treats. Reishi powder is also a great addition to soups and stews, warm sauces, and bold-flavored dips.

BONUS BENEFITS OF REISHI: Cholesterol-lowering, anti-inflammatory, antioxidant, antiaging, anti-ulcer, antitumor, antiviral, antidiabetic, heart tonic, hepatoprotective, immunomodulator, and nervine.

REISHI TAKEAWAY CHECKLIST:

✓ Promotes calm and reduces anxiety

✓ Helps reduce stress

✓ Supports better sleep

✓ Supports learning and memory

✓ Is neuroprotective and a strong detoxifier

How Can Natural Nootropics Be Both Calming and Energizing?

You may notice that some nootropics on the list of "Top 10 Natural Nootropic Foods" seem to confer contradictory benefits; for example, a nootropic might be both a stimulant as well as a calming sleep aid. Although this flexibility is partially due to a synergy of naturally occurring substances in the plant itself, it is the nootropic's role as an "adaptogen" that accounts for the duality of its effects.

Adaptogens are a special class of foods that include some superfoods and herbs. Adaptogenic foods offer the unique health advantage of supporting the endocrine system (a collection of glands that produce and regulate hormones, metabolism, sleep, and mood, among other functions) in a natural way. As their name suggests, adaptogens can literally help you adapt, or adjust, to many different kinds of stress. Although the benefits of adaptogens may sound a bit nebulous, there's nothing "magical" or "woo-woo" about them: By supporting endocrine health, adaptogens help restore your body's natural state of balance. This explains why, during certain times of the day, an adaptogen may seem to "pick you up" (for example, when you're making an important presentation), while later it can help quiet worries when your head meets the pillow.

Adaptogens have been used by most cultures around the world for thousands of years, and, given the enormously stressful climate of today's world, it's likely that we'll continue to need them more than ever. Given the many layers of benefits of smart plants, it may not come as a surprise to discover that over half the nootropic foods featured in this chapter are considered adaptogens.

SMART PLANTS NOOTROPIC ADAPTOGENS INCLUDE:

- Ashwagandha
- Goji berries
- Lion's mane
- Reishi
- Rhodiola
- Schisandra

Goji Berries —"The Well-Being Berry"

BOTANICAL NAME: *Lycium chinense, L. barbarum*

PART USED: Fruit

COMMONLY SOLD FORM: Sun-dried berries

TASTE: Tangy-sweet (the flavor is a bit like a cross between a cherry, a cranberry, a tomato and a raisin)

WHAT THEY ARE: Goji berries are a staple in traditional Chinese medicine and have been used for both healing and culinary purposes for millennia. A dried form of the small, oblong, bright red berries can be found in Asian food stores as well as most specialty food stores in North America. The natural sugars in the berry are concentrated during the drying process, resulting in a sweet, raisin-like fruit.

WHAT THEY DO: In some circles, goji berries have a great nickname: the happy berry. And while modern science hasn't definitively proven goji berries to be a mood food (capable of optimizing serotonin levels) participants in a study where goji berry juice was consumed for 14 days saw improvements in both neurological and psychological performance, including feelings of contentment, happiness, and general well-being. Other studies have suggested that the berries may indeed help improve the quality of one's sleep, while decreasing fatigue and stress. I don't know about you, but to me, getting a good night's sleep, saying goodbye to

fatigue, and feeling less stressed all sound like the ingredients for a much cheerier day!

But goji berries aren't just a way to put a smile on your face; they are exceptionally neuroprotective as well and can even enhance your mental performance, improving learning and memory. Goji berries contain a wealth of important amino acids, protective vitamins (especially vitamin C), essential minerals (particularly iron), and a range of antioxidants that have shown promise in the areas of eye health and overall immune function, while also helping to keep the blood-brain barrier from being compromised by glutamate excitotoxicity and other neurotoxic activities. Interestingly, one of the most studied compounds found in goji berries— *Lycium barbarum polysaccharides*, or carbohydrates bonded with glucose, otherwise known as "LBPs"—has been shown, in preliminary animal studies, not only to reduce the symptoms of Alzheimer's disease (through the reduction of neuron death) but to *regenerate* brain cells in the hippocampus as well.

HOW TO USE THEM: Most super-potent nootropics aren't ideal ingredients to be eaten on their own and are best hidden away in a recipe or used in capsule form, but goji berries are one of the few pleasant exceptions. In their sun-dried form, goji berries are a delightful superfood that can be snacked on (like raisins), mixed into trail mix or nondairy yogurt, and added to both sweet and savory recipes. As a nightshade, goji berries have a special flavor affinity with other nightshades, like tomatoes, eggplants, peppers, and potatoes. And as a berry, they can just as easily complement the sweet flavors of almost any kind of fruit. For mood-boosting combos that taste as great as they make you feel, try using goji berries with cacao, or add them to a berry smoothie bowl. For a simple and pure experience of the berries, you can make a traditional Chinese tea by steeping dried goji berries in hot water for a few minutes and then consuming both the sweet tea and the plumped whole berries.

A final note: Always be sure to purchase organic goji berries to avoid pesticides and other chemical residues that are sometimes used in the cultivation of the fruit.

BONUS BENEFITS OF GOJI BERRIES: Boost immune system, revitalize skin, promote longevity, support vision and eye health, boost sexual desire and fertility, and promote liver health.

GOJI BERRIES TAKEAWAY CHECKLIST:

✓ Improve learning and memory

✓ Increase feelings of well-being

✓ Protect the brain and the blood-brain barrier from excitotoxicity and other neurotoxic activities

✓ Promote neurogenesis

Purple Berries—"The Memory Fruits"

BOTANICAL NAME: n/a

PART USED: Fruit

COMMONLY SOLD FORMS: Fresh and frozen berries

TASTE: Sweet

WHAT THEY ARE: Say hello to the most common, globally accessible, and arguably longest-used nootropic on our top 10 list: purple berries. These potent, sweet fruits are part

of a broader "family" of edible berries that are characterized by their purple-ish pigment (the more saturated that pigment, the better!). Although blueberries are the most widely studied berries in this "purple" group, blackberries, bilberries, acai berries, maqui berries, and even berries with smaller amounts of "purple," like raspberries, strawberries, and cranberries, are all valued for their impressive brain-boosting benefits.

WHAT THEY DO: Long before we knew much at all about medicine, humans were eating all kinds of purple berries as an important source of energy. Now we've come to discover there's much more to this special class of superfoods.

Purple berries are a tremendous source of that all-important antioxidant group: flavonoids. While most berries contain many types of these beneficial compounds (and other antioxidants as well), purple berries are particularly rich in anthocyanins, which are often found in purple, blue, and black foods, as *cyanin* suggests. However, anthocyanins are unstable and can break down easily, and your body can only absorb a small percentage of what you consume. So, if you'd like to enjoy the antiaging benefits of anthocyanins, it is very important to obtain the most nutrient-dense sources you can find. In general, the easiest way to recognize high-antioxidant

sources is to look for natural foods that have the darkest and most vibrant colors. Scientists have found that once they are digested, anthocyanins can cross the blood-brain barrier and travel directly to the hippocampus, where they can have a beneficial impact on learning and memory.

But antioxidant advantages are not the only health benefits offered by anthocyanin-rich berries. After I interviewed Dr. Barbara Shukitt-Hale (USDA staff scientist in the Laboratory of Neuroscience and Aging, USDA-ARS, Human Nutrition Research Center on Aging [HNRCA] at Tufts University in Boston), she clarified exactly what is at work in these berries that makes them so beneficial to our health: "It's not only the antioxidant capacity that's important; it's their anti-inflammatory capacities, as well as their direct effects on the brain," Dr. Shukitt-Hale explained. "In one of our studies, we found that blueberries and strawberries increased neurogenesis, which is the process of making new neurons in the brain . . . and we also saw changes in signaling and communication in the brain—the positive signals go up while the negative signals go down. So we think that antioxidants are important, but it's not the whole story."

Research hasn't uncovered every aspect of what makes these berries so advantageous to our cognitive health, but we have discovered that improvements in the brain can occur rather quickly by simply adding them to a healthy diet. This was shown in one of Dr. Shukitt-Hale's studies with a group elderly people, who experienced improved memory after just three months of eating a healthy diet that included blueberries.

Similarly, my friend Dr. Paula Bickford, distinguished professor at the Center of Excellence for Aging & Brain Repair, Morsani College of Medicine, Department of Neurosurgery and Brain Repair, in Tampa, Florida, has also spent a large part of her lengthy neuroscience career studying blueberries, with some truly profound findings related to aging. Like Dr. Shukitt-Hale, Dr. Bickford's studies have shown that a diet enriched with blueberries can offer protection against cellular damage from oxidative stress, decrease inflammation in the brain, and enhance the health of brain cells overall. Research has also shown that blueberry consumption can improve motor skills, like balance and coordination; amplify cognition skills, like fluid intelligence (the ability to think and solve problems in a flexible way); and enhance memory. And berries aren't just useful later in life. A study showed that children aged seven to ten continued to improve their memory and problem-solving abilities proportional to the amount of purple berries

they consumed, leading researchers to conclude that eating more blueberries resulted in higher test scores.

I asked Dr. Bickford if other berries were as beneficial as blueberries, and she confirmed my hunch: *All edible berries*—and especially purple ones—are highly valuable to the health of your brain, although each kind of berry will contain a slightly different cocktail of supportive antioxidants and nutrients.

HOW TO USE THEM: Few things are more delicious than simply eating a handful of fresh berries, but there are so many other ways to enjoy them, from smoothies and desserts to salads, breakfast bowls, and so much more.

Conveniently, you can also use freeze-dried berry powders and frozen blueberries as ingredients for any number of recipes, which definitely saves money—and fear not: the nutrients in the berries are wholly retained in the freezing process. However, the anthocyanin content of berries *is* reduced when they are cooked or exposed to heat for long periods of time (although some of the con-tent does remain—it's not completely obliterated). Dr. Bickford observed that the anthocyanin content in cooked foods actually continues to diminish the longer the food sits, so if you briefly cook berries, as you would if you make the Blueberry-Chia Muffins (on page 160) for example, it's best to enjoy them soon after they're out of the oven, when the berries' nutritional benefits are at a peak.

BONUS BENEFITS OF PURPLE BERRIES: Heart-protective and improve blood circulation, can help with diabetes management, help protect bone strength, carcinopreventive, increase longevity, detoxify heavy metals, and fight obesity.

PURPLE BERRIES TAKEAWAY CHECKLIST:

✓ Improve problem solving, learning, and memory

✓ Highly neuroprotective and antiaging

✓ Help with fluidity of thought

✓ Improve coordination and balance

✓ Increase alertness and focus

✓ Enhance potential for neurogenesis

Rhodiola—"The Edge"

BOTANICAL NAME: *Rhodiola rosea*

PART USED: Herb

COMMONLY SOLD FORM: Powder

TASTE: A bit rose-like, with soapy, earthy, and bitter notes

WHAT IT IS: Rhodiola, a perennial sometimes known as "golden root" or "arctic root," has been used for a range of healing functions since ancient times. It is well documented that Pedanius Dioscorides (40–90 AD)—a Greek physician, pharmacologist, and botanist—was one of the first practitioners to use rhodiola for medicinal purposes. In fact, he featured rhodiola in his classic work *De Materia Medica*, an encyclopedia of herbal medicine, which is still considered a valuable reference for all the information it contains, almost 2,000 years after it was published.

Rhodiola thrives in dry, rocky areas of bitterly cold regions in the northern hemisphere, where it withstands intense temperature fluctuations. The history of rhodiola's uses is often recorded by cultures that are as tough as the herb itself. The Vikings, for example, used rhodiola as a tool to boost their physical strength in battle and to combat stress. Today, the herb is quite popular in Russia: Reportedly, it is used extensively in the Russian military to promote endurance, and its use was well documented in the former USSR to treat nerve-related conditions, including stress, anxiety, and depression. In Siberia, rhodiola is used to help people withstand intensely cold winter temperatures; and Russian Olympic athletes often use it to increase their stamina. Rhodiola is an adaptogen, with the ability to help balance the body overall, which explains its wide use. In fact, in traditional Chinese medicine, rhodiola is simply described as a means to encourage chi, the energy or vital force that flows through our bodies.

WHAT IT DOES: Rhodiola is one of the most effective natural nootropics for boosting mental energy, period. The herb is so popular because most people experience its effects almost immediately (some individuals may require more time to achieve the results they want). And speaking of benefits, chief among those conferred by rhodiola are improved motivation, heightened focus, and the ability to stay "in the flow" longer.

Additionally, as an adaptogen, rhodiola can help restore overall homeostasis in your body: If your energy is low and you're feeling depressed, rhodiola can give you a lift; or if you are feeling nervous and full of anxiety, it can help calm you down. In some ways, rhodiola functions much like a pharmaceutical antidepressant—without the side effects, of course—by helping to optimize mood-related neurotransmitters (serotonin,

dopamine, and norepinephrine). And, if you're overextended or burned out, the herb helps to decrease high levels of stress hormones, like cortisol, which can be neurotoxic if secreted in excessive amounts. But, as we know, the brain has the potential to be quite plastic, and even after it has been damaged by stress, herbs like rhodiola can be quite effective in restoring a normal state of function.

Rhodiola mildly energizes both your mind and your body and increases your stamina without being a stimulant. In addition to enhancing drive and attention span, it is particularly useful for all kinds of physical activities—from playing sports to hiking to washing the kitchen floor. Thanks to rhodiola's dual roles as an herbal antidepressant and a performance booster (both mental and physical), my family and I simply call it "the edge"—because that is exactly what this incredible plant has to offer.

HOW TO USE IT: On its own, rhodiola powder has a slightly odd, soapy taste that isn't altogether terrible, but it does need a little flavor "encouragement" from other ingredients. I find that it works best in sweet, fruity recipes and with chocolate. I also recommend using it in recipes that use a fair amount of fat or have a strong herbaceous flavor. Teas and tinctures are the most traditional ways of enjoying rhodiola, while smoothies are among the more recent, easy methods of incorporating the herb.

When you create your own nootropic recipes, think of rhodiola as an energizing catalyst. While it is a powerful ingredient to use on its own, rhodiola can also be combined with other nootropics to boost their effectiveness. A common nootropic "stack" is rhodiola and bacopa, a combination that is outstanding for its impact on improving memory and focus (for more information about bacopa, see page 118). When I have a challenging day ahead of me—for example, when I need to master a speech or immerse myself in complicated research and writing—I'll enjoy rhodiola in a morning beverage and take bacopa with it in capsule form. Another stack that works extremely well for reducing stress and enhancing mood is a combination of rhodiola and ashwagandha (see page 107 for more information about ashwagandha).

Unlike some natural nootropics, like purple berries, rhodiola is a "less-is-more" type of ingredient. Even though rhodiola is not a stimulant, it does increase energy, so if you are a sensitive sleeper, it may be best to use rhodiola in the morning.

Finally, although rhodiola is a natural nootropic, you'll want to obtain a standardized form of it that includes rosavin and salidroside, the active phytochemical components of rhodiola, to ensure that you get the optimum effects (quantities of these components can vary wildly in nature). Ideally, look for "3 percent rosavin and 1 percent salidroside standardized" on the label, as this 3:1 ratio appears to be a popular and effective quantity.

BONUS BENEFITS OF RHODIOLA: Adaptogen, improves endurance for physical activities, improves overall energy levels, cardioprotective, may assist in weight loss, may improve sexual function, helps keep blood sugar levels balanced, and may enhance the immune system.

RHODIOLA TAKEAWAY CHECKLIST:

- ✓ Reduces fatigue and increases energy
- ✓ Enhances mood and feelings of well-being
- ✓ Increases stamina
- ✓ Improves focus and motivation

Ashwagandha —"The Don't-Worry-Be-Happy Herb"

BOTANICAL NAME: *Withania somnifera*

PART USED: Root

COMMONLY SOLD FORM: Powder

TASTE: Bitter

WHAT IT IS: Ashwagandha, a hardy nightshade, is native to dry regions of India, Pakistan, Sri Lanka, and parts of Africa. It grows in sandy or well-drained soil and thrives in temperate, subtropical climates (for example, in the central coast of California, where I've been able to successfully grow ashwagandha in my garden). Traditionally, the roots, which contain the active compounds in the plant, are gathered in the autumn, cleaned and dried, and made into a powder or tincture.

Ashwagandha is so revered in Ayurvedic medicine that it is sometimes referred to as the "king of Ayurveda." In this traditional system of medicine, ashwagandha is classified three ways: as a general health tonic that can be used by anyone (*rasayana*); as a substance that enhances strength (*bhalya*); and as an aphrodisiac (*vajikarana*). In the West, ashwagandha is considered an adaptogen, because it can help restore the body to homeostasis.

WHAT IT DOES: Ashwagandha could easily be the subject of every page in this book because of its many beneficial effects on various areas of cognitive function. For the most part, however, ashwagandha is considered a calming adaptogen that enhances endocrine function by promoting the health of your thyroid and adrenal glands, which help regulate hormones (and the moods brought on by those hormones). Ashwagandha is often used for its beneficial effects on the nervous system, and it may also enhance GABA activity, the major downregulating neurotransmitter that suppresses stimulus response—another reason why the root helps promote a sense of tranquility. Although ashwagandha is not considered an energizing compound, it can help combat fatigue and mitigate some of the negative effects of stress caused by elevated levels of cortisol, insulin, and other unbalanced hormones. In preliminary studies, for example, ashwagandha has shown to be one of the few effective food-oriented means of helping to bring down elevated levels of cortisol.

Ashwagandha may also have a subtle effect on optimizing serotonin, dopamine, and norepinephrine activity in the brain, as well as improving epinephrine connectivity. The epinephrine (adrenaline) tie-in is particularly interesting because of the stress hormone's role in your body's fight-or-flight response, which is the very opposite of what one would consider "relaxing!" And yet, these contradictions are commonplace in the world of adaptogens, which generally support equilibrium wherever your body needs it. Perhaps this is why ashwagandha is so effective not only in reducing anxiety but also in improving mood, promoting better-quality sleep, aiding withdrawal from prescription and recreational drugs (including recovery from alcoholism), lessening the effects of obsessive-compulsive disorder (OCD), and more.

Ashwagandha may even have a future as a means of enhancing social interactions. Studies have shown that ashwagandha can dramatically improve cases of social dysfunction (one study reported a 68.1 percent improvement in social interaction while the participants were taking ashwagandha). The anxiety-reducing effects of ashwagandha can extend well beyond social events into many other aspects of life, including test-taking, public speaking, and the like. Imagine the advantage of being even 10 percent less nervous before giving your next presentation at work . . . all because your brain chemistry is

functioning a little better. As an introvert, I can personally attest to enjoying an appreciable decrease in anxiety before entering a large group situation after consuming ashwagandha—what an undervalued advantage it is to maintain a sense of inner calm!

Ashwagandha is not only a boon to brain function, but it may offer distinct neuroprotective benefits as well. Ashwagandha shows great potential as an effective Alzheimer's treatment, as it appears to both slow the progression of the disease and possibly reduce nerve cell damage. Other studies have focused on ashwagandha's potential impact on Huntington's disease and Parkinson's disease, and although the preliminary results have not shown dramatically beneficial results, it's clear that ashwagandha does, at the very least, offer some small positive effects. In addition, preliminary animal-based tests indicate that ashwagandha may also help improve memory and overall cognition, although these gains may be more apparent in cases where there is an imbalance or other disorder.

Lastly, and perhaps most exciting of all, some research has indicated that ashwagandha can affect neurogenesis—yes, your ability to make brand-new shiny brain cells. That's because ashwagandha increases the production of BDNF (brain-derived neurotrophic factor) and is one of the few edible substances on the planet that offers this benefit.

I also believe that ashwagandha can play an important role in combating the modern epidemic simply known as "burnout" by helping to reduce feelings of being overwhelmed and aiding long-term cognitive rebalance, repair, and growth. With all these benefits, it's no wonder that ashwagandha is considered such a valuable food for overall brain health (or that it merits a position of importance on this list of exceptional natural nootropics).

HOW TO USE IT: I suppose you can't have it all: Despite its powerful benefits, ashwagandha will never win any awards in the flavor category, to put it nicely. In fact, the name itself derives from Sanskrit: *ashva* (horse) and *gandha* (smell). I think we can stop the discussion of ashwagandha's pungent flavor right there! But fear not: It can be masked and hidden away quite successfully. In traditional Ayurvedic recipes, for example, ashwagandha is often prepared with ghee and honey or enjoyed as a tea. To make it even more cognitively effective, you can use it with plant-based fats like coconut oil in place of ghee and integrate it seamlessly in low-sugar lattes, smoothies, and high-fat recipes like dressings. I don't recommend baking with ashwagandha, unless you use very small quantities, as heat seems to magnify its bitter taste. It is possible, though, to use the powder in strong-flavored cookies and other sweet treats. Ashwagandha can be taken at any time of the day, but if it makes you feel "too" relaxed, try using it only in the evenings.

Ashwagandha goes very well with other nootropics that enhance its effects, and vice versa. Pairing ashwagandha with rhodiola or cacao, for example, can do wonders for enhancing mood, while a mix of ashwagandha and less potent nootropic herbs, like lavender and chamomile, can be very effective for combating anxiety as well.

BONUS BENEFITS OF ASHWAGANDHA: Anti-inflammatory, antioxidant, immune boosting, anti-tumor, nervine, antispasmodic, mild astringent, pain reliever, and diuretic. Ashwagandha has long been considered beneficial to sexual function for both men and women. (Its effectiveness in this area is likely due to the root's stress-reducing, hormone-balancing, and mood-boosting qualities.) Ashwagandha is also very rich in iron, making it important for blood health. Studies have also shown its potential benefits in the treatment of rheumatoid arthritis.

✓ Antianxiety—decreases nervousness

✓ Natural antidepressant (improves mood)

✓ Reduces stress by balancing hormones (cortisol and insulin)

✓ Soothes fatigue and neurasthenia (nervous exhaustion)

✓ Clears up cloudy thinking

✓ Helps diminish stress-induced insomnia

✓ Boosts stamina and endurance

✓ Promotes recovery from stress and helps with burnout

✓ Aids memory, focus, and concentration

Turmeric —"The Golden Root of Protection"

BOTANICAL NAME: *Curcuma longa*

PART USED: Rhizome

COMMONLY SOLD FORMS: Powder, fresh

TASTE: Pungent (yet fragrant), slightly bitter, with notes of ginger

WHAT IT IS: Turmeric is a member of the ginger family, which likely explains why the two spices are so complementary. Native to southern Asia, the tall, perennial plant is prized for its rhizome—the bulbous part of the stem. More than likely, you already have turmeric in your kitchen, and I'm happy to tell you that turmeric used for cooking and nootropic turmeric are one and the same. Although turmeric is mainly used in the West as an occasional culinary ingredient, it has been used medicinally (and as a spice) elsewhere in the world for more than 4,000 years.

Curcumin, the active (and much lauded) compound in turmeric, is a powerful substance that gives the spice its widely recognized, intense orange-yellow or "gold" color. Curcumin (diferuloylmethane) is also sold as an herbal supplement.

WHAT IT DOES: There is a tremendous amount of scientific and medical interest in turmeric and curcumin, evidenced by numerous studies and clinical trials that are currently underway. Most of the studies revolve around the effectiveness of curcumin itself, as there are indications that this unique compound is a powerful anti-inflammatory agent and highly neuroprotective.

Curcumin may inhibit depression and can act as a mood booster on several levels. First, it reduces inflammation in the brain, which is often associated with depression (the causes of depression are still a matter of debate, but the fact remains that inflammation and depression go hand in hand). Second, curcumin can help maintain optimal levels of mood-boosting serotonin, dopamine, and norepinephrine in your brain by inhibiting the action of an enzyme that can break down those mood-modulating neurotransmitters. And third, curcumin increases levels of BDNF (brain-derived neurotrophic factor)—stimulating the growth of neurons and assisting your brain in healing and "regrowing" after a bout with depression.

New research has also revealed that curcumin is associated with improved memory and learning, as well as delayed aging. In a 2018 study, consumption of high amounts of curcumin (90 mg twice a day) enhanced the participants' memory by *28 percent* over 18 months—an improvement of almost a third! And in the neuroprotective area, turmeric and curcumin have also shown distinct promise in helping to prevent Alzheimer's disease, which occurs when a protein—beta-amyloid—forms an inflammatory plaque that, in effect, strangles healthy cells in the brain. As a preventive method (not a treatment), curcumin appears to actively deter the formation of beta-amyloid plaque before it can do any damage. Researchers are now investigating whether this effect can help inhibit growth and progression in early-stage Alzheimer's as well.

Last, but not by any means least, curcumin can diminish the negative effects of "lifestyle stress," thanks to its effect on reducing cortisol levels, as well as its ability to decrease the damaging consequences of stress overall.

HOW TO USE IT: The one downside to consuming turmeric as a whole food (and not as an isolated curcumin supplement) is the unpredictable nature of its bioavailability. In other words, your body can have a difficult time digesting and utilizing turmeric effectively. However, with a bit of a smart cooking strategy, you can maximize its health benefits. Turmeric's curcumin nutrients are fat-soluble, which means they need to be combined with some kind of fat in order for your body to access the benefits, so using turmeric in recipes where it is cooked with olive oil or coconut oil is a perfect solution. Your body's absorption of curcumin is also enhanced by piperine, a compound found in black pepper, so try to combine turmeric with pepper whenever possible (fortunately, they're complementary flavors). You can use mild-tasting turmeric in just about any savory recipe, and you can even add it to smoothies, lattes, snacks, and treats. Taking a curcumin supplement to optimize its bioavailability is always an option, as well.

BONUS BENEFITS OF TURMERIC: Powerful antibacterial, antifungal, and antiviral (even helps inhibit the reproduction of the HIV virus); antiaging (reduces oxidative stress and down-regulates age-related genes); reduces chronic pain; antioxidant; anti-inflammatory; effective in preventing liver and kidney toxicity; potential treatment for skin disorders (rosacea and psoriasis), HIV, septic shock, cardiovascular disease, lung fibrosis, arthritis, and inflammatory bowel disease; anti-atherosclerotic. And that's just what we've discovered so far! In-vitro and animal studies suggest that turmeric may offer anticancer benefits as well.

TURMERIC TAKEAWAY CHECKLIST:

✓ Powerful anti-inflammatory

✓ Potent antioxidant

✓ Fights stress, boosts mood, reduces depression

✓ May improve memory

Curcumin + DHA

Curcumin can help your brain do a better job of synthesizing valuable DHA (docosahexaenoic acid, an omega-3 fat that may improve the health of your brain), so if you're taking a DHA supplement, make the most of it by pairing it with turmeric or a curcumin supplement. And don't forget to add a little bit of black pepper on the side to maximize absorption.

Schisandra —"The Focus Berry"

BOTANICAL NAME: *Schisandra chinensis*

PART USED: Fruit

COMMONLY SOLD FORM: Powder

TASTE: Mostly sour, with pungent, bitter, as well as slightly sweet, salty, and savory notes

WHAT IT IS: Indigenous to Russia, northeast China, Japan, and the Korean peninsula, schisandra is most widely cultivated today in the Republic of Korea and the People's Republic of China. A woody climbing vine, schisandra produces deep-red, edible berries. The berries are dried and ground into a fine, blackish-purple powder and used as both a food and a remedy to heal a wide range of ailments in Russia and various parts of Asia. Schisandra is also revered in traditional Chinese medicine. Additionally, in Nepal and other areas of the world (including North America), schisandra is considered a superfood and is used as a culinary ingredient.

WHAT IT DOES: Schisandra is most commonly used to treat insomnia, and its benefits have been confirmed by several animal studies showing that it helps reduce anxiety and enhance sleep—not only increasing the total hours of sleep but also improving the *quality* of rest by augmenting the amount of restorative, deep, slow-wave sleep.

But because schisandra is considered an adaptogen, it doesn't just chill you out and help get you tucked in at night; it can also boost your performance while you are awake. Animal studies have shown that the active component of schisandra berries improves memory (in some cases it has even reversed memory impairment) by helping to modulate acetylcholine neurotransmitter levels. Schisandra also supports the synthesis of neural adenosine triphosphate—otherwise known as ATP (aka "brain energy"). What's more, special compounds in schisandra are considered antiaging as well and actively protect the brain from oxidative stress and functional deficits like dementia.

I find schisandra to work rather quickly as a cognitive boost—it's not something that has to build up in your system over days or weeks to deliver the benefits. And it turns out that I'm not the only one. A recent double-blind, placebo-controlled, randomized (albeit small) human study confirmed my personal experience to a tee, along with so much more. Forty women, aged 20 to 68, who claimed to live a lifestyle that left them exposed to frequent high-stress situations, participated in the study. First, the pilot study participants were exposed to a test created to mentally exhaust them. Then some participants were given a formula consisting of a standardized combination of schisandra and rhodiola, while others just received a placebo. Just two hours later, all participants were exposed to a second test specifically designed to assess cognitive function. The results of taking a *single dose* of the formula were impressive, to say the least. According to a 2010 article in the medical journal *Phytomedicine*, the schisandra-rhodiola group experienced a significant improvement in attention, speed, quality, and accuracy, all without side effects!

Schisandra checks the boxes for almost every quality you could want from a nootropic: It can help keep you calm and lower anxiety, while also keeping you alert, attentive, and in the flow—thereby increasing your productivity. And, yes, it may actually make you smarter, or at least improve the quality of your work. I look forward to the continued study of schisandra as a nootropic; I believe there is still much to learn about this plant.

HOW TO USE IT: Schisandra is every bit as fascinating from a culinary standpoint as it is from a health point of view. In traditional Chinese medicine, schisandra is known as *wu wei zi*, which means "five flavors fruit," because it hits all five Chinese flavor markers: sweet, sour, bitter, pungent/spicy, and salty. (These characteristics are then linked with health benefits for the five yin organs: spleen, liver, heart, lungs, and kidneys, respectively.) As you might imagine from that description, the flavor of the schisandra berry is quite adaptable: It can hang out as innocuously as a wallflower in sweet smoothie bowls, or it can add a bit of interest to savory vegetable recipes or soups. The overall flavor of schisandra is a little like nutmeg, so while you may not want to use it in large quantities as the focal flavor of a dish, it can be an interesting and exciting ingredient to use as an add-in "spice."

Unless you find yourself in one of the regions where schisandra is a native plant, most likely you'll find it only in powdered form. I'll be the first to admit that it is not exactly a common ingredient in most grocery stores, but you should be able to find it in natural food stores or online. For information about where to buy schisandra, check out the Resources Guide (page 265). Just be sure to purchase a certified organic brand (usually sourced from China).

BONUS BENEFITS OF SCHISANDRA: Adaptogen (balances stress); improves cardiovascular health; normalizes blood pressure and circulation; protects the liver; improves physical performance and combats fatigue; bolsters the respiratory system; helpful in soothing stomach disorders and ulcers; enhances the immune system. Currently, research is underway to test the effectiveness of schisandra in preventing cancer.

SCHISANDRA TAKEAWAY CHECKLIST:

✓ Promotes calm, reduces stress, relieves anxiety

✓ Helps with duration and quality of sleep

✓ Good for memory

✓ Enhances brain energy and mental activity

✓ Boosts attention and work performance; speeds reflexes

✓ Neuroprotective

USING NATURAL NOOTROPICS IN RECIPES

Adding natural nootropics to your diet may be easier than you think. While most of the recipes in this book (beginning on page 127) are centered on "everyday" neuroprotective smart plants, some contain a few of the "easier to find and use" nootroopic ingredients as well, such as fresh purple berries, turmeric, dried goji berries, cacao, and matcha. Using these simpler nootropic boosts is a wonderful way to begin gaining an extra cognitive edge, along with some culinary inspiration.

Cooking with some of the more "uncommon" natural nootropics—like lion's mane, reishi, ashwagandha, rhodiola, and schisandra —may not feel as intuitive at first, but you'll likely find the practice simple to pick up.

These lesser-known foods can often be used like spices (or simply blended in and hidden among bolder recipe flavors), as they are all found in powder form and are functionally potent, even when used in very small quantities. While most of the recipes in this book do not include these less common nootropics, you can find easy ways to incorporate them by following the Brain Boost suggestions that accompany each recipe. And if you're ready to make all nootropics a part of your daily wellness plan, head over to the Rituals section (page 238), where you'll find a full suite of nootropic-rich, brain-boosting recipes that will give you the opportunity to explore the entire gamut of natural nootropics in delicious ways.

Keep in mind that every natural nootropic offers different advantages. To make things simple, you can use the Natural Nootropics by Function list below as a guide to fine-tune your personal cognitive goals. These "functions" include the five main benefits of nootropic brain optimization: **Calm** (antianxiety, improves sleep, relieves stress), **Flow** (promotes creative thought and encourages mental clarity), **Mood** (supports a sense of well-being and motivation), **Memory** (helps with recollection and aids learning), and **Focus** (aids concentration and improves attention span).

NATURAL NOOTROPICS BY FUNCTION

FUNCTION ▸	Calm	Flow	Mood	Memory	Focus
	Ashwagandha	Matcha	Ashwagandha	Ashwagandha	Ashwagandha
	Cacao*	Purple Berries	Cacao	Cacao	Cacao
	Goji Berries	Reishi	Goji Berries	Goji Berries	Lion's Mane
	Lion's Mane	Rhodiola	Lion's Mane	Lion's Mane	Matcha
NOOTROPIC ▸	Matcha*	Schisandra	Reishi	Matcha	Purple Berries
	Reishi		Rhodiola	Purple Berries	Rhodiola
	Schisandra		Turmeric	Reishi	Schisandra
	Turmeric			Schisandra	
				Turmeric	

*Note: While matcha and cacao have been studied for their stress-relief and antianxiety effects, they contain a small amount of caffeine (especially matcha) and should not be used as a sleep aid if you are sensitive to caffeine.

THE WORLD OF NOOTROPICS

Natural nootropics are the superfoods in the world of brain optimization. Not only do these powerful ingredients maintain and protect neurological function; they can actually *enhance* your cognitive performance, too.

- Natural nootropics are loaded with benefits for the brain (and often the body, as well!). Avoid so-called "brain-boosting" chemical compounds, which can have adverse health consequences.

- Identify your personal cognitive goals and match them with natural nootropics that meet your needs.

- Use everyday smart plants as the base ingredients in recipes, and add natural nootropics for an extra boost.

CHAPTER 7

Mind-Enhancing Supplements

"It is by logic that we prove, but by intuition that we discover."

HENRI POINCARÉ, French mathematician, theoretical physicist, philosopher of science, and engineer

There are hundreds of plants that could be considered nootropics, although they vary in potency and availability. So while the small collection of nootropics you'll find in this chapter may come in the form of a pill, rest assured that they are still plant-based! At the moment, these special plants are either only available as a supplement, or they simply don't work well in recipes as ingredients because of their flavor. Nevertheless, once you take note of their incredible benefits, you'll likely conclude that these supplements may be worth seeking out. Consider this part of the book a peek into the future of "what's next" for natural nootropics—and another opportunity to take brain optimization to the next level.

BACOPA MONNIERI (BRAHMI): It pains me to kick a powerful nootropic like bacopa down to our list of supplements (rather than including it with prime natural nootropic recipe ingredients), but unfortunately there's not much I can do about it. When I first found bacopa in a powdered form, I celebrated by immediately buying two large bottles of the stuff and prepared to go on a bacopa recipe-testing marathon. After three mind-blowingly hideous, cannot-be-fixed, there's-no-way-to-even-try-and-drink-this smoothie tests, I realized I'd finally met my match: a superfood that tastes so bad, it simply cannot be masked. (Fresh bacopa, which has a milder flavor than the powder, is sometimes used as a vegetable in

Indian cooking, but is not readily available in North America. Conversely, the more accessible, powdered form of bacopa has an otherworldly bitterness.) So although I don't usually say this about a food, when it comes to bacopa, just buy the capsule.

Even though many of us may be unfamiliar with bacopa, the herb is, in fact, considered to be among the oldest of all known nootropics—its use in India, in Ayurvedic medicine, goes back more than 4,000 years. While the Indian government has supported an enormous amount of research into the relationship between bacopa and cognitive function, study of the herb in the West has begun only recently—in the last ten years or so. Therefore, despite the tremendous number of papers published on bacopa, there have not been enough human clinical trials to cement its place in Western medical practice. That said, having personally experienced the real benefits of this herb, I, for one, can't wait for bacopa to earn its place in the spotlight.

Traditionally known as brahmi, bacopa is a voracious creeping herb that grows in and around watery places, such as marshy wetlands, riverbanks, and tidal pools. Although it is native to India and Sri Lanka, bacopa is now grown in Australia, Florida, the Gulf Coast, and, most recently, in my own backyard in California, much to my delight. If you grow the herb yourself, be aware that there are a number of bacopa subspecies, but only *Bacopa monnieri* contains nootropic and brain-sharpening properties.

Although bacopa has been used to treat illness in the past, it appears that the herb can also be used for all-around cognitive improvement. Bacopa enhances working memory, long-term memory, focus, and information processing speed and also reduces anxiety. Bacopa is one of my favorite natural nootropics for all these reasons, and, for me, it begins to produce tangible results within a week of taking it. Others may find that its effects are not as immediate, but after a month or so of consistent use, they'll discover that both their short- and long-term memory have been turned up considerably. Be sure to buy organic bacopa, as the plant can easily absorb unwanted contaminants, like lead and nitrates, if it is grown in polluted water.

Stack It!

Bacopa and rhodiola are a particularly good nootropic pair for enhancing drive, focus, and memory—and they're a great team for boosting work-related performance! Whether you take bacopa and rhodiola together or at different points in the day, you'll still gain the synchronistic benefits.

Be Careful with Dopamine Precursors

Mucuna pruriens is a great example of a plant that can effectively increase dopamine levels in your brain (which explains why it is often marketed as a nootropic). This plant, also known as "velvet bean," contains unusually large quantities of naturally-occurring L-Dopa—the direct precursor of dopamine—with levels as high as 9 percent potency (and even higher in concentrated formulas). *Mucuna pruriens* also enhances lucid dreaming and sex drive, which makes it easy to see why it's such a sought-after "superfood." However, caution is advised.

Thanks to the nutrients they contain, most brain-boosting foods can help optimize how you process dopamine. But these nutrients have many other uses in the body as well. For example, the amino acid tyrosine, which your body can convert into L-Dopa *if needed,* can also be used for many other functions, such as making thyroid hormones. But foods containing L-Dopa signal just one thing to your brain: Produce more dopamine! Make no mistake: This direct impact on neurotransmitters is essentially self-medication, and it comes with great risk. You really don't want to go out of your way to disrupt dopamine balance, which can have a dangerous domino effect on your mental microclimate.

So while *Mucuna pruriens* can be helpful in cases of Parkinson's, where dopamine is compromised, it doesn't mean it's good for someone who is healthy. In that light, it would be wise to steer clear of taking L-Dopa-rich ingredients, like *Mucuna pruriens*, on a regular basis. When I asked Dr. Andrew Hill (the cognitive neuroscientist and creator of the Peak Brain Institute, with whom I spoke at the beginning of my own brain optimization journey) about "velvet bean," he looked me straight in the eye and said, "I'd be very careful with this one." Given the long list of potential side effects caused by L-Dopa (or too much dopamine), I'm inclined to agree and would therefore not rely on the foods that contain it as nootropics.

Fortunately, L-Dopa is naturally found in very few edibles, other than tamarind (probably the most common natural source, albeit much less potent than *Mucuna pruriens*) and a few rarely used herbs, including senna and moth bean. Outside of its medical uses to treat people suffering from diseases or those in a catatonic state, it's probably not something you want to actively seek out on your own.

CBD OIL: Nope, hemp-sourced CBD oil (short for cannabidiol) won't get you high—it doesn't contain THC (or any other psychoactive compounds, for that matter). However, CBD can be a real boon to the health of your brain, as well as your body overall. CBD oil is strongly anti-inflammatory and neuroprotective and is a potent antianxiety supplement that may also boost mood. Despite its many benefits, at the time of this writing, CBD oil is only legal in some states in the United States, which is why you won't see CBD oil as an ingredient in any of the recipes in this book. If you do have legal access to it, you can easily add some drops of CBD oil directly to a smoothie, salad dressing, or other uncooked food (heated applications of CBD result in nutrient loss). CBD oil has a somewhat nutty taste, with a faint but pleasant background flavor of marijuana.

PANAX GINSENG: As a revered root, panax is one of a slew of ginseng varieties that belong to the same botanical family. Although each kind of ginseng offers slightly different effects, all of them enhance energy. However, panax ginseng is most often used as a cognition booster and is known for its ability to increase mental and physical reaction time and accuracy, as well as reduce mental fatigue. It is also a very popular herb for enhancing feelings of well-being and happiness.

GOTU KOLA: Gotu kola is consumed as a leafy green food in many Eastern countries, but in the West, it is taken as a supplement. Typically advertised as a gentle way to help calm the nervous system, gotu kola can help decrease anxiety and promote feelings of well-being. Some people use the supplement as a kind of "beginner's nootropic" because of it's mild yet generally positive

effects. Whether or not you see any tangible improvements in your mood, you can be confident that significant upgrades are likely occurring in the background, as gotu kola is known to stimulate the growth of new neurons and protect the brain against toxins.

HOLY BASIL: *Tulsi* is another name for holy basil, a strong antioxidant and adaptogen that offers multiple benefits to your body as a whole—including cognitive enhancements—while helping to reduce stress and manage anxiety. While you can take holy basil as a supplement, it is also available as a tea, which some find especially relaxing and enjoyable before going to bed and as a great way to calm the mind.

ARTICHOKE EXTRACT: While you may be tempted to enjoy a batch of fresh artichoke hearts for therapeutic reasons (and they certainly are good for you), eating the vegetable by itself is unlikely to make much of a change in your cognitive state. However, using a condensed artichoke extract (in either a capsule or tincture form) will give you a more potent dose of the vegetable's active compounds, which can improve short-term memory and recall. And, because artichoke is a natural prebiotic, it supports balanced gut flora as well.

ST. JOHN'S WORT: Of all the nootropics, St. John's wort is perhaps best known for its successful use as a potent antidepressant. In fact, the herb is so effective that in Germany it outsells chemically derived antidepressant medications many times over. Be aware, though, that St. John's wort interacts with many prescription drugs—including pharmaceutical antidepressants—so you should only use this herb under a physician's supervision.

CURCUMIN: If you're not into having a turmeric latte every day or need a higher and more effective dose of turmeric than the spice you're cooking with, a curcumin supplement is where it's at. Many cognitive health experts recommend taking curcumin every day as a form of "cheap insurance," because of the herb's effectiveness in protecting the brain from inflammation and degeneration.

ASTAXANTHIN: Although it's not a nootropic per se, astaxanthin is such a powerful brain protectant that it earns an honorable mention on the list of "mind-enhancing supplements." Astaxanthin, which can be sourced from algae (as well as fish and krill), is a highly potent carotenoid antioxidant that helps preserve cognitive function as you age by reducing oxidative stress and inflammation. It has many other benefits, too— I've personally taken it to improve joint health after running injuries, and it's offered impressive results.

NOOTROPIC HERBS & SPICES

We've covered some of the most powerful and unique natural nootropics in the world, but there are plenty of common plants that offer minor nootropic effects as well—many of which may already be waiting in your kitchen in the form of herbs and spices! While their effects may be mild, I like to think that these little doses of brain-boosting micronutrients add up—like putting extra pennies in the "greater cognitive good" jar. So don't hesitate to add these flavorful foods to your recipes because, when it comes to nutrient variety, the more the merrier. You'll definitely see most of the ingredients in the following chart pop up in the recipes in this book, starting on page 127.

Herb/Spice	Brain Benefits	Culinary Use
Black Pepper	Helps overall brain functioning and clear thinking. Mild antidepressant. The active compound in black pepper, piperdine, can also amplify the absorption of other nootropics.	Savory foods, salads, fresh fruit
Chamomile	Highly calming. May improve sleep quality and reduce anxiety and depression.	Tea, desserts
Cinnamon	Can enhance cognition, learning potential, and recognition-oriented memory. Has shown beneficial effects on neurodegenerative diseases like Alzheimer's and Parkinson's.	Fruits, grains, winter squash, desserts
Cloves	Naturally high in manganese (an essential mineral for brain function). May decrease oxidative stress in the brain.	Baked goods, cooked fruits, sweet vegetables
Fenugreek	Packed with choline (an essential brain nutrient); can help with brain development, memory, nerve-cell signaling, and mood disorders.	Cooked vegetables, legumes, rice
Garlic	Overall neural protectant. May help shield the brain from neurodegenerative disorders, including Alzheimer's, Parkinson's, and Huntington's diseases.	Savory meals & snacks of all kinds
Ginger	Contains a special compound called zerumbone, which may help prevent brain tumors, inhibit inflammatory responses, and improve reaction time and working memory.	Roots & tubers, fruits, creamy foods
Lavender	Induces calm and promotes relaxation.	Tea, nuts, summer fruits, desserts
Lemon Balm	May help modulate mood and cognitive function. Helps fight stress, promotes calm focus, and aids with information processing.	Tea, light salads, berries
Licorice	In small quantities, licorice may be neuroprotective and improve sleep.	Tea, desserts
Peppermint	May increase cognitive performance and mood, as well as enhance brain alertness and quicken reflexes.	Tea, smoothies, desserts, fruits, salads
Rosemary	May promote mild memory improvement, through consumption and aroma.	Beans & legumes, Mediterranean vegetables, nuts & seeds
Sage	Can help improve memory and overall cognitive performance.	Beans, grains & pasta, soups, winter squash
Vanilla	Mild antidepressive effects. Aroma can positively affect electrical activity of the brain.	Smoothies, baked goods, desserts, fruits

It's true: There is no best diet for everyone. There's only the best diet for *you*, as you are right now—and even that may change. Consequently, while we've covered general guidelines in previous chapters, you won't find anything in the way of black-and-white prescriptive doses in this book. "The Golden Rule of Brain Optimization" isn't extreme or a gimmick, either. If anything, the golden "rule" is closer to the homespun wisdom you've likely heard so many times before: **Balance is key.**

- Balance your dietary choices by eating food that makes your brain *and your whole body* feel good, which will support a long, healthy life.

- Balance your nutrition by eating a wide variety of plants that support your lifestyle and biological needs. Eating seasonally will help.

- Balance the quantity of the foods you consume by respecting the potency of all foods, and keep moderation in mind—even the healthiest foods can become toxic when they are eaten in excess. For optimal health (and to make it easier to balance nutrition),

eat "close to the earth" by relying on real foods, rather than supplements, as much as possible.

- Balance your lifestyle. A healthy diet will only go so far and does not replace the importance of nurturing and supporting your whole being. Whether it's a matter of getting more sleep, exercising, hydrating, meditating, setting goals, trying new things, falling in love, or even simply using a new nonallergenic laundry detergent—yes, absolutely, do it! Your diet will help you immensely, but your lifestyle will most certainly enhance (or hinder) your overall experience.

To be alive and to experience being human is a gift. And with this gift comes an immense opportunity to learn, explore, create, help, and make a positive impact. Nourishing your brain through healthy whole foods and natural nootropics will groom you for success on so many levels: It will give you the most solid base on which to build and live your life to the fullest . . . as the most balanced, abundant version of yourself.

Maybe I've seen too many sci-fi movies, but I'll admit, sometimes the question still tugs at me: If we continue to perfect our understanding of nutrition, is there a possibility that we could someday have the ability to become "limitlessly" smarter? Alas, as exciting as the notion of never-ending genius may be, the reality is that there will always be an end point to what any single human being can achieve, physically and cognitively, during the course of a lifetime.

But. If you're like most people, chances are you haven't yet reached the peak of what you *can* achieve. And just imagine all the cognitive "money" you're currently leaving on the table . . . money which could be so easily grasped with a few simple dietary tweaks. Limitless brainpower may be a wild fantasy, but being and feeling your best can easily become your new normal. Can you honestly say you're currently at the very top of your personal cognitive game? And, if not, what are you waiting for? You now have a whole world of smart plants to try, and their reward is right at your fingertips: the opportunity to experience the true potential of your own incredible mind.

Chapter Cheat Sheet:
MIND-ENHANCING SUPPLEMENTS

There are hundreds of varieties of plant-based nootropics, with each offering a unique range of benefits to help fine-tune your brain's performance. While some nootropics can be used as ingredients in recipes, others are best consumed as supplements, either because of limited availability or poor flavor.

- Use natural nootropic supplements to bolster a healthy, brain-boosting diet. Supplements cannot replace a well-rounded diet or the practice of a holistic lifestyle, but they can help support any of your positive efforts.

- Include nootropic spices and herbs in your cooking and celebrate every cognitive-friendly "win," however small.

- Follow the golden rule for long-lasting wellness that has stood the test of time: balance. A balanced brain is an optimized brain.

Part Two

THE
RECIPES

Smart Plants recipes are all about ensuring the most brain-healthy foods are as utterly irresistible to your taste buds as they are to your brain. So to help you make the healthiest— and tastiest—choices when you're at the farmer's market or in the produce aisle of your local supermarket, the recipes in this book are divided into seasons. The sections—Spring, Summer, Fall, and Winter—offer simple recipes for all kinds of seasonal dishes for every meal of the day, from breakfast to dessert to everything in between. (You'll also find a complete list of Recipes by Meal on page 262.)

The Mind Meter key at the bottom of each recipe gives you insight into the cognitive benefits each recipe has to offer. If you want to gain even more healthy-brain benefits from the recipes, the Brain Boosts offer powerful ingredient options. And if you're ready to make the world of nootropics part of your everyday lifestyle, head over to the Rituals section (page 238). There you'll find highly functional recipes packed with nootropics that can easily fit into your daily routine.

INSPIRATION FOR EATING SEASONALLY

Although nutrition is a deeply complex subject, what we know without a doubt is that enjoying a varied diet is an essential part of meeting your brain's needs. Incorporating the breathtaking diversity of seasonal foods is a wonderful way to ensure this variety, as each food offers its own beneficial alchemy of nutrients. You'll also find that the practice of buying seasonal foods from local sources is both favorable to the environment and important for the requirements of your own biochemistry, which can vary or even depend on where you live. (For example, a fruit-prominent diet may be more nutritionally fitting for someone living in Hawaii, while a fat- and protein-centered diet might be more appropriate for someone living in Alaska.)

Perhaps most importantly, eating seasonally will help you to cultivate a deeper appreciation for plant foods in general, as you explore a delicious range of flavors, bright colors, and appealing textures. As a result, you'll likely find you begin to crave these "treats of the season" as they come around, while improving the way you think and feel at the same time.

HOW TO USE THE MIND METER KEY

Mind Meters indicate which of the five main benefits of nootropic brain optimization and which of the Three Ps of Brain Building (shown below in italics) each recipe offers. Here's a breakdown of these benefits and their attributes:

Calm: Helps manage anxiety, improves sleep quality, and provides stress relief.

Flow: Helps encourage mental clarity and promotes creativity.

Mood: Helps balance the mind, promotes a sense of well-being and positivity, and supports motivation.

Memory: Helps with working memory (short-term) as well as memory recall (long-term) and aids learning.

Focus: Helps stimulate reaction time and alertness, enhances concentration, and improves stamina.

Priming: Optimizes the brain's everyday activity and maintenance.

Protection: Defends the brain against the factors that cause cognitive impairment and disease.

Plasticity: Promotes the brain's ability to continuously adapt to changes and learn new things (neuroplasticity), and encourages the growth of new brain cells (neurogenesis).

SPRING

The first roots and shoots of spring are harbingers of lush times to come in the world of produce: Chartreuse sprouts poke out of gardens, a few berries stud the foliage of rejuvenated plants with pops of color, new onions make their way delicately to the surface, and the feathery fronds of carrots and radishes peek out of the ground, reminding us that hibernation is over. Spring is a true plant-lover's season, and the luminous colors and flavors it offers align beautifully with intentions of eating clean and feeling clear.

Berry-Almond Amaranth Porridge

What a vastly underused pseudo-grain amaranth is, despite its impressive complete-protein status and gluten-free bragging rights. Once this toothsome porridge is cooked, I like to stir in something creamy, like yogurt, which offers gut-friendly probiotics and also nicely complements the texture of the grain.

To make this porridge even healthier, it's finished off with a delicious, saucy compote of super-tender fruits that burst with their own juices, simply by allowing frozen fruit to defrost, then spooning it over the porridge. This method of making a compote is easy and, because the berries are uncooked, you get the maximum benefit from brain-healthy antioxidants in the fruit.

SERVES 2

½ cup amaranth

2 cups water

2 cups frozen mixed berries (such as strawberries, blueberries, and blackberries)

2 tablespoons maple syrup*

⅛ teaspoon ground cinnamon

½ cup vanilla nondairy yogurt, unsweetened

½ teaspoon almond extract (optional)

2 tablespoons slivered almonds (optional)

*To make this recipe sugar-free, use 2 tablespoons monk fruit sugar as a substitute.

1. In a small pot, mix together the amaranth and water and place the pot over high heat. Bring the mixture to a boil, and then reduce the heat to low. Let the mixture simmer gently for 15–20 minutes, uncovered, or until the amaranth is chewy and tender and a thick porridge has formed. Stir the mixture frequently during the last few minutes of cooking to avoid burning.

2. Meanwhile, place the berries in a separate small pan over very low heat for a couple minutes, until the fruit has completely defrosted and is juicy. Remove the pan from the heat and stir in the maple syrup and cinnamon. Cover the pan to keep the berry mixture warm. In a bowl, whisk together the yogurt and almond extract, if using.

3. Divide the amaranth porridge into two bowls and swirl in the yogurt mixture, along with the berries and their juices. Top with the almonds and serve warm.

Brain Boost: Top each bowl with 1 tablespoon of goji berries.

Mind Meter

Fl	Mo	Me	Fo	Pri	Pro	Pl

Red Pepper Frittata Cups

Although these healthy, completely plant-based mini fritattas make a fantastic savory breakfast, they can be enjoyed—warm or cold—at any time of the day (don't be surprised if you sneak one in for an afternoon snack), and they are also an ideal "company's coming for brunch" go-to. Serve them with a simple tossed salad of baby greens in a light vinaigrette for a well-rounded meal, and feel free to substitute the vegetables (in the ingredient list) with other favorites, such as broccoli, peas, and mushrooms.

MAKES 8 FRITTATA CUPS /
SERVES 4

Cooking oil spray

1 ¼ cup garbanzo
bean flour

1 tablespoon
nutritional yeast

¾ teaspoon sea salt

1 cup unsweetened
almond milk

2 tablespoons fresh
lemon juice

1 tablespoon fresh
thyme leaves, minced

2 tablespoons olive
oil, divided

1 large yellow onion,
halved and thinly
sliced

4 large cloves garlic,
minced

2 cups baby arugula

(continued on following page)

1. Preheat the oven to 350°F. Spray 8 of the cups in a muffin pan with cooking oil spray.

2. In a large bowl, mix together the garbanzo bean flour, nutritional yeast, and salt. Add the almond milk, lemon juice, thyme, and 1 tablespoon of the olive oil, and whisk the mixture into a smooth batter.

3. Warm the remaining 1 tablespoon olive oil in a large sauté pan over medium heat. Add the onion slices and sauté for 5 minutes, until they're very soft. Add the garlic and sauté for 30 seconds longer, stirring constantly. Add the arugula and cook, stirring, just until the leaves are wilted—about 1 minute longer. Remove the pan from the heat. Fold the vegetables into the garbanzo flour mixture, along with the roasted bell peppers and walnuts, mixing well. Transfer the mixture to the prepared muffin cups and fill them evenly, almost to the brim (don't fret, the fritattas will barely rise). Once the cups have been filled, lightly tap the muffin pan on the counter to make any protruding vegetables sink under the batter—the tops should appear fairly flat. Bake the frittata cups for 23–28 minutes, or

(continued on following page)

Mind Meter

2 roasted red bell peppers (fresh or jarred),* cut into 1/2-inch dice

1/3 cup finely chopped walnuts

*Note: For a super-quick version of this recipe, nothing beats the convenience of using jarred roasted red bell peppers—all you have to do is drain and chop them. But if you'd like to make your own roasted peppers, it's fairly simple: Roast two fresh bell peppers directly over a gas flame or under the oven broiler until the skin is charred on all sides. Let the peppers cool in a sealed paper bag. Peel off the skin, remove the stem and seeds, and then cut the peppers into 1/2-inch dice.

until the tops are slightly golden and the centers feel set to the touch.

4. Remove the muffin pan from the oven, and let the frittata cups cool in the pan for a minimum of 5 minutes before extracting them with a knife. The frittata cups may be enjoyed hot or cold. You can also refrigerate them for up to 4 days and then reheat them, if you like.

Brain Boost: Add 1 tablespoon of lion's mane powder to the garbanzo bean flour when you mix in the nutritional yeast and salt.

FOOD FOR THOUGHT: Bell Peppers ⸻

All types of bell peppers—red, orange, yellow, and even green—are brimming with an array of brain-friendly carotenoids, including beta-carotene, alpha-carotene, lutein, and zeaxanthin. These antioxidants are thought to not only protect your brain against damage and disease, but may even improve cognitive function, particularly in older adults. Bell peppers also supply many other essential vitamins for your brain, including vitamin B_6 and vitamin C. Research indicates that organic bell peppers contain significantly higher levels of these important micronutrients than non-organic varieties, so aside from avoiding harmful pesticides, you now have yet another reason for choosing organic produce when picking your peppers!

Cauliflower-Leek Soup

Sorry, potato-leek soup, this simple variation, which uses cauliflower instead of potatoes, offers so much more, including a raft of healthy nutrients. The amount of seasoning you add at the end of the cooking time will depend on the kind of vegetable broth you use (for example, if you're using a low-sodium broth, add about ½ teaspoon each of sea salt and ground black pepper). Be sure to wash the leeks very well before using them, as they can be quite sandy.

MAKES 6 CUPS / SERVES 4

2 tablespoons olive oil

3 medium leeks, trimmed, white and light green parts sliced thin (about 4 cups)

1 medium head cauliflower, cut into 1-inch florets (about 5 cups)

4 cups vegetable broth

1 cup water, plus more if needed

1/3 cup raw cashews

1 tablespoon fresh lemon juice

Sea salt and ground black pepper

1. In a heavy-bottomed pot, warm the olive oil over medium heat. Add the leeks and sauté, stirring occasionally, until they're well softened, about 7–8 minutes. Add the cauliflower florets, vegetable broth, water. Set the heat to high and bring the mixture to a boil. Cover the pot, leaving the lid open a small crack, and reduce the heat to low. Simmer the mixture for 15 minutes. Add the cashews, cover the pot again, and simmer for 5 minutes longer.

2. Take the pot off the heat, stir in the lemon juice, and let the soup cool for a moment before transferring it to a blender. Process the mixture in batches, if necessary, until it is smooth. The soup should be creamy, but if it becomes too thick, add a little extra water. Season the soup to taste with salt and pepper, and then ladle it into bowls. Serve with a little freshly ground black pepper on top.

VARIATION: Add a generous handful of baby spinach to the soup mixture right before blending it to make a vibrantly green variation that tastes just as great!

Brain Boost: After the soup is blended, add 1 teaspoon schisandra powder and briefly blend until it is incorporated.

Mind Meter

Baby Greens Salad with Chia-Herb Vinaigrette

Chia does a great job of thickening the vinaigrette in this tender salad so that it hugs the leaves with a fresh, herbaceous flavor. Chia seeds also burst with important amino acids, good fats, and a wide range of minerals. Sometimes I like to add a little bit of fruit (such as sliced strawberries or a chopped apple) to the mix for extra sweetness and color.

SERVES 4

½ cup chopped fresh parsley

½ cup chopped fresh mint

1 small clove garlic, minced

3 tablespoons olive oil

2 tablespoons tamari

2 tablespoons fresh lemon juice

2 tablespoons chia seeds, divided

5 ounces baby lettuce greens (about 6 cups, packed)

3 medium radishes, trimmed and sliced thin

1 cup shelled edamame*

1 large avocado, sliced

*Either fresh or frozen (and defrosted) shelled edamame may be used.

1. First, make the dressing. In a mortar and pestle or a mini blender, combine the parsley, mint, garlic, olive oil, tamari, and lemon juice, and blend into a green sauce. Stir in 1 tablespoon of the chia seeds and refrigerate the dressing for a minimum of 15 minutes to thicken a bit before serving.

2. To make the salad, combine the lettuce, radishes, and edamame in a large bowl. Just before serving, add as much dressing as desired, and toss gently until the leaves are lightly and evenly coated. To serve, top the greens with the avocado slices and sprinkle with the remaining 1 tablespoon chia seeds.

Brain Boost: Add 1 cup of fresh sliced strawberries to the salad.

FOOD FOR THOUGHT: Edamame

Edamame, the fresh green form of soybeans, is an ideal source of plant-based protein—shelled edamame offers about 18 grams per cup and contains *all* essential amino acids. For the brain, there's even more good news: Edamame is also an excellent source of cognition-supportive micronutrients like folate, choline, magnesium, calcium, and vitamin K, which may help explain why there is a lower incidence of age-related brain disorders in populations that consume large amounts of soy, such as those in East Asia.

Mind Meter

| Ca | Mo | Pri | Pro | Pl |

French Lentils with Roasted Radishes

The French countryside, with its romantic rolling hills, painterly skies, and centuries-old villages is one of my favorite places to visit. And with family living there half the year, I try and make those visits as frequent as possible. We love cooking and eating and chatting the day away, and we always make good use of seasonal specialties from the local markets in impromptu recipes. This brain-healthy dish is the result of one such spontaneous supper, which has since reappeared many times in my kitchen back in California.

SERVES 4

1 1/2 cups Puy (French) lentils, or black lentils

1 bay leaf

Sea salt and ground black pepper

3 cups radishes

3 tablespoons olive oil, divided

3 large cloves garlic, pressed

2 tablespoons minced fresh mint

1/4 cup minced fresh chives

3 tablespoons hemp seeds, divided

2 tablespoons fresh lemon juice

2 cups (packed) mâche or baby spinach

1/2 cup Almond Ricotta (page 145)

1. Preheat the oven to 450°F.

2. In a medium saucepan over high heat, combine the lentils and the bay leaf with about 5 cups of water. Bring to a boil, and then reduce the heat to medium-low. Simmer gently until the lentils are tender but not mushy, about 15–20 minutes. Drain the lentils in a colander over the sink, and remove the bay leaf. Transfer the lentils to a bowl and season them with 1/2 teaspoon salt and 1/2 teaspoon ground black pepper. Cover the bowl to keep the lentils warm.

3. Meanwhile, clean and trim the radishes, removing the stems, while leaving their tails intact. Halve the radishes lengthwise, and quarter any large halves. Warm 1 tablespoon of the olive oil in an ovenproof sauté pan* over medium-high heat. When the oil is hot, add the radishes to the pan in a single layer (flat side down as much as possible), season generously with salt and pepper, and

(continued on following page)

*If you don't have an ovenproof sauté pan, use a regular skillet and then transfer the cooked radishes to a baking sheet before roasting them in the oven.

Mind Meter

Brain Boost: Mix
1 tablespoon of reishi
powder or lion's mane
powder into the lentils
after you've cooked and
drained them.

cook for 2–3 minutes to lightly sear the bottoms. Remove the pan from the heat, stir in the garlic, distributing it well, and transfer the pan to the oven. Roast the radishes for 7–12 minutes (depending on their size), until they are vibrantly red and lightly golden on the edges. Remove the pan from the oven.

4. In a large mixing bowl, combine the cooked lentils, roasted radishes and their cooking juices, and the remaining 2 tablespoons of olive oil. Add the mint, chives, 2 tablespoons of the hemp seeds, lemon juice, and the mâche or baby spinach to the bowl. Toss the mixture to combine and season to taste with additional salt and pepper as desired. Add the Almond Ricotta to the mixture in small dollops and fold it into the mixture gently, retaining the dollops as much as possible. Sprinkle the remaining tablespoon of hemp seeds on top, and serve warm or at room temperature.

Seared Asparagus with Olives

Approximately 1 million years ago, a friend who was in culinary school showed me this super-quick method of making gorgeous "roasted" asparagus without even turning on the oven, and I've been cooking asparagus this way ever since . . . while enjoying all kinds of fun ingredient adjustments along the way. Seared asparagus makes a fantastic side dish, but if you'd rather turn it into a main course, just serve it on top of a bed of quinoa with a little extra lemon, and voilà!

You can also use other nuts, like walnuts or almonds (or hemp seeds), instead of the cashews, or even toss the asparagus with some Almond Ricotta (page 145) at the end.

SERVES 4-6

2 pounds asparagus
(about 2 bunches)

2 tablespoons olive oil

Sea salt and ground
black pepper

¼ cup cashews, finely
chopped

½ cup pitted
kalamata olives

2 tablespoons fresh
lemon juice

FOOD FOR THOUGHT:

Asparagus ———

Asparagus is loaded with folate, offering a whopping 67% of an adult's daily requirement in every cup. And with its stores of other B-complex vitamins, a good supply of choline, and high amounts of tryptophan, this simple vegetable is a powerhouse of brain protection.

— Trim the asparagus by snapping off the woody ends (or slice off the ends where they start to turn white). In the largest sauté pan you have, warm the olive oil over medium heat. Add the asparagus spears to the pan and spread them out into the flattest layer possible; some of the spears may overlap, but that's okay. Cover the pan, and cook the asparagus for about 5 minutes. Uncover the pan and season the asparagus with a little salt and black pepper. Using tongs, give the asparagus spears a light toss around the pan to cook evenly. Sear the asparagus for another 2–5 minutes, uncovered and without tossing, until the asparagus is tender-crisp and bright green, with a little bit of browning. Stir in the cashews, olives, and lemon juice and remove the pan from the heat. Adjust the salt and pepper, if desired. Transfer the mixture to a serving dish and enjoy warm or at room temperature.

Brain Boost: Whisk 1 tablespoon of lion's mane powder into the lemon juice before adding it to the asparagus.

Mind Meter

Almond Ricotta

The best nondairy cheeses (and best dairy cheeses, too, for that matter) are developed slowly through a meticulous fermentation process that can take days, weeks, and even months. I've eaten them; I've made them; I've loved them. There is a hack, however, for making nondairy cheese a lot more quickly: Add already-fermented products, such as miso and yogurt, to the recipe. This simple trick gives the cheese the tangy taste you crave, satisfies your gut's need for digestion-friendly good bacteria, and allows you to start a cheese in the morning and have it ready for dinner (an unheard-of time frame in the cheesemaking world). You can use this easy-to-make nondairy ricotta as a dip for vegetables, a spread for wraps, or a topping for salads or pasta.

MAKES 2 CUPS

1 ½ cups blanched, slivered almonds, soaked in water for 4–6 hours

2 tablespoons fresh lemon juice

¾ teaspoon sea salt

1 ½ teaspoons yellow miso paste

¼ cup unsweetened coconut-milk yogurt, or other unsweetened nondairy yogurt

2–4 tablespoons unsweetened almond milk

1. Rinse and drain the almonds very well in a colander over the sink, shaking out as much excess moisture as possible. Place the nuts in a blender, along with the lemon juice, salt, miso, yogurt, and 2 tablespoons of the almond milk. On low speed, process the mixture into a ricotta-like puree, stopping the machine as needed and scraping down the sides to push the cheese down toward the blades. (You may need to do this several times, and it will likely take a few minutes to make the puree.) Add additional almond milk, 1 tablespoon at a time, only if needed to blend—the cheese mixture should be very thick. Once it is smooth and ricotta-like, transfer the mixture to a bowl. Cover the bowl and refrigerate the cheese for a minimum of 4 hours before serving, to allow the flavors to meld and the cheese to set.

2. The finished ricotta can be refrigerated and enjoyed for up to 7 days.

Brain Boost: While this recipe is not particularly friendly to the addition of powdered nootropics due to its delicate flavor, it's phenomenal served with fresh berries like blueberries and blackberries.

Mind Meter

Tamari Tempeh with Broccoli & Sesame

On its own, tempeh can be as unassuming as it gets, but, like a chameleon, it will gladly take on the colorful personality of the seasonings and sauces that surround it. Serve this protein-rich dish with a side of rice, or just enjoy it all on its own. Giving the tempeh a nice sear in the pan, before you add the liquid, will add a delectable texture.

SERVES 2–3

1 cup vegetable broth

1 cup apple juice

2 tablespoons tamari

¼ cup rice vinegar

2 large cloves garlic, pressed

1 tablespoon peeled fresh ginger, grated

¼ teaspoon red pepper flakes

4 cups broccoli florets, cut in 1–2-inch pieces

1 tablespoon toasted sesame oil

2 tablespoons sesame seeds, divided

Sea salt

2 tablespoons olive oil

8 ounces tempeh

1. In a medium bowl, whisk together the vegetable broth, apple juice, tamari, vinegar, garlic, ginger, and red pepper flakes. Set the mixture aside.

2. In a large pot (about 4 quarts), bring 1 inch of water to a boil. Set a steamer basket in the pot, and place the broccoli in the steamer basket. Cover the pot, and briefly steam the broccoli for 3–4 minutes, until it is bright green. Transfer the broccoli to a bowl, and toss it with the sesame oil, 1 tablespoon of the sesame seeds, and a pinch of sea salt. Cover the bowl to keep the broccoli warm.

3. Empty the pot you just used for steaming, wiping away any moisture, and return it to the stove. Pour in the olive oil and warm it over medium heat. Crumble the tempeh into large, bite-size pieces, directly into the pan. Sear the tempeh, stirring it occasionally, until it is golden-brown, 3–5 minutes. Pour in the vegetable broth mixture you set aside, and after the steam has died down, bring the liquid to a simmer. Reduce the heat to low and let the liquid continue to simmer, uncovered, until it has reduced to approximately ⅓ cup at the bottom of the pan, 10–15 minutes. Once the mixture has reduced, fold the steamed broccoli into the tempeh and sauce, and take the pot off the heat. Transfer the contents—extra sauce and all—to a large serving dish and garnish with the remaining sesame seeds.

VARIATION: In place of (or in addition to) the broccoli, you can easily use other steamed vegetables in this dish—just keep the total quantity of vegetables to around 4–5 cups. Try broccoli rabe, thinly sliced carrots, sliced red bell peppers, or small shiitake mushrooms.

Brain Boost: Add ½ teaspoon schisandra powder to the broccoli while tossing it with the sesame oil and sesame seeds.

Mind Meter

Carrot & Pea Farro Risotto

This risotto, which is made with nutrient-rich farro (instead of risotto rice) and combined with pureed sweet carrots (instead of cheese) probably errs more on the side of a warm, savory porridge than anything else, but it is, nevertheless, comfortingly elegant. Serve it with a nice green salad and consider doubling the recipe for another day as—unlike traditional risotto recipes—this one reheats very well for an almost instant ready-made dinner.

SERVES 3-4

1 pound carrots

5 tablespoons olive oil, divided

Sea salt

½ cup shallots, finely diced

5-6 cups vegetable broth, divided

2 tablespoons apple cider vinegar

2 teaspoons yellow miso paste

1 tablespoon nutritional yeast

1 cup farro, rinsed

2 tablespoons minced fresh parsley, divided

2/3 cup frozen peas

¼ cup raw walnut halves

1. Peel and trim the carrots. Cut one medium-size carrot into ¼-inch dice. Place the diced carrot in a bowl and toss with 1 tablespoon of the olive oil. Add a couple pinches of salt, and set the bowl aside. Slice the remaining carrots into ¼-inch rounds.

2. In a medium saucepan, warm 2 tablespoons of the olive oil over medium-low heat. Add the sliced carrot rounds and shallots to the pan. Sprinkle the mixture with a pinch of salt and sauté for 5–6 minutes, until the shallots are translucent. Stir 2 cups of the vegetable broth and all of the apple cider vinegar into the pan. Set the heat to high, bring the mixture to a boil, and then reduce the heat to medium-low. Simmer the mixture for 20–25 minutes, or until the liquid is reduced by about half. Remove the pan from the heat and let the mixture cool slightly for a couple minutes before transferring it to a blender. Add the miso and nutritional yeast to the blender, and process until the mixture is smooth. Add a little extra broth, if needed, to create a thick, smooth puree. Cover, and set the mixture aside.

(continued on following page)

Mind Meter

Carrots are famous for their high beta-carotene content (your brain converts beta carotene to vitamin A), which helps to protect against cognitive decline. And by adding a bit of healthy fat like olive oil to carrots, you'll increase the bioavailability of the carotenoids even more.

────────

3. Place the farro and 3 cups of the vegetable broth in a large saucepan. Bring the mixture to a boil; reduce the heat to medium-low and let the mixture simmer for 30–35 minutes, or until the farro is very tender—the liquid should be mostly evaporated, although a little should remain in the pan to keep the farro from burning. Stir the carrot puree and 1 tablespoon of the olive oil into the farro and season with salt to taste. Check the consistency: It should have a risotto-like texture—a bit like porridge, but not too thick. If the consistency is too thick, add a little more vegetable stock, and if it is too thin, simply cook the mixture over low heat for a minute or two longer. Fold 1 tablespoon of the minced parsley into the farro, and cover the saucepan to keep the farro warm.

4. Warm the remaining tablespoon of oil in a medium saucepan over medium heat. Add the diced carrots, sautéing them for 3–5 minutes or until they're almost tender. Stir the peas into the pan and cook them for 2–3 minutes more or until the peas are warmed through and bright green.

5. When you're ready to serve the risotto, mix the carrots and peas into the farro mixture and make any final adjustments to the consistency, if needed. Ladle the risotto into bowls and use an extra-fine grater to shave the walnuts on top of each bowl. Garnish with the remaining parsley.

Brain Boost: Sprinkle the finished dishes with schisandra powder—about 1 teaspoon total for the recipe as a whole, or ¼ teaspoon per serving.

Chimichurri Mushroom Tacos

These flavorful, colorful, and almost meaty-tasting tacos feature succulent marinated mushrooms, vibrant pickled shallots, crisp cabbage, and an herbaceous chimichurri sauce (a traditional Argentinean green sauce). You'll want to assemble each of the components in the recipe several hours ahead of time, but once the prep work is done, the actual dish itself can be assembled in mere minutes. For a lighter version of the tacos, you can use butter lettuce leaves in place of tortillas to make a wrap.

SERVES 4-6

2 cups chopped fresh parsley

2 cups chopped fresh cilantro

8 large cloves garlic, sliced

1/2 cup olive oil

3/4 cup red wine vinegar, divided

4 teaspoons dried oregano

1 teaspoon red pepper flakes

Sea salt

1 pound (about 4 large) portobello mushrooms, cut into 1-inch cubes

1 large shallot, thinly sliced

(continued on following page)

1. To make the chimichurri, place the parsley, cilantro, garlic, olive oil, ½ cup of the red wine vinegar, oregano, red pepper flakes, and 1 teaspoon sea salt in a food processor. Blend the ingredients into a pesto-like marinade. Transfer the mixture to a large bowl, and toss with the mushrooms. Cover the bowl and refrigerate for a minimum of 2 hours (or overnight) to allow the mushrooms to marinate.

2. While the mushrooms are marinating, place the sliced shallots in a small mason jar with a lid. Add the blueberries, the remaining ¼ cup red wine vinegar, and ¼ teaspoon sea salt. Tightly screw the lid on the jar and shake vigorously to combine. Keep the jar at room temperature until the blueberries have defrosted, and then refrigerate for a minimum of 1 hour (or until ready to use) to allow the blueberries to release their juices and the shallots to pickle.

3. A few minutes before serving, place a large skillet over medium-high heat. Using a slotted spoon, transfer the marinated mushrooms to the hot pan. Reserve any

(continued on following page)

Mind Meter

Fl	Mo	Me	Fo	Pri	Pro	Pl

½ cup frozen blueberries*

8–10 small (6-inch) organic corn tortillas, warmed

½ medium head green cabbage, thinly shredded

¼ cup hemp seeds

¼ cup fresh mint leaves, thinly sliced

*Note: If possible, use frozen wild blueberries, which are smaller than cultivated "regular" blueberries and pick up more flavor in the pickled shallot mixture.

chimichurri remaining in the bowl as a sauce for the tacos. Let the mushrooms cook for a couple minutes without stirring them, to lightly sear the bottoms, then use a spatula to flip and sear the mushrooms on the other side—about 5–6 minutes total. Remove the pan from the heat.

4. To assemble, spoon some of the cooked mushrooms onto each of the warm tortillas, and lightly drizzle them with some of the reserved chimichurri sauce. Top with the shredded cabbage, a few slices of pickled shallots and blueberries, a pinch of hemp seeds, and a sprinkle of mint.

Brain Boost: Add 1 teaspoon of reishi powder to the food processor while blending the ingredients to make the chimichurri.

FOOD FOR THOUGHT: Parsley

Parsley isn't just a garnish—it's a healing, brain-boosting blessing. The herb contains a special antioxidant compound called apigenin, which is known to decrease inflammation, help reduce anxiety, fight stress, and improve your mood!

Savory Chickpea Protein Bars

This mouthwatering combination of chickpeas, omega 3–rich nuts and seeds, and a savory spice mix makes low-sugar snacking both convenient and deeply satisfying.

MAKES 10 BARS

Cooking oil spray

3 tablespoons flaxseed powder

1/2 cup water

2 cups crispy rice cereal*

1 cup raw walnut halves

1 cup cooked or canned chickpeas (unsalted), drained and patted dry

1/4 cup tahini

2 tablespoons maple syrup

1 tablespoon yellow miso paste

1 tablespoon harissa seasoning or chili powder blend

1/2 teaspoon salt

1/4 cup raw sunflower seeds

1 tablespoon chia seeds

*Look for brands that contain little to no added sugar.

1. Preheat the oven to 350°F. Line a 9 × 9–inch baking pan with parchment paper, allowing a little extra paper to flop over the two lateral sides to make it easy to remove the bars. Spray lightly with cooking oil spray.

2. In small cup, whisk together the flaxseed powder and water.

3. In a food processor, combine the rice cereal and walnuts. Pulse until the walnuts are partially ground, about the size of gravel. Add the chickpeas, tahini, maple syrup, miso paste, harissa seasoning, salt, and flaxseed mixture to the food processor, and blend until the ingredients are well distributed and stick together like a dough. Add the sunflower seeds and chia seeds, and pulse until the seeds are just incorporated without grinding them down too much. Spread the dough into the prepared pan, press firmly into a compact layer. Bake for 20–22 minutes, or until the top looks dry and the edges turn golden. Transfer the pan to a wire rack. When cool, use the parchment flaps to remove the contents, and then cut into bars.

4. If desired, individually wrap the bars in plastic, or store them in an airtight container. The bars will keep at room temperature for one week, or freeze them for several months.

Brain Boost: Add 2 teaspoons of schisandra powder or reishi powder to the food processor while adding the chickpeas and other ingredients.

Mind Meter

Matcha Custard with Berries

Although this recipe is exceptionally easy, you'll want to pay close attention while cooking it to get the right consistency. For the first couple minutes of stirring the liquid on the stovetop, it stays rather thin, and you may think that the recipe is a bust. But just as you're giving up hope, the arrowroot will suddenly transform the consistency of the custard, beautifully thickening it, and you'll want to take it off the heat before it becomes *too* thick. The timing of that moment may vary by a few minutes depending on your stove, so stay close by while the pan is on the heat, and use your best judgment to avoid a custard that's overly thick or too loose (although it will taste delicious either way).

SERVES 6-8

1 cup raw cashews, soaked in water overnight

4 cups hot water

1 teaspoon matcha powder

7 tablespoons maple syrup

2 teaspoons vanilla extract

½ teaspoon sea salt

6 tablespoons arrowroot powder

1 ½ cups fresh blueberries or blackberries

Brain Boost: Top each serving with ½ teaspoon cacao nibs.

1. Rinse and drain the cashews, and then place them in a blender. Add the hot water to the blender, along with the matcha powder. If the top of your blender has a removable center cap, remove it to help release steam, and then cover the top with a kitchen towel. Blend the ingredients into a smooth milk.

2. Pour 1 cup of the matcha milk into a medium bowl and set it aside.

3. Pour the remaining matcha milk into a medium pot. Whisk in the maple syrup, vanilla extract, and salt.

4. Add the arrowroot powder to the reserved matcha milk in the bowl and whisk the mixture into a slurry. Add the slurry to the matcha milk in the pot and warm it over medium-low heat. Whisking continuously, cook the mixture for 4–5 minutes or until it begins to thicken into a loose, pudding-like consistency. Once the consistency has thickened, take the pot off the heat immediately—the custard will continue to solidify slightly as it cools. Pour the custard into a large container or 6–8 individual small cups (ramekins work well). Serve the custard warm or cold, topped with plenty of fresh berries.

VARIATION: Orange blossom water, a natural extract often used in Moroccan cuisine (and available in natural food stores and online), is a wonderful addition that adds a sensual, floral flavor to the custard. To use it, add 1½ teaspoons of orange blossom water to the matcha milk while you're adding the maple syrup, vanilla extract, and salt to the pot.

Mind Meter

| Ca | Fl | Mo | Me | Fo | Pri | Pro | Pl |

SUMMER

The sheer abundance of summer produce is enough to make a person feel rich. Colorful, gem-like fruits—such as plumped-up peaches, plums, mangos, melons, and berries—overflow the farmer's markets, luring you to experience their natural sugars and flavorful juices. Savory low-sugar fruits like tomatoes, avocados, and olives are at their prime as well, along with peppery arugula, refreshing cucumbers, and crunchy broccoli. All of this summertime treasure is bursting with flavor and saturated with nutrients, ready to satisfy your taste buds and nourish your brain with exactly what it craves.

Blueberry-Chia Muffins

Whenever a long weekend rolls around, the urge to make muffins strikes. Easy to prepare and with a quick reward in store, muffins are simply a happy food on all levels, and these berry-full, omega 3–boosted muffins make a good situation even better.

This recipe calls for frozen "wild" blueberries because their small size adds up to better distribution in the batter, ensuring every bite delivers a delicious burst of blueberry goodness.

MAKES 12 MUFFINS

Cooking oil spray

1 ¾ cups spelt flour or gluten-free baking blend

1 tablespoon baking powder

½ teaspoon sea salt

¾ teaspoon ground cinnamon

½ teaspoon ground cardamom

3 tablespoons chia seeds, divided

6 tablespoons coconut oil

¾ cup unsweetened almond milk

7 tablespoons maple syrup

1 teaspoon vanilla extract

1 ½ cups frozen wild blueberries

1. Preheat the oven to 350°F. Lightly coat a 12-cup muffin pan with cooking oil spray.

2. In a large bowl, stir together the flour, baking powder, salt, cinnamon, cardamom, and 2 tablespoons plus 2 teaspoons of the chia seeds in a large bowl.

3. In a small saucepan, gently melt the coconut oil over the lowest heat until it is completely liquid. Turn off the heat, add the almond milk, maple syrup, and vanilla extract, and whisk well.

4. Add the wet mixture to the dry ingredients and mix together until just combined. Add the frozen berries, and gently fold them into the batter—just enough to incorporate them. (If you overmix, juice from the berries will stain the batter.) As the coconut oil hardens, the batter may begin to solidify a bit, so work as quickly as you can to spoon the batter equally into the 12 prepared muffin cups, pressing them lightly into shape if needed. Sprinkle the muffin tops with the remaining chia seeds. Bake the muffins for 25–30 minutes, or until the tops begin to turn golden brown and a toothpick comes out clean when inserted into a muffin. Let the muffins cool for a few minutes before serving.

5. Once the muffins are completely cool, you can store them in an airtight container for up to 3 days.

VARIATION: Use MCT oil in place of the coconut oil, and whisk together the wet ingredients in a separate bowl, instead of in a warm saucepan.

Brain Boost: Add 2 teaspoons matcha powder while mixing together the dry ingredients.

Mind Meter

Fl Mo Me Fo Pri Pro Pl

Arugula & Peach Salad with Almond Ricotta

This refreshing and bright salad, with just a hint of spice, is the essence of summer. If you're in a hurry, you can substitute the Almond Ricotta with ½ cup of blanched slivered almonds. You can also enjoy this salad as a main meal by simply doubling the amount of dressing and adding 2 cups of cooked and cooled quinoa to the dish, just before serving, for extra protein.

SERVES 4

5 ounces arugula (about 6 packed cups)

2 large yellow peaches, pitted and sliced into thin wedges

1 yellow or orange bell pepper, finely diced

2 tablespoons olive oil

2 tablespoons balsamic vinegar

¼ teaspoon sea salt

⅛ teaspoon cayenne pepper

½ small orange

½ cup Almond Ricotta (page 145)

1. To make the salad: Combine the arugula, peaches, and bell pepper in a large bowl.

2. To make the dressing: Combine the olive oil, balsamic vinegar, salt, and cayenne pepper in a separate bowl. Grate ½ teaspoon of zest from the orange peel and add it to the bowl. Squeeze the juice from the orange and add 1 tablespoon of juice to the bowl as well. Use a whisk to combine all the ingredients.

3. Just before serving, toss the salad with the dressing and top it with small dollops of Almond Ricotta. Toss once or twice gently, and serve.

VARIATION: Got the grill going? (Or just looking for an excuse to fire it up?) Here's how to make a fantastic grilled version of this salad: Slice the peaches into very wide wedges and cut the bell pepper into thick strips. Brush them with olive oil and grill for a few minutes on each side. You may want to add rounds of sliced red onion to the grill, as well, for extra savory flavor. When the fruit and vegetables are nicely seared, place them on the dressed salad greens and top with Almond Ricotta.

Brain Boost: Add ½ teaspoon of ashwagandha powder to the dressing, along with 1 extra tablespoon of orange juice.

Mind Meter

Chamomile Lemonade

Floral, soothing, and utterly refreshing, chamomile makes for a delicious iced drink—perfect for warm-weather weekends when the most important thing on the agenda is to relax. Even though it's pleasantly sweet, this drink is impressively low in sugar, thanks to the use of stevia.

MAKES ABOUT 2 QUARTS / SERVES 8

8 cups water, divided

6 chamomile tea bags

½ cup fresh lemon juice

1 tablespoon maple syrup

50-60 drops liquid stevia, or to taste

Ice, for serving

— Bring 3 cups of water to a boil in a saucepan. Remove the pan from the heat and add the tea bags. Let them steep for 10 minutes to brew a very strong tea, then remove and discard the tea bags. Let the tea cool to room temperature (you can add a little bit of ice to the tea, if you like, to help cool it down). Pour the tea into a large pitcher when it's cool, and stir in the lemon juice, maple syrup, and remaining 5 cups of water. Add about 50–60 drops of stevia (or sweeten to taste), and serve with a generous amount of ice. The tea will keep for up to 1 week in the refrigerator.

Brain Boost: Add 1 cup frozen blueberries or frozen raspberries to the tea when you add the stevia. As the berries melt, they will release their antioxidant-rich juices and add a little fun texture to the tea.

FOOD FOR THOUGHT: Chamomile ——————

As a healing herb, chamomile has enjoyed one of the longest histories of use in the canon of plant medicine and is as popular today as it has been for centuries. Gentle, yet effective, chamomile contains flavonoids and oils that make it particularly useful as a mild sedative that helps soothe anxiety, reduce stress, calm the mind, settle mood, and offer relief to those with sleep disorders.

Mind Meter

Roasted Beet Salad with Blackberry Vinaigrette

While you can just as easily use other types of berries in this recipe, the tartness of blackberries complements the beets especially well. If you're looking to save time, you can buy cooked beets instead of making them yourself (vacuum-packed cooked beets will offer better flavor than jarred beets).

SERVES 4

8 small beets*, trimmed and peeled

4 tablespoons olive oil, divided

Sea salt

¾ cup dry quinoa

1½ cups water

1½ cups blackberries, divided

1 lemon

5 ounces baby spring greens mix (about 6 packed cups)

2 tablespoons minced fresh mint, plus a few leaves for garnish

¼ cup roasted macadamia nuts, chopped

*If only large beets are available, you'll only need 4–5 for the recipe.

1. Preheat the oven to 425°F.

2. Halve the beets and then cut them into ½-inch-thick wedges. Place the beets in a mixing bowl and toss the wedges with 1 tablespoon of the olive oil and a good pinch of salt. Transfer the beets to a baking sheet and roast them for 25–30 minutes, or until the beets are tender, tossing them once or twice while they're cooking. Remove the beets from the oven and place them in a bowl to cool.

3. While the beets are in the oven, mix together the quinoa and the water in a medium saucepan and bring the mixture to a light boil over medium-high heat. Reduce the heat to low and gently simmer the mixture, uncovered and without stirring, until all the water has evaporated, about 15 minutes. Remove the pan from the heat and let the quinoa stand for 5 minutes. Fluff the quinoa with a fork, and then transfer it to a bowl. Let the quinoa cool to room temperature before adding it to the salad.

4. To make the dressing: Place half the blackberries in a small bowl and mash them thoroughly with a fork. Use an extra-fine grater to zest the lemon over the bowl, then cut the

(continued on following page)

Mind Meter

Brain Boost: Add
3 tablespoons of
dried goji berries to
the salad garnishes.

lemon in half and squeeze 1 tablespoon of the lemon juice into the bowl. Add the remaining 3 tablespoons of olive oil, as well as ½ teaspoon salt, and mix well.

5. To serve: Place the greens in a large bowl. Add the mint, cooked quinoa, and as much dressing as desired (add a little at a time), and toss well. Slice the remaining blackberries in half and scatter them over the salad. Top with the roasted beets and macadamia nuts, and garnish with a couple extra mint leaves.

FOOD FOR THOUGHT: Beets

Thanks to plentiful levels of folate, vitamin B_6, vitamin K, magnesium, potassium, valuable antioxidants, fiber, and much more, beets are a gold-star brain food. They can even reverse the effects of aging on your brain by encouraging healthy blood flow, tissue oxygenation, and neuroplasticity. (And when coupled with exercise, the root's beneficial effects are enhanced even more!)

White Bean Pesto Dip

I don't know about you, but once I have a batch of pesto hanging around, I always find more than one way to use it. And although this recipe originally began as a simple vegetable-and-bean pilaf, everyone who ate it agreed that it was the marriage of beans and pesto that really stole the show. This discovery made me move the vegetables to the side and focus on turning the star of the recipe—the beans—into a protein-rich, hummus-like dip. Slather this delicious spread on carrots, celery, and broccoli florets as a snack, or enjoy it with sandwiches and veggie burgers.

MAKES ABOUT 1½ CUPS / SERVES 8

1½ cups cooked cannellini beans, or other white beans (or 1 [15-ounce] can, rinsed and drained)

2 tablespoons fresh lemon juice

2 tablespoons tahini

Sea salt

3 tablespoons Broccoli Pesto (page 177), or store-bought basil pesto

¼ cup celery, thinly sliced on a diagonal

¼ cup raw walnuts, finely chopped

Olive oil, flaked salt, ground black pepper, and garden herbs, for serving

1. In a food processor, combine the canellini beans, lemon juice, tahini, and ¼ teaspoon salt. Blend the ingredients into a very smooth, thick puree. Taste and adjust the salt as desired.

2. Transfer the puree to a shallow serving bowl or plate and use the back of a spoon to spread it evenly over the bottom. Make a crater in the middle of the puree and fill it with the pesto. Sprinkle the top with the sliced celery and walnuts, and finish with a drizzle of olive oil, flaked salt, ground black pepper, and additional herbs, like parsley or chives.

Brain Boost: Add 2 teaspoons of reishi powder while blending the beans, lemon juice, tahini, and salt in the food processor.

Mind Meter

Creamy Tomato-Miso Soup

The mild sweetness of goji berries balances the flavor of this creamy, extra-luxe soup. For the best flavor, enjoy it while tomatoes are at their peak during the hottest months, when the soup can be served either warm or chilled.

MAKES ABOUT 5 CUPS / SERVES 4

2 tablespoons olive oil

1 medium yellow onion, diced

2 pounds Roma tomatoes, diced (about 5 cups)

Sea salt

3 tablespoons dried goji berries

1/4 teaspoon crushed red pepper flakes

2 1/2 cups water, plus more if needed

1/2 cup raw cashews

2 tablespoons yellow miso paste

1. Warm the oil in a heavy-bottomed pan over medium heat. Add the onion and sauté for 5 minutes to soften. Stir in the tomatoes, add a couple of big pinches of salt and sauté for 15 minutes, until the tomatoes are mostly broken down. Add the goji berries, red pepper flakes, and water, and bring to a boil over high heat. Reduce the heat to low, and simmer the mixture for 20 minutes, uncovered.

2. Remove the pan from the heat. Let the mixture cool for a minute or two, and then transfer it to a blender. Add the cashews and miso paste, and blend until the mixture is completely smooth. The resulting soup should have a nice thickness to it, but additional water may be added, if needed, to thin it. Season the soup with additional salt to taste and serve warm or chilled.

Tip: If you're in a hurry, use 1 (28-ounce) can of crushed tomatoes, instead of fresh tomatoes, and skip the step of sautéing them for 15 minutes!

Brain Boost: Toss in 1 teaspoon of schisandra powder while adding the miso paste to the blender.

Mind Meter

Mediterranean Quinoa Bowl

With all its protein, greens, good fats, and antioxidants, this bowl is a fully balanced meal—and a fabulous one at that. Wilting the arugula at the end of the cooking tames the feisty green's bitterness and makes it deliciously tender, while the fresh corn and cucumbers add pops of crunch. A dash of za'atar, an aromatic Middle Eastern spice mix (available at most supermarkets or online), makes this recipe come alive with flavor, but you can just as easily tune up the bowl with additional salt and pepper instead, if you'd prefer.

MAKES 4 SERVINGS

1 cup dry quinoa

2 cups water

1 ear organic white corn, or 1 ½ cups frozen corn kernels, defrosted

2 cups Persian cucumber (or other variety), halved and sliced thin

⅓ cup pitted kalamata olives, halved

¼ cup (packed) fresh basil, finely chopped, plus extra for garnish

2 tablespoons (packed) fresh mint, finely chopped

⅓ cup hemp seeds

2 tablespoon fresh lemon juice

2 tablespoons olive oil, divided

(continued on following page)

1. In a medium saucepan, mix together the quinoa and water. Bring the mixture to a light boil over medium-high heat, and then reduce the heat to a low simmer. Continue to cook the quinoa, uncovered and without stirring, until all the water has evaporated, about 15 minutes. Remove the pan from the heat and let the quinoa stand for 5 minutes. Fluff the quinoa with a fork, and then transfer it to a large mixing bowl. Let the quinoa cool to room temperature.

2. If you are using fresh corn, cut the kernels off the corncob with a chef's knife, and add them to the quinoa in the large mixing bowl. (Alternatively, use defrosted corn kernels.) Add the sliced cucumber, olives, basil, mint, and hemp seeds to the bowl. Drizzle the mixture with lemon juice and 1 tablespoon of the olive oil, and season with ½ teaspoon salt, ½ teaspoon ground black pepper, and the za'atar seasoning. Toss all the ingredients to combine them.

3. Add the remaining tablespoon of olive oil to a large, deep skillet and warm it over medium heat. Once the pan is hot, add the tomatoes and a pinch of salt. Cook the tomatoes for 1-2 minutes, just to soften them a little.

Sea salt and ground
black pepper

1 teaspoon za'atar
spice mix (optional)

1 cup cherry
tomatoes, halved

5 ounces arugula
(about 6 packed
cups)

Add the arugula to the pan, a large bunch at a time, stirring constantly—as the arugula begins to shrink a bit, add more. Toss the arugula in the pan just to wilt it (it shouldn't be in the pan for more than a minute), and then transfer the mixture to the quinoa bowl. (The arugula will continue to wilt outside the pan, so it's quite all right to err on the side of undercooking it.) Toss the mixture well, taste for seasoning, and adjust salt and pepper if desired. Top the quinoa with the additional basil, just before serving.

Brain Boost: Add ¾ teaspoon of schisandra powder while mixing in the za'atar seasoning.

FOOD FOR THOUGHT: Arugula ————————————

In addition to boasting large amounts of brain-friendly magnesium, vitamin K, and folate, arugula is also a great source of highly protective carotenoid compounds like beta-carotene, lutein, and zeaxanthin. These "super nutrients" not only play a role in developing and maintaining brain function; they may also enhance learning and memory.

Mind Meter

Rotini with Broccoli Pesto, Olives & Lemon

This is a quick dish I like to make for people who claim not to like vegetables, because here the veggies are tucked away in the sauce, out of sight and out of mind. And while we're on the subject of being sneaky, making this rotini dish gives you an opportunity to explore some of the new, incredible pasta products that are on the market these days—from gluten-free, to vegetable-based, to superfood-infused varieties. Take advantage of these newcomers whenever a pasta craving strikes—your brain will love the bonus benefits, as you enjoy the flavor in every bite.

SERVES 4

12 ounces rotini or fusilli

1 recipe Broccoli Pesto (page 177), or 1½ cups store-bought basil pesto

½ cup pitted and sliced kalamata olives

¼ teaspoon red pepper flakes

Zest of 1 lemon

Olive oil, for serving (optional)

Flaked salt, for serving (optional)

— In a large pot, cook the pasta according to the manufacturer's directions. Drain the pasta and return it to the pot. Stir in the pesto, olives, red pepper flakes, and lemon zest. While it is warm, serve the pasta with a drizzle of olive oil and a sprinkling of flaked salt on top, if desired.

Brain Boost: Use the Brain Boost listed in the Broccoli Pesto (page 177).

FOOD FOR THOUGHT: Broccoli

Like other cruciferous vegetables, broccoli contains high amounts of sulforaphane, a highly neuroprotective—and potentially even neuroregenerative—natural compound. Broccoli also contains plenty of choline to support memory, as well as folate to support mood and overall brain function.

Mind Meter

Broccoli Pesto

Talk about a super brain-optimizing pesto sauce! The olive oil in this recipe offers performance-boosting monounsaturated fats, cheesy-tasting nutritional yeast provides many of your brain's favorite B vitamins, and broccoli adds an array of cognitive-sharpening nutrients. You can also use this pesto to add extra nutrition to all kinds of dishes, from roasted vegetables and sandwiches to soups and so much more. Because it so versatile, I suggest doubling the recipe and freezing half of it in ice cube trays to defrost and use whenever you need it.

MAKES ABOUT 1 ½ CUPS

2 cups broccoli florets, cut into 1½-inch pieces*

2 tablespoons pine nuts

½ cup (packed) fresh basil, finely chopped

1 clove garlic, peeled and sliced

⅓ cup olive oil

2 tablespoons fresh lemon juice

1 tablespoon nutritional yeast

½ teaspoon sea salt

¼ teaspoon red chili flakes

Water

*Note: You can also substitute fresh broccoli with frozen broccoli florets. Simply defrost the broccoli and use it in the recipe (there's no need to steam it, so you can skip the first step in the instructions).

1. First, steam the broccoli: Fill a large pot with an inch of water and bring it to a boil. Place a steamer basket inside the pot and add the broccoli. Cover the pot and steam the broccoli for 8–10 minutes, or until it is very tender. Remove the broccoli and let it cool to room temperature.

2. Toast the pine nuts in a dry pan over low heat for 3–5 minutes until they turn golden brown and smell fragrant, stirring them frequently to avoid burning. Remove the pan from the heat and transfer the nuts to a plate to cool.

3. In a food processor or a high-speed blender, combine the broccoli, basil, garlic, olive oil, lemon juice, nutritional yeast, salt, and chili flakes. Blend into a thick paste. Add the pine nuts and just enough water (about 2–3 tablespoons) to make a completely smooth sauce, and then blend once more. Refrigerate the pesto until you're ready to use it.

Brain Boost: Add 1 tablespoon of either reishi powder or lion's mane powder to the food processor while blending the broccoli, basil, garlic, and olive oil, etc.

Mind Meter

Sesame Rice with Dulse & Avocado

The Inn of the Seventh Ray, one of the most romantic restaurants you'll ever visit, is quietly tucked into the Santa Monica Mountains next to an old oak-lined riverbed. Although the restaurant is best known for dinners enjoyed under twinkling lights, the Inn's Sunday brunch buffet is equally enchanting, with its wide and tempting assortment of everything from flavorfully dressed vegetable ribbons to cinnamon rolls fresh out of the oven. But among all the wonderful choices, my favorite is a very simple dish: seaweed rice. In fact, I'm so deeply obsessed with it that I've created a homemade version, so I can now enjoy this ideal feel-good food—with it's mineral-rich seaweed and smart fats from avocado and sesame—whenever I crave it.

SERVES 3-4

1 cup short-grain brown rice

½ cup (packed) dried dulse,* lightly torn

2 tablespoons olive oil

2 tablespoons fresh lemon juice

1 tablespoon rice vinegar

1 tablespoon tamari

2 tablespoons toasted sesame seeds (regular or black), plus extra for topping

1 large avocado, pitted, peeled, and cubed

*Note: Use dried organic dulse that comes in large pieces, not dulse "flakes." Because of their small size, dulse flakes add too much seaweed to the dish and oversaturate it with flavor.

1. Rinse the rice very well in a strainer, and then place it in a heavy-bottomed pot, along with water. Stir to distribute the rice. Over high heat, bring the mixture to a boil, and then lower the heat to a simmer. Cook the rice for 30 minutes, uncovered.

2. Over the sink, pour the rice back into the strainer and drain it. Return the rice to the warm pot (do not turn on the stove) and fold in the dulse—some large clusters of dulse are okay. Cover the rice and let it sit for 10 minutes longer to tenderize, and then fluff it with a fork. Add the olive oil, lemon juice, vinegar, tamari, and 2 tablespoons of the sesame seeds. Stir to combine. Gently fold in the avocado and transfer the mixture to a serving bowl. Garnish with a pinch of extra sesame seeds and enjoy the dish either warm or cold.

Brain Boost: Add 3 tablespoons of dried goji berries to the warm rice after it has been cooked.

FOOD FOR THOUGHT: Dulse Seaweed

As a seaweed, dulse is the epitome of nutrient density, with its high quantities of minerals (like iron, magnesium, and zinc) and vitamins (like vitamin C, and many of the Bs) that all help promote cognitive and psychological balance. It also contains a wealth of neuroprotective antioxidants and bioactive compounds, including fucoidan, which has been studied for its effects on reducing inflammation in the brain and protecting against cognitive disorders.

Mind Meter

Ca   Mo   Me   Pri   Pro

Lentil-Beet Burgers

Rich in earthy umami flavor, these protein-laden burgers, made from plant-based superfoods, can be prepared either in a skillet or on the grill. Black lentils give the burgers a firmer texture than green lentils and also offer additional brain-protective antioxidants.

MAKES 6-8 BURGERS

1 cup black lentils

2½ cups mushroom broth, or vegetable broth

3 medium beets

1 tablespoon olive oil, plus more for cooking

4 cloves garlic, minced

½ cup minced yellow onion

1 teaspoon minced fresh rosemary

¾ cup hulled raw sunflower seeds

1 tablespoon red wine vinegar

2 tablespoons yellow miso paste

3 tablespoon ground chia seed powder, or ground flaxseed powder

Ground black pepper

¼ cup hemp seeds

Sea salt

1. Rinse the lentils and sort through them to remove any small pebbles. In a medium saucepan, combine the lentils and the broth, and bring the mixture to a boil over high heat. Cover the pan, leaving the lid open a crack. Reduce the heat to a low simmer and cook the lentils until they are tender, 25–30 minutes. (Do not overcook the lentils or they will become too soft.) Remove the pan from the heat and pour the lentils into a colander over the sink to drain any excess liquid. Let the lentils cool for a few minutes.

2. Meanwhile, prepare the beets: Wash the roots well, trim the ends, and peel off the outside skin. Use a grater to create 1½ cups of beet shavings. (If there are any beets left over, you can save them to add to a side salad.)

3. In a medium nonstick sauté pan, warm 1 tablespoon of olive oil over medium heat. Add the garlic and cook it for 30 seconds. Add the onion and rosemary, and cook the mixture, stirring often, for 3–4 minutes, or until the onions are translucent. Add the beets and cook them until they've softened, about 3–4 minutes longer.

4. Transfer the hot mixture to a food processor and add the sunflower seeds, vinegar, miso, chia seed (or flaxseed) powder, ½ tablespoon ground black pepper, and half of the lentils. Process briefly until a slightly chunky mixture

(continued on following page)

Mind Meter

Brain Boost: Add
1–2 tablespoons of
lion's mane powder or
reishi powder to the
food processor with
the sunflower seeds,
vinegar, and remaining
ingredients.

that sticks together easily has formed—do not overprocess or the burgers will become mushy. Add the remaining lentils and the hemp seeds, and pulse several times to incorporate, while leaving a little bit of texture. Taste, and adjust salt and pepper, if desired.

5. Transfer the mixture from the food processor to a large bowl. Shape the mixture, ⅓–½ cup at a time, into 6–8 compact balls, and then press them into ½-inch-thick patties.

6. To prepare the burgers for cooking, brush both sides of the patties lightly with olive oil and season each side lightly with salt and pepper. Brush a sauté pan with a little oil as well, and warm it over low heat. Place a few patties in the pan (however many can comfortably fit), and cook them for 5–6 minutes on each side, or until lightly browned. Serve warm, as desired (see suggestions below).

7. Lentil-Beet Burgers can be made up to three days ahead of time. Wrap the raw patties separately in plastic, and keep them refrigerated until you're ready to cook them.

Healthy-Brain Serving Suggestions for Burgers:

- Whole grain buns, or butter lettuce leaves to use as wraps
- heirloom tomato slices
- avocado slices
- baby leafy greens, such as arugula or sprouts
- fermented vegetables, such as a good sauerkraut
- mustard and/or sugar-free ketchup

Avocado Potato Salad

The only thing that's better than a regular potato salad is this avocado-infused variation! Rich with avocado sauce, creamy avocado chunks, fiber-filled chia seeds, and loaded with vibrant fresh herbs, this may be the smartest potato salad you'll ever meet.

SERVES 4–6

1½ pounds red potatoes, scrubbed and cut into 1-inch chunks

2 large avocados, divided

¼ cup unsweetened almond milk

2 tablespoons fresh lemon juice

1 tablespoon Dijon mustard

½ teaspoon sea salt

¼ cup minced fresh chives

¼ cup minced fresh dill

¼ cup minced dill pickles (about 2 spears)

1 tablespoon chia seeds

1. Bring a large pot of salted water to a rapid boil. Add the potatoes and cook them until they're tender when pierced with a knife, about 8–10 minutes. Drain the potatoes in a colander over the sink and rinse them with cold water. Let the potatoes continue to drain and cool in the colander while working through the next steps.

2. Scoop the flesh of one avocado into a large bowl. Use a fork to mash it into a smooth paste. Add the almond milk, lemon juice, mustard, salt, chives, and dill to the bowl. Mix well. Add the potatoes, pickles, and chia seeds to the bowl and toss to combine with the avocado "sauce." Pit, peel, and dice the remaining avocado, and gently fold the small chunks into the potato salad. Transfer the salad to a serving dish and enjoy immediately, or refrigerate for up to 1 day, covered.

Brain Boost: Add 1 teaspoon of schisandra powder while mixing the mashed avocado with the almond milk, lemon juice, mustard, salt, chives, and dill.

FOOD FOR THOUGHT: Avocados

If you don't already love avocados for their incredible taste and texture, here's yet another reason to love them: Avocados supply tyrosine, the amino acid that is a precursor nutrient to dopamine, your mood-boosting and motivation-inducing neurotransmitter.

Mind Meter

Watermelon Slushie

This slushie is the kind of quick, healthy dessert you make on a whim, and it's guaranteed to elicit grateful "ahhs" during the dog days of summer. That's exactly why I keep a zippered plastic bag full of chopped watermelon in the freezer as soon as the mercury starts to rise. Fruit (nature's sugar) is always the best ingredient for dessert, and the chia seeds in this simple recipe help to slow down the release of sugar in your blood, thanks to the healthy fiber and omega-3 fats they supply.

SERVES 4

4 cups seedless watermelon, cut into 1-inch cubes, frozen overnight

6 tablespoons fresh lime juice

1 cup water

2 tablespoons chia seeds

20 drops liquid stevia, or to taste

— Place the frozen watermelon cubes in a high-speed blender,* breaking apart any cubes that may have frozen together. Add the lime juice, water, and chia seeds, and sweeten with stevia. Blend into a thick, frosty mixture, using the blender's tamper, if needed, to incorporate all the chunks. Taste the mixture for sweetness—depending on the natural sugar content of the watermelon, you may need to add a few more drops of stevia. Once you're satisfied with the flavor, transfer the slushie to serving glasses and enjoy immediately.

VARIATION: If you have a little fresh mint on hand (or a lot of fresh mint that may be taking over your garden!), throw a handful into the watermelon slushie while blending it for a bit of extra cooling power.

Brain Boost: Add a handful of fresh or frozen blueberries to the mix. Or, if you have some acai powder or another form of purple or red berries, you can add it to the slushie blend as well.

*If you don't have a high-speed blender, you can use a food processor instead—just be sure to stop the machine and scrape down the sides a few times as you're processing.

Mind Meter

FALL

All hail the harvest season! Among the showy canopies of trees with brilliantly colored leaves lies the real magic of fall: its produce. With the advantage of a lengthy spring and summer growing season, autumn crops develop deeper flavors and stores of powerful nutrients. Seasonal fruits like figs, grapes, and last-chance berries turn vitamins and minerals into absolute treats. Leafy greens are also at their best, as luscious Swiss chard and kale grow into giant plants; incredible mushrooms pop up everywhere, as if eager to be featured in savory delicacies; and hearty squashes and tubers begin to make their debut, including ever-popular pumpkins and sweet potatoes. Even late-ripening tomatoes and avocados are still around and some might even say are at their best. In essence, fall gives us a wonderful problem: the feeling that there are almost too many good things to eat.

Mindful Matcha Granola

With all its treasure-filled bits and pieces, this grain-free granola is full of brain-supportive function—complete with healthy fats, micronutrients, and nootropic benefits. Be sure to use big coconut flakes for this recipe (not shredded coconut) to give it a nice clustery texture.

MAKES 6½ CUPS /
18 SERVINGS

2 cups unsweetened coconut flakes

2 cups sliced almonds

1 cup chopped raw walnuts

½ cups pumpkin seeds

¼ cup sesame seeds

¼ cup ground flaxseed powder

3 tablespoons cacao nibs

2 teaspoons matcha powder

½ teaspoon sea salt

¾ teaspoon ground cinnamon

¼ cup coconut oil

6 tablespoons maple syrup

1 teaspoon vanilla extract

Brain Boost: Add 2 teaspoons of lion's mane powder while mixing together the dry ingredients.

1. Preheat the oven to 250°F. Line a baking sheet with parchment paper or a silicone baking mat.

2. In a large bowl, combine the coconut flakes, almonds, walnuts, pumpkin seeds, sesame seeds, flaxseed powder, cacao nibs, matcha powder, salt, and cinnamon—and mix well.

3. Place the coconut oil, maple syrup, and vanilla into a small saucepan and set it over low heat. Stir the mixture until the oil has completely melted and the mixture is slightly warm.

4. Add the liquid ingredients to the dry ingredients in the bowl, and stir until fully incorporated. Spread the mixture onto the prepared baking sheet in an even layer. Bake the granola for 40–45 minutes or until it is slightly golden, tossing the mixture once halfway through the cooking time. When the granola is done, remove it from the oven.

5. Let the granola cool in the pan for about 20 minutes—it will continue to harden as it sits. When the granola is room temperature, transfer it to an airtight container until you are ready to enjoy it. The granola should be stored out of direct sunlight and will last up to 1 month.

VARIATION: I know what you're probably thinking, and—yes!—feel free to switch up the nuts and seeds and/or add additional spices to make this the granola of your dreams. For best results, keep the quantity of coconut flakes as is.

FOOD FOR THOUGHT: Pumpkin Seeds

Pumpkin seeds (also called "pepitas") are a fabulous source of brain-healthy zinc, which helps protect the brain from inflammation and may even act as a mild antidepressant. Zinc is more easily absorbed by the body when it's consumed with vitamin C—a complimentary nutrient, which you can get by tossing in some goji berries.

Mind Meter

Ca	Fl	Mo	Me	Fo	Pri	Pro	Pl

Mocha Muffins

Although I don't drink coffee very often, I do love the taste, and since caffeine does have cognitive-stimulating benefits, I can attest that these coffee-infused muffins are some serious bites of "go time." These muffins are not too sweet, but if you have a sweet tooth (and want to make the muffins less of a snack and more of a treat), you can replace the cacao nibs and walnuts with ½ cup mini chocolate chips. Either way, between the coffee, MCTs, cacao, and omega 3s from the walnuts and flax—and optional lion's mane—these muffins are sure to seriously light you up!

MAKES 10 MUFFINS

Cooking oil spray

1¼ cups unsweetened cold-brew coffee*

2 tablespoons ground flaxseed powder

1½ cups spelt flour, or gluten-free baking blend

3 tablespoons cacao powder

1 tablespoon baking powder

½ teaspoon sea salt

¼ teaspoon ground cinnamon

3 tablespoons cacao nibs

⅓ cup finely chopped raw walnuts

6 tablespoons coconut sugar, divided

½ cup melted coconut oil, or MCT oil

*If you can't find cold-brew use a strong batch of your favorite coffee at room temperature.

1. Preheat the oven to 375°F.

2. Spray 10 cups of a 12-cup muffin pan with cooking oil spray.

3. In a large mixing bowl, whisk together the coffee and flaxseed powder. Set the mixture aside.

4. In a medium bowl, combine the flour, cacao powder, baking powder, salt, and cinnamon. Mix well. Add the cacao nibs and walnuts, and mix to distribute. Set the bowl aside.

5. Stir 5 tablespoons of coconut sugar into the large bowl with the coffee-flaxseed powder mixture. Add the melted coconut oil (or MCT oil) and whisk very well.

6. Add the dry mixture to the wet mixture, and stir it just enough to incorporate the ingredients—do not overmix. Divide the batter evenly among the 10 oiled cups in the muffin pan, and then sprinkle the tops of the muffins with the remaining 1 tablespoon of coconut sugar.

Brain Boost: Add 1 tablespoon of lion's mane powder to the dry ingredients.

7. Bake the muffins for 15–18 minutes or until a toothpick comes out mostly clean. Take the pan out of the oven and let the muffins rest for several minutes in the pan, then transfer the muffins to a baking rack to continue to cool. Enjoy the muffins warm or at room temperature.

8. Once the muffins are completely cool, they may be stored in an airtight container to retain their moisture and will keep well for up to 3 days.

FOOD FOR THOUGHT: Walnuts

Its resemblance to the brain has made the walnut a symbol of intelligence, wisdom, and knowledge—and for good reason. The high amount of omega 3 fats in walnuts supports everyday brain health and maintenance; the vitamin E content is highly neuroprotective; and the naturally occurring polyphenolic compounds in walnuts reduce inflammation, improve nerve signaling, increase neurogenesis, and defend the brain against toxicity and neurodegenerative diseases.

Mind Meter

| Ca | Mo | Me | Fo | Pri | Pro | Pl |

Spinach, Mushroom & Tofu Scramble

This exceptionally hearty, high-protein, and mineral-rich scramble is a must-have for savory breakfast lovers. What's more, you can easily switch up the vegetables like using red bell peppers in place of mushrooms, for example, or kale instead of spinach. The secret ingredient in this scramble is tahini, which makes a little bit of a mess in the pan at first (be sure to use a non-stick pan), but soon it transforms the tofu pieces into irresistible hits of flavor.

SERVES 2–4

1 (14-ounce) package extra-firm tofu, drained

¼ cup nutritional yeast

¼ teaspoon ground turmeric

¼ teaspoon crushed red pepper flakes

2 tablespoons tahini

Sea salt and ground black pepper

1 tablespoon coconut oil

½ red onion, minced

2 cups cremini mushrooms, sliced thin

1 garlic clove, minced

4 cups (packed) spinach

3 tablespoons hemp seeds

Sliced green onions, cubed avocado, and lemon wedges, for serving

1. Wrap the tofu in several layers of paper towel and squeeze gently to remove as much water as possible; repeat once or twice if needed. Discard the towels.

2. In a mixing bowl, crumble the tofu into large chunks—the chunks should be about the size of scrambled egg pieces. Sprinkle the nutritional yeast, turmeric, and red pepper flakes into the bowl. Next, add the tahini, along with ¾ teaspoon salt and ¼ teaspoon ground black pepper. Gently combine to coat the tofu pieces.

3. In a large, nonstick skillet, warm the coconut oil over medium heat. Add the onion and mushrooms, and season them with a couple of pinches of salt. Sauté the vegetables until they are well softened, about 7–8 minutes, stirring occasionally. Stir in the garlic and cook for 30 seconds longer. Add the tofu mixture and toss well. Let the mixture cook until the tofu becomes a little more fluffy, about 5 minutes, mixing it now and again—a bit of tofu that sticks to the bottom of the pan is par for the course, but you can use a wooden spoon to scrape up the browned bits and toss them back into the scramble (they will actually add to the flavor). Add the spinach to the skillet and cook for just 1–2 minutes longer, until the spinach has wilted. Remove the pan from the heat, stir in the hemp seeds, and season generously with salt and pepper to taste.

Brain Boost: Add 1 tablespoon of lion's mane powder to the tofu mixture along with the nutritional yeast, turmeric, and red pepper flakes.

4. Serve the scramble warm, piled with green onions and lots of avocado. Garnish with a few lemon wedges and give them a quick squeeze over the dish just before enjoying.

Mind Meter

| Ca | Mo | Me | Pri | Pro | Pl |

Fig & Hazelnut Wild Rice Salad

I don't know about you, but I'm always looking for an excuse to bring home a couple baskets of figs from the market whenever I see them—they're such a wonderful late-summer/early fall treat. But if you've already missed fig season, feel free to substitute other fruits for the figs in this recipe—halved grapes, a sliced pear, or strawberries work beautifully here as well. The simple, French-style dressing for this wild rice salad is at its best once it's had a chance to sit, so make the most out of your schedule by whisking it together while the rice is cooking, and the dish will come together in a flash.

SERVES 4-6

1 cup dry wild rice blend

2/3 cup hazelnuts

1/4 cup olive oil

1/4 cup apple cider vinegar

2 teaspoons Dijon mustard

1/4 cup minced shallots

1 teaspoon sea salt

5 ounces baby arugula (about 6 packed cups)

2 tablespoons fresh parsley, minced

1/2 cup fennel, sliced paper-thin

3 cups fresh juicy figs, cut into small wedges

1. Cook the rice blend according to the manufacturer's directions (directions will vary by brand and mix). Once cooked, let the rice cool to room temperature.

2. Meanwhile, heat the oven to 350°F. Toast the hazelnuts on a rimmed baking sheet for 8–10 minutes—tossing them halfway through the cooking time—until they're golden brown and fragrant. Let the nuts cool, rub off the skins, and then coarsely chop the nuts.

3. To make the dressing: Combine the olive oil, vinegar, mustard, shallots, and salt in a small mason jar with a lid. Seal the jar, shake it well, and refrigerate the dressing for a minimum of 30 minutes, or until you are ready to use it.

4. To serve: Combine the cooled cooked rice, arugula, parsley, fennel, and most of the chopped hazelnuts in a large bowl (reserve a small handful of the nuts for garnish). Shake the dressing well, and add as much as desired to the salad, tossing everything together. Add the figs and gently toss just to incorporate, taking care not to bruise the fruit. Transfer the mixture to a serving dish and sprinkle with the reserved hazelnuts.

Mind Meter

Brain Boost: Add 1 teaspoon of schisandra powder to the dressing.

Ginger Kabocha Soup

If kabocha is unavailable at your local store, you can also use acorn squash or butternut squash to make this nourishing, soul-satisfying soup.

MAKES 6 CUPS / SERVES 4

1 tablespoon coconut oil

½ white onion, diced

2 cloves garlic, thinly sliced

1 tablespoon fresh ginger, peeled and minced

2½ pounds kabocha squash, peeled, seeded, and diced into 1-inch cubes (about 6 cups)

⅓ cup dried goji berries

1 bay leaf

3 cups water, plus more if needed

Sea salt and ground black pepper

2 tablespoons yellow miso paste

1 cup full-fat canned coconut milk, plus more, for serving

1. Place the coconut oil in a heavy-bottomed pot and warm it over medium-low heat. Add the onion and sauté for 5 minutes. Add the garlic and ginger and sauté for 1 minute longer, stirring constantly. Add the diced squash, goji berries, bay leaf, 3 cups of water, ½ teaspoon salt, and ½ teaspoon ground black pepper to the pot. Bring the mixture to a boil over high heat. Cover the pot, reduce the heat to low, and let the mixture simmer for 20 minutes.

2. Take the soup off the heat, remove the bay leaf, and add the miso paste and coconut milk. Working in batches, if needed, ladle the soup into a blender and process until the texture is completely smooth. (Alternately, use a handheld immersion blender to puree the soup directly in the pot). Squash soups tend to thicken when they cool, so while you want the soup to be rich and creamy, you can add a small amount of water, a few tablespoons at a time, if the consistency of the soup becomes too thick for your liking. Ladle the soup into bowls and give each serving a light swirl of extra coconut milk. Top the soup with a little ground black pepper and enjoy it while it's warm.

Brain Boost: After the soup is fully blended, add ¾ teaspoon schisandra powder and blend once more, briefly. After ladling the soup into bowls, sprinkle each serving with a light pinch of additional schisandra and experience the enlivening flavor of this special nootropic!

Mind Meter

Lentil-Vegetable Stew

Humble as it may be, there are few things that are more appealing to me (an unabashed lentil lover) than a hearty lentil stew, thick with protein-rich legumes and studded with tender vegetables. In my version of this stew, I like to use small black lentils or French lentils because of their superior texture (they're far less mushy than larger brown or green lentils) and high antioxidant content.

If you're looking at the vegetables and spices in the ingredients list and thinking, "Could I add ____," the answer is yes, yes, yes! You can use any kind of root or tuber you may have on hand in place of sweet potatoes or carrots. Feel free to mix in some of your favorite herbs or add a handful of green vegetables, like chopped spinach or broccoli florets, at the end of the cooking time to get some bonus nutrients, too.

MAKES 8 CUPS / SERVES 6

2 cups black lentils or French (Puy) lentils

2 tablespoons olive oil

½ yellow onion, finely diced

1 stalk celery, finely diced

1 large carrot, finely diced

5 large cloves garlic, minced

1 tablespoon fresh thyme leaves, chopped

1 medium sweet potato, peeled and cut into ½-inch dice (about 2 cups)

2 bay leaves

8 cups water

Sea salt and ground black pepper

1. Rinse the lentils and sort through them to remove any small pebbles.

2. In a large, heavy-bottomed pot, warm the olive oil over medium heat. Add the onion, celery, and carrot, and sauté for 5 minutes, stirring occasionally. Add the garlic and thyme, and cook for 30 seconds longer, stirring constantly. Add the lentils, sweet potato, bay leaves, and water. Turn the heat up to high and bring the mixture to a boil. Cover the pot and then reduce the heat to a low simmer. Cook the soup for 30–35 minutes, or until the lentils are very tender. Remove the pot from the heat and discard the bay leaves. Add 1 teaspoon salt and ¼ teaspoon ground black pepper to the soup and stir it well. Taste the soup and adjust the seasonings, if desired. Keep the pot covered until you're ready to serve, and enjoy it warm.

Brain Boost: Add 1–2 tablespoons of lion's mane powder to the pot when you add the water.

Mind Meter

Lasagna with Swiss Chard & Navy Beans

There's really only one rule to keep in mind when you make lasagna—and that's to make enough for leftovers. Lasagna always takes a bit of effort, so it's nice to enjoy it for at least one extra meal! This brain-friendly, all-veggie recipe makes great use of high mineral greens, omega 3–rich hemp seeds, and savory white beans that offer important amino acids and fiber.

MAKES 1 (12 × 9-INCH)
PAN OF LASAGNA /
SERVES 8

1½ cups cooked navy beans or other white beans (or 1 [15-ounce] can, rinsed and drained)*

6 tablespoons hemp seeds, divided

3 tablespoons coconut oil, divided

2 cups leeks (about 1–2), trimmed, halved, and thinly sliced

8 ounces cremini mushrooms, sliced (about 3 cups)

6 cups (packed) Swiss chard leaves (about 2 large bunches), stems removed and finely chopped

(continued on following page)

*For the best flavor, use salted beans. If you are using unsalted beans, add ¼ teaspoon of salt to the bean-and-hemp-seed mixture.

1. Preheat the oven to 350°F. Place a baking rack in the center of the oven.

2. In a small bowl, mix the beans and 5 tablespoons of the hemp seeds in a small bowl and set it aside.

3. In a large pot, warm 1 tablespoon of the coconut oil over medium heat. Add the leeks and sauté them for 1 minute. Add the mushrooms and cook them for 5 minutes to soften, stirring often. Add the Swiss chard and cook it for 2 minutes, stirring constantly. Remove the pot from the heat and transfer the vegetables to a bowl. Mix in ¼ teaspoon salt and ¼ teaspoon ground black pepper, and set the bowl aside.

4. In a blender, combine the cashews, water, garlic powder, nutritional yeast, arrowroot powder, 1 teaspoon salt, and the remaining 2 tablespoons of coconut oil. Blend until smooth. Pour the mixture into a medium saucepot and warm it over medium-low heat, stirring occasionally. Once the mixture begins to bubble, reduce the heat to low, and whisk for 4–5 minutes, stirring constantly, or until the mixture has thickened substantially and has reduced almost by half (it should almost have the consistency of a fondue). Remove the pot from the heat.

(continued on following page)

Mind Meter

Sea salt and ground black pepper

1⅓ cup raw cashews

3 cups water

1 tablespoon garlic powder

¼ cup nutritional yeast

2 tablespoons arrowroot powder

3 cups Goji-Tomato Marinara (page 202), or store-bought marinara sauce

9 no-boil, whole-grain lasagna noodles

Brain Boost: The marinara sauce in this recipe is the perfect place to add extra nootropics, whether you're using Goji-Tomato Marinara (page 202) or just looking to elevate a store-bought marinara sauce. Simply mix 1 tablespoon of lion's mane or reishi powder into the sauce.

5. To assemble the lasagna, spread 1 cup of the marinara sauce over the bottom of a 12 × 9–inch casserole dish. Place 3 noodles over the sauce, making sure they don't touch one another or the sides of the dish. Spread half of the vegetable mixture over the noodles and then sprinkle half of the bean mixture over the vegetables. Lightly press the top so that there is an even layer. Drizzle ⅓ of the cashew cream on top, spreading it out gently. Add another layer of 3 lasagna noodles and spread half of the vegetable mixture over them. Then add half of the bean mixture, spreading it evenly. Drizzle ⅓ of the cashew cream over the bean mixture. Place the remaining 3 noodles on top and spread the whole surface with the remaining 2 cups of marinara sauce. Drizzle the remaining cashew cream over the surface in large swatches—do not spread it.

6. Cover the dish tightly with foil and bake the lasagna on the oven's center rack for 40 minutes. Remove the foil and bake for 20 minutes longer. Set the oven temperature to broil and bake for 2–4 minutes to lightly brown the cashew sauce on top. Remove the lasagna from the oven, and sprinkle the remaining 1 tablespoon of hemp seeds on top. Let the lasagna rest for a minimum of 10–15 minutes, to set. Cut it into 8 slices and serve.

7. To store any leftovers, wrap the pan tightly and refrigerate the lasagna for up to 5 days. It reheats beautifully.

VARIATION: While cremini mushrooms will certainly do the trick in this recipe, you can also use chanterelles, shiitake, and oyster mushrooms, all of which take the flavor of this lasagna to new heights. If you're not a mushroom fan, you can use 2 cups of chopped roasted red bell peppers instead.

Goji-Tomato Marinara

My favorite flavor pairing for goji berries is actually a savory one: tomatoes. And what better way to utilize this combo than in a marinara sauce, where the inherent sweetness of antioxidant-rich goji berries takes the place of sugar (which is commonly added to some marinara recipes). As a bonus, goji berries also help absorb a bit of the extra liquid from the tomatoes while the sauce is cooking, so you can put together a massively beneficial (not to mention delicious) sauce faster than ever. Use this versatile marinara in all kinds of pasta dishes, mixed with roasted vegetables and quinoa, or as a dip for baked sweet potato fries.

MAKES ABOUT 6 CUPS

2 (28-ounce) cans whole plum tomatoes, preferably unsalted

½ cup dried goji berries

2 tablespoons olive oil

1 medium yellow onion, finely diced

Sea salt

2 tablespoons garlic, minced (about 5-6 cloves)

½ teaspoon dried oregano

2 tablespoons fresh basil, minced

1. Place the entire contents of the canned tomatoes, including the juice, into a blender, along with the goji berries. Blend briefly—you can leave the sauce a little chunky or puree it until it is completely smooth, depending on the texture you prefer.

2. In a large heavy-bottomed pot, warm the olive oil over medium-low heat. Add the onion, a big pinch of salt, and sauté for 7–10 minutes, until the onion is golden brown. Add the garlic and oregano, stirring frequently, and sauté for about 1 minute, until the garlic is fragrant. Pour the tomato-goji puree into the pot. Bring the sauce to a simmer, and cook it over low heat for 20–25 minutes, uncovered, stirring occasionally, to reduce and slightly thicken the sauce. Stir in the basil and add a generous amount of salt to taste (usually around 1 teaspoon or more if you're using unsalted tomatoes, and about ½ teaspoon if you're using salted tomatoes). If you want a smooth sauce, you can return the mixture to the blender and fully puree it. Or just leave the marinara chunky if you prefer a more textured sauce.

SERVING SUGGESTION: Add this sauce to your favorite pasta with a heap of steamed broccoli on the side.

Brain Boost: Mix 1 tablespoon of lion's mane powder or reishi powder into the sauce after cooking.

FOOD FOR THOUGHT: Tomatoes

Tomatoes (as well as goji berries) are an incredible source of lycopene, an antioxidant that helps protect vital and sensitive brain lipids from damaging inflammation. Lycopene is more absorbable by your body once it has been heated, so look to cooked tomato sauces as an especially beneficial way to boost brain function.

Canned or Fresh?

Using canned tomatoes in sauce recipes is a massive time-saver that helps create a flavorful marinara quickly and easily. But if your schedule permits (or your tomato garden is exploding), you can use fresh tomatoes instead! First, you'll want to remove their slightly bitter skins by lightly cutting a small x into the surface of the tomatoes and then submerging them in boiling water for about 1 minute to loosen the skins. Then dunk the tomatoes immediately in an ice-water bath, and the skins will peel away easily. You can then proceed with the recipe as usual, but you'll want to cook the tomatoes longer—about 45 minutes to an hour—or until you have a rich and dark sauce. You'll need about 3 ½ pounds of fresh tomatoes to substitute the two 28-ounce cans to make this Goji-Tomato Marinara recipe.

Mind Meter

| Ca | Mo | Me | Pri | Pro | Pl |

Chopped Kale Salad

For me, this balanced, nutrient-dense, cognition-friendly salad is an absolute staple. And as much as I love this salad as a side dish, you can add some chickpeas or baked tofu, along with some slivered almonds or sunflower seeds to make it into a satisfying main meal. Dressed kale salads actually improve in texture as they sit, so this salad can last for several days in the refrigerator—it's a great make-ahead dish for parties or potlucks, or just to have on hand for a quick and healthy bite anytime.

SERVES 4

¼ cup tahini

¼ cup red wine vinegar

2 tablespoons olive oil

2 tablespoons tamari

1 small shallot, minced

1 medium fennel bulb

Juice of ½ lemon

1 large bunch curly kale, stemmed and coarsely chopped

1 medium carrot, shredded

1 medium sweet crisp apple (such as Gala), cored and cut into ¼-inch dice

Sea salt and ground black pepper

1. First, make the dressing: In a small bowl, whisk together the tahini, vinegar, olive oil, and tamari. Once the mixture is smooth, stir in the shallot. Let the dressing sit at room temperature for at least 10 minutes, allowing the flavors to meld.

2. Meanwhile, trim the fennel (if there are some fronds attached to the bulb, keep a few on hand for garnish). Cut the bulb in half and use a mandoline to make very thin shavings (alternatively, use a knife to cut the bulb, slicing as thinly as possible). Place the shavings in a sieve, dunk them into a bowl of ice water, and add the lemon juice. Let the fennel chill for several minutes until it becomes very crisp, and then drain it.

3. To assemble the salad: Place the kale, carrot, apple, and fennel into a large bowl. Add as much dressing as desired— the quantity will vary, depending on the size of your bunch of kale, so a good place to start is with about half of the dressing. Toss the salad by hand, gently massaging the kale to tenderize it. Add more dressing if needed, as well as a little salt and pepper to taste. Garnish the salad with a few fennel fronds . . . because you're fancy like that.

Brain Boost: Mix 1 tablespoon of lion's mane powder into the dressing, along with the tahini, vinegar, olive oil, and tamari.

Mind Meter

Spicy Cacao Black Beans & Turmeric Rice

I'll admit, when I'm making dishes that include small amounts of black beans, I often succumb to the convenience of just popping open a can, rather than soaking the beans overnight. But the truth is, making a big batch of your own beans means you'll eat like royalty for days to come: You'll enjoy beans in bowls, beans in wraps, beans on toast, and so much more. In short, nothing beats really great homemade beans, and this is truly a recipe for a good mood, thanks, in part, to the addition of cacao, which gives the dish more of an earthy, spicelike undertone (rather than the chocolate flavor you might expect).

You can consider this recipe "slightly spicy," on the heat scale. If you're not really a spice fan, simply cut the amount of chipotle in half; if you're a major heat lover, add extra chipotle, to taste, when the beans have finished cooking. Don't be afraid to fine-tune these beans, or, as I like to say, "Don't worry, bean happy."

SERVES 8

2 tablespoons olive oil

1 medium red onion, diced

3 cloves garlic, minced

1 jalapeño pepper, seeded and diced

1 pound black beans, soaked overnight, drained and rinsed

⅛ teaspoon baking soda

¼ cup cacao powder

1 teaspoon ground cumin

1 teaspoon ground cinnamon

½ teaspoon chipotle powder

(continued on following page)

1. In a large, heavy-bottomed pot, warm the olive oil over medium heat. Add the onion, garlic, and jalapeño, and sauté until softened, about 5 minutes. Add the beans, baking soda, cacao powder, cumin, cinnamon, chipotle, and 1½ teaspoons of salt. Pour enough water into the pot to cover the beans by an inch—about 5 or 6 cups (if in doubt, start with less water and add more halfway through cooking, if needed). Bring the mixture to a boil, and then reduce the heat to a low simmer and cover. Cook the beans for 1 hour, or until they are very tender.

2. Transfer 1 cup of the cooked beans to a small bowl and add the lime juice, coconut sugar, and tahini. Smash the beans into a paste with a fork. Return the mashed mixture to the pot, mix it well, and taste the mixture, adjusting the amount of salt, as desired. Let the beans rest for a minimum of 15 minutes, uncovered, before serving to allow the flavors to meld.

3. Serve the beans over of a bed of rice to absorb all the flavorful liquid, and top with as much salsa and cilantro as

Sea salt

2 tablespoons fresh lime juice

1 tablespoon coconut sugar

1 tablespoon tahini

4 cups Turmeric Rice (below) or 4 cups cooked rice

Fresh salsa and cilantro, for serving

you like. The beans will last, refrigerated, for up to 1 week (where they will continue to improve in flavor), or store them in the freezer for up to a couple of months.

Brain Boost: Add 1 teaspoon of ashwagandha powder to the beans while mashing them with the lime juice, coconut sugar, and tahini for extra-happy beans!

FOOD FOR THOUGHT: Black Beans

Black beans are a perfect protein-filled food for boosting cognition. An excellent source of zinc, a cup of cooked black beans supplies roughly two-thirds of the mood-balancing and disease-preventing folate that your body requires every day. What's more, their dark color signals the presence of valuable phytonutrients—an array of anthocyanin antioxidants that encourage better memory function, enhance learning, and stimulate neurogenesis.

Turmeric Rice

This rice may taste like "regular" rice . . . but it looks much prettier and offers bonus brain-protective benefits, too!

MAKES ABOUT 4 CUPS

1 cup long-grain brown rice

1 teaspoon ground turmeric

1¾ cups water, plus more if needed

Sea salt

Place the rice, turmeric, water, and a couple big pinches of salt in a medium pot. Bring the mixture to a boil over medium-high heat, and then cover the pot and reduce the heat to a low simmer. Cook the rice for 45–50 minutes, or until the water has evaporated and the rice is tender. Remove the pot from the heat, fluff the rice with a fork, and let it sit, covered, for 10 minutes longer to steam and improve the texture. Serve the rice warm or cool with your favorite proteins and/or vegetables piled on top. Turmeric Rice will last up to 4 days in the refrigerator.

Mind Meter

Citrus Sweet Potatoes

Sweet potatoes truly are superheroes: They're full of brain-healthy nutrients, they promote longevity, and they taste so good they're downright crave-worthy. Could you also use different types of sweet potatoes, like pretty purple ones, in this dish? You bet! The more colors, the merrier.

SERVES 4

2 pounds small sweet potatoes

3 tablespoons olive oil, divided

1 teaspoon ground cumin

¼ teaspoon ground cinnamon

Sea salt and ground black pepper

2 tablespoons fresh lime juice

1 teaspoon sriracha sauce

1 large navel orange

1 tablespoon unsweetened shredded coconut

Handful of arugula or fresh herbs like cilantro, parsley, or mint, for garnish

Brain Boost: Whisk ¼ teaspoon of rhodiola powder into the dressing before adding the orange segments.

1. Preheat the oven to 400°F.

2. Peel the sweet potatoes, and slice them on a diagonal into ½-inch pieces—if some of your potatoes have a greater diameter, cut the larger slices in half.

3. In a large bowl, toss together the sweet potato slices with 2 tablespoons of the olive oil, cumin, cinnamon, ½ teaspoon salt, and ¼ teaspoon ground black pepper, until the slices are well-coated. Arrange them on a baking sheet in an even layer. Roast the sweet potatoes for 25–30 minutes—tossing them halfway through the cooking time—or until the edges begin to brown.

4. Meanwhile, make the citrus dressing: In a small bowl, whisk together the remaining 1 tablespoon of olive oil with the lime juice, sriracha sauce, and ¼ teaspoon salt. Using a paring knife, carefully cut away the peel and outside pith of the orange and slice it into small segments. Fold the segments into the dressing, and let rest for 10 minutes.*

5. Once the sweet potatoes are done, arrange them on a serving platter and drizzle the dressing and orange segments over the top. Just before serving, sprinkle the dish with coconut and a little arugula or herbs.

*Note: As tempting as it may be, do not squeeze the orange juice from the segmented orange into the dressing, as it will make the dressing too watery. You can, however, squeeze it into a glass and enjoy it yourself!

Mind Meter

Pri Pro

Chocolate Beet Brownies

I make these special brownies often, for friends or events, and they have become one of my most requested "secret" recipes over the years. Striking the perfect balance between super-moist and slightly cakey, these brownies have some major brain-boosting ingredients—like cacao, beets, avocado, chia, and MCT oil—and come together like magic (in fact, they may blow your mind . . . but in a good way). Although you don't need to cook the beets before putting them in the batter, the trick to making them "disappear" in the brownies is to use a fine grater to shred the beets; once they're cooked, no one will ever detect the secret ingredient.

MAKES 16 BROWNIES

Cooking oil spray

2 tablespoons ground chia seed powder

1/3 cup water

3/4 cup spelt flour, or gluten-free baking blend

1 teaspoon baking powder

1 teaspoon baking soda

1/2 teaspoon sea salt

6 tablespoons cacao powder

3 tablespoons cacao nibs

1/3 cup mini chocolate chips

1/2 cup pureed avocado

1/4 cup MCT oil, or melted coconut oil

1 cup coconut sugar

1 cup peeled and finely shredded beets

1. Preheat the oven to 375°F. Spray a 9 × 9–inch baking pan with cooking oil spray, and line it with an 8 × 16–inch piece of parchment paper, pressing the paper into the pan and allowing it to fold over two sides to create flaps.

2. In a small bowl, whisk together the chia seed powder and water. Set the bowl aside to allow the chia to swell into a thick gel.

3. In a medium bowl, mix together the flour, baking powder, baking soda, salt, and cacao powder. Stir in the cacao nibs and chocolate chips.

4. In a large bowl, whisk together the avocado, MCT oil or melted coconut oil, and chia gel until the mixture is very smooth. Add the coconut sugar, mixing it well with the wet ingredients in the bowl, and then stir in the beets. Add the dry ingredients to the wet ingredients in the bowl and mix them until they're fully combined—the batter will be thick.

5. Transfer the batter to the prepared pan and spread it out evenly, using the back of a spoon or your fingers to evenly smooth out the surface. Bake the brownies for 35–40 minutes, or until a toothpick comes out mostly clean (a few moist crumbs are fine). Let the brownies rest in the pan for 10 minutes and then use the parchment flaps

Tip: If you use a fork to mash the avocado, be sure to mash it until it is very smooth—there should be no lumps. For the best results, use a handheld immersion blender to whip the avocado into a perfectly smooth puree.

Brain Boost: Mix 1 tablespoon of lion's mane powder into the dry ingredients.

to lift the brownies onto a baking rack to cool completely. Cut them into 16 squares.

6. Kept in an airtight container or tightly wrapped at room temperature, the brownies will stay fresh for up to 4 days.

VARIATION: While these brownies do contain coconut sugar (and should be considered a "special treat with benefits"), you can reduce some or all of the sugar by using a monk fruit 1:1 sugar substitute (see page 266 for recommendations). Replacing half of the sugar with this monk fruit sweetener is a great way to slash the sugar without sacrificing taste.

Mind Meter

| Ca | Mo | Me | Fo | Pri | Pro | Pl |

WINTER

While the markets in winter may offer a pared-down selection of goods, the season nevertheless offers a bounty of hearty foods, like orange squashes, starchy potatoes, and sweet roots. There are still plenty of greens to be had, too, in the form of kales and cabbages (such as Brussels sprouts, which are at their best!); tree nuts like hazelnuts and pecans are at their freshest; and choice fruits like apples, pears, pomegranates, and persimmons brighten the grayest days. Even at this time of year, the world of plants offers comfort and cheer, ensuring that your body feels warm and satisfied, while your mind stays sharp and bright.

Golden Oatmeal with Currants and Pears

Thanks to a mere half teaspoon of turmeric, the oats turn a deep yellow while they cook, making this hearty oatmeal truly look—and feel—like a bowl of golden sunshine on a cold morning. I like using currants in this recipe because their tiny size makes for better distribution throughout the oatmeal, and I appreciate seasonal pears because they're so soft and sweet. You can also substitute other fruits as you like, such as raisins and apples. Although this recipe makes a single serving, it's easy to multiply; just be sure to increase the size of the pot you cook with to prevent any spillover from the bubbling oats.

SERVES 1

1 cup water

1/2 teaspoon ground turmeric

1/4 teaspoon ground ginger

1/8 teaspoon finely ground black pepper

Pinch sea salt

3/4 cup rolled oats

1/2 very soft and ripe pear, cut into 1/2-inch dice

2 tablespoons dried currants

2 teaspoons coconut sugar

Unsweetened vanilla almond milk and chopped raw walnuts, for serving

1. Combine the water, turmeric, ginger, ground black pepper, and salt in a small saucepan. Cover, and bring the mixture to a boil. Stir in the oats, cover the pan, and reduce the heat to medium-low. Cook the oats, without stirring them, for 5 minutes, or until they are tender.

2. Remove the pan from the heat and fold in the diced pear, currants, and coconut sugar. Transfer the oatmeal to a bowl and pour as much almond milk as desired on top. Sprinkle the oatmeal with walnuts and serve it warm.

Brain Boost: Sprinkle 1 tablespoon of cacao nibs over the bowl as a topping.

FOOD FOR THOUGHT: Oats

Oats, one of the best grains for cognitive support, are packed with all kinds of beneficial nutrients, including B vitamins, manganese, and magnesium, as well as plenty of fiber for a happy gut. Oats also contain unique antioxidants called avenanthramides, which can fight inflammation throughout the body and the brain.

Mind Meter

Rosemary-Roasted Walnuts

These easy-to-dress-up walnuts are so versatile, they go with just about everything, whether you serve them as a snack with cocktails or as a topping for a savory dish. Between all the healthy fats in the walnuts and the medicinal properties of the rosemary, this simple recipe adds up to quite an impressive brain food.

MAKES 2 CUPS /
SERVES 8

2 tablespoons
coconut oil, melted

1½ tablespoons
minced fresh
rosemary

½ teaspoon sea salt

¼ teaspoon cayenne
pepper

1 tablespoon coconut
sugar

2 cups raw walnut
halves

1. Preheat the oven to 350°F. Line a baking sheet with parchment paper.

2. In a medium bowl, mix together the coconut oil, rosemary, salt, cayenne, and coconut sugar. Add the walnuts to the bowl and toss until well coated. Spread the mixture onto the prepared baking sheet and bake for 10–15 minutes, or until the walnuts are golden brown and fragrant. Let the walnuts cool before serving.

3. Roasted nuts can last several weeks at room temperature in an airtight container but are best kept refrigerated to preserve their fats over the long term.

Brain Boost: Before you add the walnuts to the bowl, toss them with 1 teaspoon of reishi powder.

FOOD FOR THOUGHT: Rosemary

When Shakespeare wrote, "There's rosemary, that's for remembrance," he may have been alluding to the common practice of leaving sprigs of rosemary at gravesites as a symbol of remembrance and loyalty. But modern cognitive research has shown that Shakespeare's words can be taken literally, as well as symbolically. And, as it turns out, you don't even need to eat rosemary to gain its benefits; merely smelling the herb can cause a slight uptick in acetylcholine, which can offer improved memory and brain function.

Mind Meter

Garlicky Butter Bean Soup with Greens

If you need proof that "simple" can equal "oh-so good," you'll find it in a batch of this nourishing soup, which can easily be doubled for a great make-ahead meal. The recipe is wonderfully versatile, too: You can use any dark leafy green, whether it's spinach, kale, chard, or collards.

**MAKES 6 CUPS /
SERVES 4**

2 tablespoons olive oil

1 yellow onion, finely diced

1 packed tablespoon pressed garlic (from about 5–6 cloves)

4 cups vegetable broth, plus more if desired

3 cups cooked butter beans (or 2 [15-ounce] cans, rinsed and drained)

1/2 teaspoon ground turmeric

1/2 teaspoon red pepper flakes

Sea salt and ground black pepper

2 cups dark leafy greens (any variety), torn

1 tablespoon fresh lemon juice

1/4 cup hemp seeds

1. In a large, heavy-bottomed saucepan, warm the olive oil over medium heat. Add the onion and sauté for 5 minutes. Add the garlic and sauté for 30 seconds longer, stirring constantly. Pour the vegetable broth into the pan with the onion and garlic, and then stir in the beans, ground turmeric, red pepper flakes, 1/4 teaspoon salt, and 1/4 teaspoon ground black pepper. Bring the mixture to a boil, reduce the heat to low, and simmer for 10 minutes.

2. Remove the pan from the heat and stir in the greens and lemon juice. Let the soup rest for about 5 minutes, covered, to allow the greens to wilt and become tender. Adjust the seasoning to taste, if desired, and add a little water or extra broth to the soup if you prefer a thinner consistency. Serve it warm, topped with hemp seeds.

Brain Boost: Add 1 tablespoon of reishi powder to the vegetable broth when you add the ground turmeric.

Mind Meter

Ca	Fl	Mo	Me	Fo	Pri	Pro	Pl

Butternut Hummus

If there were hummus police, officers would likely shut down this recipe, because it contains very little of the time-honored formula. But for what it lacks in tradition, this hummus more than compensates with its super-creamy texture and slightly sweet, "goes-with-everything" flavor. It plays particularly well with crudités like carrots, celery, and jicama and makes a delicious spread for whole-grain crackers and rice cakes. It also makes a great spread for wraps and sandwiches.

SERVES 8

1 pound butternut squash, peeled and cut into 1-inch dice (4 cups)

1½ cups cooked unsalted garbanzo beans (or 1 [15-ounce] can, rinsed and drained)

⅓ cup tahini

1 clove garlic, sliced

½ teaspoon red pepper flakes

¼ cup red wine vinegar

Sea salt

2 scallions, trimmed and sliced thinly on a sharp diagonal

Pomegranate seeds, hemp seeds, and extra-virgin olive oil, for serving (if desired)

1. Bring 1 inch of water in a large heavy-bottomed pot to a boil. Place a steamer basket inside the pot and fill it with the butternut squash. Cover the pot, and steam the squash for about 10 minutes, or until it is very tender when poked with a knife. Remove the squash from the pot and let it cool to room temperature.

2. Place the squash in a food processor, along with the garbanzo beans, tahini, garlic, red pepper flakes, red wine vinegar, and ¾ teaspoon sea salt. Puree the mixture until it is very smooth (this may take a few minutes). Taste and make any adjustments to the seasoning, adding additional vinegar or salt, or even more garlic, if desired. Swirl the hummus in a serving bowl and sprinkle the scallions on top. If desired, garnish the hummus with a handful of pomegranate seeds and hemp seeds, and drizzle a little olive oil over the top, just before serving.

FOOD FOR THOUGHT: Butternut Squash

Butternut squash is very high in antioxidants and phytonutrients and has more beta-carotene than pumpkins. It offers many of the B-complex vitamins as well—all of which help to protect your brain from oxidative stress. Don't be shy about buying several gourds at time—a butternut squash can last up to 3 months when stored in a cool, dry place.

Brain Boost: Add 1 tablespoon of lion's mane powder to the food processor while pureeing the squash, garbanzo beans, tahini, and other ingredients.

Mind Meter

| Ca | Mo | Me | Pri | Pro | Pl |

Orange-Farro Salad with Kale & Dried Fruit

Some salads are so satisfying, you feel you could eat them forever. For me, this flavorful salad, with its complementary chewy and soft textures and festive colors, is one of them. Don't worry if the farro seems a little dressing-heavy when you first mix it. The addition of bountiful greens and fruit will balance it out, but make sure you add them right before serving.

SERVES 2–4

1 cup dry farro

⅓ cup dried goji berries

⅓ cup dried cranberries (preferably sweetened with apple juice)

½ cup pumpkin seeds

3 tablespoons olive oil

1½ tablespoons balsamic vinegar

1 tablespoon Dijon mustard

Sea salt and ground black pepper

2 oranges

5 ounces baby kale (about 6 packed cups)

¼ cup minced fresh chives

1. Rinse the farro, and place it in a medium saucepan with about 4 cups of water. Bring the mixture to a boil, and then reduce the heat to medium-low. Simmer for 30 minutes or until the farro is tender. Drain any remaining water out of the pan and transfer the farro to a large mixing bowl. Mix the goji berries, cranberries, and pumpkin seeds into the warm farro.

2. In a small bowl, combine the olive oil, balsamic vinegar, Dijon mustard, ¾ teaspoon salt, and ½ teaspoon ground black pepper. Use an extra-fine grater to create 1 teaspoon of zest from one of the oranges, and then extract 3 tablespoons of juice from the same orange. Add the juice and orange zest to the dressing and mix well. Add the dressing to the farro and toss. Cover and refrigerate until the farro is cool.

3. When you're ready to serve the salad, peel and remove the pith from the remaining orange, and cut it into bite-size pieces (or supremes), removing any seeds. Add the orange pieces to the bowl with the farro, along with the kale and chives. Gently toss the mixture, adjust the salt and pepper, if desired, and serve.

Brain Boost: Add ¼ teaspoon of rhodiola powder to the dressing.

Mind Meter

Riced Cauliflower Bowl with Chickpeas & Pistachio Dukkah

The neutral flavor of lightly cooked, "riced" (ground) cauliflower serves as an ideal backdrop for warming spices, proteins, and other vegetables. This utterly comforting dish also supplies other ingredients (like turmeric and spinach) that read like a "best-of" list for your brain.

SERVES 3-4

1 cup unsweetened coconut-milk yogurt

2 tablespoons fresh lemon juice

Sea salt

6 cups cauliflower florets (about 1 medium head)

1 tablespoon coconut oil

2 cloves garlic, minced

2 tablespoons water

1 teaspoon ground turmeric

Ground black pepper

1½ cups cooked (or 1 [15-ounce] can) garbanzo beans, rinsed, drained, and patted dry

4 cups (packed) baby spinach

1-2 tablespoons Pistachio Dukkah (page 224)

1. To make the dressing: In a small bowl, mix together the yogurt, lemon juice, and ¼ teaspoon of salt. Refrigerate the dressing until you are ready to use it.

2. Place the cauliflower florets in a food processor. Pulse several times until the cauliflower has been broken down into small bits that resemble rice. Transfer the riced cauliflower to a large bowl, and set it aside.

3. In a large skillet with a tight-fitting lid, melt the coconut oil over medium heat. When the oil is hot, add the garlic and cook it for 30 seconds. Add the cauliflower and water and season with the ground turmeric, ¾ teaspoon salt, and ¼ teaspoon ground black pepper. Mix well. Cover the skillet, and steam the cauliflower mixture over very low heat for 10 minutes. Remove the lid, toss the mixture, and continue to cook it for 5–6 minutes, uncovered, stirring occasionally, until all the excess moisture has evaporated and the cauliflower has dried out slightly (it should resemble fluffy rice). Mix the garbanzo beans and spinach into the cauliflower and cook for 2–3 minutes more until the spinach is wilted and the beans are warm. Remove the mixture from the heat.

(continued on following page)

Mind Meter

Ca	Fl	Mo	Me	Fo	Pri	Pro	Pl

4. To serve, spoon the cauliflower rice mixture into 3–4 bowls. Drizzle each bowl with 2–3 tablespoons of the yogurt dressing, and sprinkle the top with 1–2 tablespoons of Pistachio Dukkah (use more of both toppings, if you like). Serve the dish warm or at room temperature.

Pistachio Dukkah

This Middle Eastern spice blend is like magic dust; it enlivens just about any dish it touches. There are quite a few iterations of dukkah, each of which uses different spices, herbs, and nuts, but I like this simple pistachio variation for its versatility and visual appeal. Try it with salads, grain dishes, soups, and roasted vegetables, like cauliflower and sweet potatoes, or just sprinkle it on top of your avocado toast.

MAKES ABOUT ²/₃ CUP

1 tablespoon fennel seeds

1 tablespoon cumin seeds

½ cup unsalted toasted pistachios (shelled)

2 tablespoons toasted black sesame seeds

½ teaspoon sea salt

Brain Boost: Mix in 1 teaspoon of schisandra powder to the blend after the nuts have been ground down.

In a small pan over medium heat, toast the fennel and cumin seeds for 2–3 minutes, or until they are fragrant. Remove the seeds from the pan and let them cool for 1–2 minutes, and then use a spice grinder or a mortar and pestle to grind the seeds into a powder. Add the pistachios, sesame seeds, and salt. Grind the mixture a little bit more, leaving in some texture. Store the dukkah in an airtight container in the refrigerator for up to 3 months.

Seared Tofu with Kale & Whole-Grain Mustard

It is a little unnerving to think that I spent my entire childhood believing that the sole purpose of mustard is to adorn hot dogs (and also that it has to be an electric shade of yellow). In truth, mustard can bring recipes to life, just as it does in this dish. In this recipe we use both Dijon and whole-grain mustard for an extra bold flavor that enhances every bite of succulent kale and tender tofu.

SERVES 4

1 (14-ounce) package extra-firm tofu

3 tablespoons olive oil, divided

2 cloves garlic, pressed

1 tablespoon Dijon mustard

1 teaspoon maple syrup

1 tablespoon white wine vinegar

Sea salt

1 bunch lacinato kale or another variety of kale, stemmed and coarsely chopped

1 small sprig rosemary

1 teaspoon red pepper flakes

½ cup yellow onion, thinly sliced

1 tablespoon whole-grain mustard

2 tablespoons chopped flat-leaf parsley

1. Press the tofu between several layers of paper towels to extract as much moisture as possible. Halve the tofu widthwise, and then cut the pieces into 1-inch cubes.

2. To make the marinade: Place 2 tablespoons of olive oil, the garlic, Dijon mustard, maple syrup, vinegar, and ½ teaspoon salt in a large bowl. Mix very well, and then add the tofu. Gently toss the tofu cubes by hand, making sure they're well-coated with the marinade. Place the tofu in a single layer in a large nonstick skillet over medium heat, leaving any excess marinade in the bowl (reserve for step 3). Cook the tofu cubes, turning them every few minutes, until they're deeply golden on each side. Transfer the tofu to a large serving bowl, along with any tofu "skin" left in the pan. Season the tofu with a small pinch of salt and cover to keep warm.

3. Toss the kale and ¼ teaspoon salt in the bowl with the reserved marinade, using your hands to thoroughly massage the leaves with the mixture.

4. Give the skillet you just used a quick clean and return it to the stove over medium heat. Warm the remaining

(continued on following page)

Mind Meter

Brain Boost: Mix 1 teaspoon of the reishi powder into the marinade with the olive oil, garlic, and Dijon mustard, etc.

tablespoon of olive oil in the skillet, and add the rosemary sprig and red pepper flakes. Let the mixture sizzle for about 30 seconds, until it is fragrant. Add the onion and cook, stirring often, for about 5 minutes, until the onion has softened. Reduce the heat to medium-low and add the kale and any remaining marinade. Cook until the kale is well wilted, stirring often for about 3–5 minutes or until tender.

5. Remove the skillet from the heat and stir in the whole-grain mustard. Transfer the vegetables to the bowl with the tofu, lightly toss the ingredients together, and sprinkle with fresh parsley. (You can use the rosemary sprig for garnish as well.) Serve warm or at room temperature.

VARIATION: Go big and sprinkle a handful of Rosemary-Roasted Walnuts (page 217) on top of this dish—a perfect pairing!

FOOD FOR THOUGHT: Mustard

Hippocrates (460–375 BCE), often referred to as the "father of medicine," used mustard seeds in various treatments. Even the legendary Dr. Edward Bach (1886–1936), famous for developing flower remedies as a form of alternative medicine (his formulas are still used today), incorporated mustard extracts to treat nerve tension and depression. While modern Western medicine does not overtly promote mustard as a brain-boosting compound, the seed's strong anti-inflammatory and digestion-promoting properties have been shown to help create a balanced system for the mind to function at its best.

Turnip, Apple & Freekeh Pilaf

I like to make this whole-grain pilaf instead of stuffing for holiday dinners . . . and if there's any left over, it's great to warm up for breakfast the next day. Freekeh, an ancient grain that's packed with fiber, minerals, and essential nutrients, has become increasingly popular in recent years. (If your local store doesn't carry freekeh, you can use barley instead; just add ¼ cup of water to the broth in which you cook the barley.)

SERVES 6–8

4 cups vegetable broth

Sea salt

2 tablespoons olive oil

½ yellow onion, minced

2 stalks celery, minced

1 pound turnips, trimmed, peeled, and cut into ¼-inch dice

1 large sweet apple (such as Gala), cored and cut into ¼-inch dice

1½ cups dry freekeh

2 big sprigs fresh thyme

1 bay leaf

Ground black pepper

¼ cup dried currants

3 green onions, trimmed and thinly sliced on a diagonal

1. Pour the vegetable broth into a medium-size pot (1½ quarts or larger). Add a couple big pinches of salt if the vegetable broth is sodium-free or low-sodium. Cover the pot, bring the broth to a low simmer, and then remove the pot from the heat. Keep the pot covered.

2. Meanwhile, add the olive oil to a large, heavy-bottomed pot and place it over medium heat. Add the onion, celery, turnips, and apple, and sauté for 5–7 minutes or until the ingredients have softened. Add the freekeh to the pot and cook the mixture for 1–2 minutes longer, stirring it often.

3. Pour the hot broth into the pot and add the thyme, bay leaf, ½ teaspoon salt, and ½ teaspoon ground black pepper. Bring the mixture to a simmer, cover the pot, and reduce the heat to low. Cook the freekeh for 20–25 minutes, or until it is tender and the broth has fully cooked away. Remove the pot from the heat and let the freekeh rest, covered, for 5 minutes. Add the currants and green onions, and fluff the mixture with a fork. Discard the bay leaf and thyme stems. Add salt and plenty of ground black pepper to taste, and serve the freekeh warm or at room temperature.

Brain Boost: Stir 1–2 tablespoons (depending on how "strong" a boost you desire) of lion's mane powder into the hot broth before adding it to the freekeh.

Mind Meter

Roasted Brussels Sprouts with Pecans

Even those who profess to hate Brussels sprouts will come around when they get a taste of these juicy, tender sprouts in their crispy, caramelized coats. If you're feeding a crowd (or even just a couple people who are extra-big fans of Brussels sprouts), you may want to double the recipe because your guests are definitely going to ask for seconds. Sometimes I mix cooked white beans or farro into the sprouts to make them a balanced, full meal.

**SERVES 3–4,
AS A SIDE DISH**

⅓ cup raw pecans

2 tablespoons fresh lemon juice

1 tablespoon maple syrup

1½ tablespoons olive oil

1 teaspoon fresh thyme leaves, lightly minced

1 pound Brussels sprouts, trimmed and halved

1 tablespoon avocado oil, or another oil with a very high smoke point, like algae oil*

Sea salt and ground black pepper

1 tablespoon water

*Note: Avocado oil and culinary algae oil (which is now increasingly available at natural food stores) are the healthiest high-heat cooking oils on the market.

1. Preheat the oven to 500°F. While the oven is warming up, spread the pecans onto a baking sheet and toast them in the oven for about 5 minutes or until they're lightly browned and fragrant (keep a close eye on them so they don't burn). When they're done, set them aside.

2. To make the dressing: Place the lemon juice, maple syrup, olive oil, and thyme in a large mixing bowl, and whisk them together. Set the bowl aside (later, you'll add the sprouts to the bowl, after they're cooked).

3. On a baking sheet, toss the Brussels sprouts in the avocado oil (or another oil that is well suited to high-heat cooking), ¼ teaspoon salt, and ¼ teaspoon ground black pepper until the sprouts are well-coated. Add 1 tablespoon of water to the pan and spread the Brussels sprouts in a single layer, flat side down. Cover the pan very tightly with aluminum foil. Roast the Brussels sprouts for 10 minutes, remove the foil, and then roast for 10–15 minutes longer, or until the Brussels sprouts are nicely browned. Transfer the sprouts to the mixing bowl with the prepared dressing, add the pecans, and toss well. Sprinkle the sprouts with additional salt and pepper, as desired, and serve warm or at room temperature.

Brain Boost: Add 2 tablespoons of goji berries to the cooked Brussels sprouts while tossing them in the dressing with the pecans.

Mind Meter

Turmeric-Roasted Roots

This colorful root-based dish is a wonderfully healthy way to enjoy "starchy foods," whether as a finger food, a side dish, or a fancy shared plate. What's more, you can easily turn it into a main meal by serving these delicious roasted roots on a bed of cooked grains, like quinoa, along with a few dark salad greens like baby kale or spinach for good measure. To give the dish even more color (and a wider array of antioxidants), use rainbow carrots, if they're available.

SERVES 4, AS A SIDE DISH

1 pound small carrots, peeled and trimmed

1 pound small parsnips, peeled and trimmed

2 tablespoons olive oil

1 tablespoon maple syrup

½ teaspoon ground cumin

½ teaspoon ground turmeric

¼ teaspoon ground cinnamon

Sea salt and ground black pepper

½ cup unsweetened coconut-milk yogurt (or another nondairy variety)

Zest and juice of 1 lime

2 tablespoons hemp seeds

2 tablespoons torn fresh mint leaves

1. Preheat the oven to 425°F.

2. You'll want the carrots and parsnips to be about ½-inch thick and 4–6 inches long, so depending on the size of the roots, leave them whole or slice them into halves, quarters, or evenly sized sticks.

3. Place the cut roots into a mixing bowl, along with the olive oil, maple syrup, cumin, turmeric, cinnamon, ½ teaspoon salt, and ¼ teaspoon ground black pepper. Spread the roots on a baking sheet in an even layer and roast for 25–35 minutes, tossing once or twice during the cooking time, or until the roots are tender and lightly browned.

4. While the roots are cooking, combine the yogurt, lime zest, lime juice, and ½ teaspoon salt in a small bowl. Mix well and refrigerate until you're ready to serve.

5. When the roots are fully roasted, spoon most of the yogurt sauce over a platter, add the roots, and drizzle the remaining spoonfuls of sauce on top (for a less-dramatic presentation you can also just toss everything together). Sprinkle the roots with hemp seeds and mint, and serve warm.

Brain Boost: Toss the roots with ½ teaspoon of schisandra powder after they've been roasted.

Mind Meter

Rich Chocolate Fruit Dip

You would never guess that sweet potatoes are the main ingredient in this ultra-decadent (yet remarkably healthy) chocolate dip! Indeed, the process of slow-roasting sweet potatoes at a low temperature enhances their natural sweetness, enabling you to make a dessert that satisfies your sweet tooth without adding much sugar to the recipe. I love serving this rich dip with fresh fruit, like apple slices and strawberries, for potlucks and holiday parties (it's always gone in a flash), but I can also attest that it is wickedly delicious as a pudding. However you serve it, you'll find yourself scraping the bowl clean—for all the right reasons.

MAKES ABOUT 2 ½ CUPS / SERVES 6

1 pound small sweet potatoes, any variety

½ cup cacao powder

¼ teaspoon ground cinnamon

¼ teaspoon sea salt

2 tablespoons roasted almond butter

¼ cup maple syrup

½ cup unsweetened vanilla almond milk, or more as needed

2–3 cups sliced fresh fruit, such as apples, crisp pears, or strawberries, for serving

1. Preheat the oven to 350°F. Wash and dry the sweet potatoes, and prick them a couple times with a fork. Place the sweet potatoes on a pie plate or small baking sheet, and bake for 45–60 minutes, or until they're extremely soft. Remove the sweet potatoes from the oven and let them cool at room temperature or in the refrigerator.

2. When the sweet potatoes are cool, remove and discard the skins, and place the sweet potato flesh into a blender. Add the cacao powder, cinnamon, salt, almond butter, maple syrup, and vanilla almond milk. Blend until completely smooth, stopping the machine if needed and scraping down the sides before blending once more. If needed, blend in a little extra almond milk, 1–2 tablespoons at a time, to create a smooth whip that looks like frosting. Transfer the mixture to a serving bowl and refrigerate it until you are ready to serve. Enjoy it as a dip with sliced fresh fruit, or as a pudding, with fresh fruit on top.

Brain Boost: Make this dip an even happier one by adding ¼ teaspoon of ashwagandha powder to the blender with the other ingredients. (You can add up to ½ teaspoon of ashwagandha, if you don't mind the herb's strong flavor.)

Mind Meter

Almond Gingersnap Cookies

These chewy, lightly spiced, and slightly crisp cookies are a great treat for the holidays. In fact, they are the essence of "sugar and spice and everything nice," *without* all the unhealthy fats, refined flours, and empty sugars in traditional recipes. Instead, these cookies call for coconut sugar, which has a subtle caramel flavor (and is much lower on the glycemic index than cane sugar or molasses); as well as wholesome spelt and almond flour; and coconut or MCT oil. With less than a teaspoon of sugar per cookie, I like to think that these cookies fall into the sweet gray area of moderation in a brain-healthy diet, but if you want to lower the sugar content even more, you can swap out half the coconut sugar with a monk fruit sugar substitute (see page 266 for suggestions) without really changing the flavor of the cookies.

MAKES ABOUT 40 COOKIES

⅓ cup melted coconut or MCT oil

¼ cup unsweetened almond milk

¼ cup unsweetened almond butter

1 teaspoon vanilla extract

1 cup plus 1 tablespoon coconut sugar, divided

1¼ cup spelt flour

¾ cup almond flour

2 teaspoons baking powder

¼ teaspoon sea salt

1 teaspoon ground cinnamon

1 tablespoon ground ginger

½ teaspoon ground black pepper

1. Preheat the oven to 375°F. Line 2 baking sheets with parchment paper or silicone baking mats.

2. In a large bowl, whisk together the coconut oil or MCT oil, almond milk, almond butter, and vanilla until the mixture is smooth. Add 1 cup of coconut sugar to the wet ingredients in the large bowl, and mix to combine.

3. Place the spelt flour, almond flour, baking powder, salt, cinnamon, ginger, and ground black pepper in a medium bowl. Mix well. Add the dry ingredients to the wet ingredients in the large bowl, and mix until fully incorporated.

4. Use a melon baller or a tablespoon to make about 42 dough balls. Place the remaining 1 tablespoon coconut sugar in a small bowl. Dip one side of each of the balls into the coconut sugar and place it sugar side up on the

(continued on following page)

Mind Meter

Ca	Fl	Mo	Me	Fo	Pri	Pro	Pl

baking sheet. Once all the cookies have been rolled in the sugar, use the flat bottom of a glass to press the balls into ¼-inch-thick disks. Bake the cookies for 11–13 minutes, or until the bottoms are lightly golden. Transfer the cookies to a wire rack and let them cool and crisp up.

Tip: If you'd like to get a head start on cookie prep, you can refrigerate the dough for up to 2 days ahead of time, or freeze it for up to 1 month and defrost it for 30 minutes before baking.

How to Blend Melted Coconut Oil with Other Ingredients in Recipes

Coconut oil is solid at room temperature, and even when it is in liquid form, it will quickly solidify if combined with cold liquids, which can make it difficult to use in some recipes, especially those that require baking. To keep it liquid, gently warm the coconut oil in a small saucepan, over the lowest heat, until it has fully melted. Then, if you are adding a cool liquid to the recipe, such as chilled almond milk, add it to the saucepan to warm it up a bit as well. Once all the liquid ingredients are slightly warm, proceed with the recipe.

RITUALS

Rituals aren't recipes that you save for a special occasion or a specific season, and they certainly don't require much fuss. Rather, rituals are recipes that are a part of your daily brain-building practice, and their regular consumption can be a key component in advancing your personal cognitive goals.

Don't let the simplicity of the rituals fool you: These simple yet profoundly effective recipes are designed, first and foremost, with function in mind. Each is enriched with top-notch natural nootropics (see page 86 for more information on the details of these ingredients) and **custom-formulated to offer specific cognitive gains**. The key on page 129 describes each of the benefits. But there's even more to the power of these recipes: Beyond their primary benefits, they are gently helpful for almost every aspect of cognition covered in this book, as many nootropics and plant-based foods are multitasking by nature. Consequently, there are no Mind Meters for the recipes in these pages, as each recipe contains virtually every benefit they measure—plus an additional cognitive boost!

Whether you choose to incorporate one or some of the delicious smoothies, lattes, and energy bites (or even the incredible MCT butter) into your daily lifestyle, you'll enjoy the full potential of natural nootropic foods that can truly boost your brainpower. Consider these "advanced" nootropic recipes as a bit of extra credit in your pursuit of cognitive improvement, including sharper thinking and focus, a calmer mindset and better sleep, easier access to creative flow, and enhanced memory and mood.

MCT Butter

As a delicious heart-healthy substitute for dairy butter and margarine, this buttery spread, with its rich load of brain-healthy nutrients like MCTs and choline, is almost too good to be true. A big part of what makes MCT butter so magical is the addition of sunflower lecithin. Make sure that the lecithin you use is fresh, in order to prevent the butter from separating. If your lecithin looks gummy, that's a sign that it's time to buy a new supply. (I usually keep lecithin in the refrigerator to extend its shelf life.)

MAKES ABOUT 1 ½ CUPS

½ cup room temperature water

2 tablespoons sunflower lecithin granules

1 teaspoon sea salt

¾ cup coconut oil, melted*

6 tablespoons coconut MCT oil

½ teaspoon apple cider vinegar

*If the coconut oil is solid, let it melt gently in a double boiler or place it in a small saucepan, over the lowest possible heat, for a very brief time (the butter will last much longer if the oil does not get too hot).

— Place the water, lecithin granules, and sea salt in a blender. Add the coconut oil, MCT oil, and apple cider vinegar. Start the blender on a low speed to mix the ingredients, and then increase the speed to high, blending until the mixture resembles a whip. Pour the mixture into an airtight container and refrigerate for about 1 hour or until it is firm. Keep the MCT butter refrigerated (it will soften at room temperature); it will last for up to 3 weeks.

VARIATIONS: There are several variations of MCT Butter that can add nootropics in the first step of the recipe. Try 1 teaspoon of ground turmeric + ¼ teaspoon of ground black pepper for an anti-inflammatory turmeric butter; use ½ teaspoon of ashwagandha powder for a butter that has a gentle positive effect on your mood; or add 1 teaspoon of matcha powder to turn this recipe into a focus-enhancing spread.

FOOD FOR THOUGHT: Sunflower Lecithin ————————————

Sunflower lecithin is an excellent source of choline, an important micronutrient that's directly linked to memory, learning, and neurotransmitter maintenance (1 tablespoon/250 mg supplies about half of your daily choline needs). Sunflower lecithin is also full of brain-friendly vitamins and minerals, like vitamin E and calcium. (For information on sourcing sunflower lecithin, see page 266.)

Banana-Nib Smoothie

This milkshake-like smoothie has a bit of a peanut-butter-and-banana flavor (without actually including peanuts in the ingredients) and makes an excellent morning-time drink to start the day with a feeling of calm. Cacao is high in relaxation-inducing magnesium, but if you are sensitive to the mildly excitatory phytochemicals in the bean, just leave out the cacao nibs—you'll still have a great-tasting drink. (I also recommend adding the greens in the recipe variation below for an extra dose of magnesium.)

MAKES 3 CUPS / SERVES 2

1 banana

5 Brazil nuts

2 tablespoons cacao nibs

2 Medjool dates, pitted

1 tablespoon hemp seeds

¼ teaspoon ashwagandha powder

¼ teaspoon ground cinnamon

1 cup unsweetened almond milk

1 cup ice

Liquid stevia, to taste (optional)

— Place all the ingredients, except the ice and stevia, in a blender and process until smooth. Add the ice and blend once more into a thick and frosty drink. Taste the smoothie; depending on the sweetness of the banana, you may want to add a couple drops of liquid stevia to balance the flavor.

VARIATION: Make it green! Add a handful of baby spinach for an extra dose of magnesium and other important minerals.

FOOD FOR THOUGHT: Brazil nuts

Although selenium is only a trace mineral, a deficiency of this micronutrient is no small matter: A lack of selenium is associated with cognitive decline and can contribute to depression. Fortunately, one of the most saturated food sources of selenium is the Brazil nut. In fact, a single large Brazil nut can offer up to twice your daily minimum needs of this important micronutrient!

The Magic of Stevia

While stevia won't boost your brainpower in and of itself, it *can* help you reduce your consumption of refined sugar (which can have a deleterious affect on cognition). Although stevia is 200–300 times sweeter than sugar, this natural sweetener contains no sugars, no calories, and has no effect on your glycemic levels—it only tastes sweet!

Stevia can be used very effectively to increase the sweetness of recipes, especially beverages. Even so, for the best flavor results use stevia to reduce the quantity of another form of sugar in a recipe (including fruit), rather than replacing it entirely.

There are many forms of stevia, but the liquid form, sold in small vials with a little dropper inside, offers the easiest way to calibrate the amount of stevia you use and also control its potent sweetness.

Matcha-Berry Smoothie

Get into your creative groove with this creamy medley of berry flavors; the taste of matcha may blend into the background, but the flow-state benefits it offers will definitely keep your ideas in the forefront of your mind.

MAKES 3 CUPS / SERVES 2

1 cup frozen mixed berries (such as raspberries, blueberries, and strawberries)

2 tablespoons raw cashews

2 Medjool dates, pitted

1 teaspoon matcha powder

1 teaspoon vanilla extract

1½ cups unsweetened almond milk

½ cup ice

Liquid stevia, to taste (optional)

— Place all the ingredients, except the ice and stevia, into a blender and process until smooth. Add the ice and blend once more into a thick and frosty drink. Taste the smoothie; depending on the sweetness of the fruit, you may want to add a couple drops of liquid stevia to balance the flavor.

Blueberry-Almond Smoothie

If your tastebuds ran the show, they'd probably forget that there's lion's mane mushroom powder in this fruity, luscious, well-balanced smoothie. (You can't taste it!) But with so many potent memory boosting, brain-protective nootropics packed into every drop, you'll surely remember to keep adding it every time you make this blend!

MAKES 2 CUPS /
SERVES 2

1 banana

½ cup frozen
blueberries

Handful fresh baby
spinach

2 tablespoons
roasted almond
butter

1 teaspoon ground
cinnamon

2 teaspoons lion's
mane powder

¾ cup coconut water

1 teaspoon vanilla
extract

1 cup ice

Liquid stevia, to taste
(optional)

— Place all the ingredients, except the ice and stevia, into a blender and process until smooth. Add the ice and blend once more into a thick and frosty drink. Taste the smoothie; depending on the sweetness of the banana, you may want to add 8–10 drops of liquid stevia to balance the flavor.

Chocolate & Greens Smoothie

Loaded with mood-boosting ingredients—including cacao, goji berries, lion's mane, and more—it's hard to tell what brings more joy: the beneficial biochemistry of the natural nootropics in the ingredients or the indulgently creamy chocolate taste of the smoothie itself!

MAKES 2 CUPS / SERVES 2

¼ cup raw cashews

1 frozen banana

1 large handful baby spinach

2 tablespoons goji berries

2 tablespoons cacao powder

1 teaspoon lion's mane powder

1 Medjool date, pitted

¾ cup coconut water

1 teaspoon vanilla extract

1 cup ice

Liquid stevia, to taste (optional)

— Place all the ingredients, except the ice and stevia, into a blender and process until smooth. Add the ice and blend once more into a thick and frosty drink. Taste the smoothie; depending on the sweetness of the banana you may want to add 4–6 drops of liquid stevia to balance the flavor.

Freezing Bananas

If you have frozen bananas on hand, you can always make professional-quality frosty shakes any time you please! (Freezing is also the perfect way to rescue a bunch of rapidly browning bananas and save them from the compost bin.) To prepare frozen bananas (very ripe bananas will taste best), first peel and cut the bananas into quarters or sixths and then freeze them in a flat layer inside a zippered plastic bag. Frozen bananas will keep for months, until you're ready to use them.

Creamy Mango Smoothie

The amount of focus-promoting nootropics in this smoothie may seem minuscule, but make no mistake: These ingredients are potent! You can double the amount for a stronger effect, but the flavor of the nootropics will become more pronounced . . . and not necessarily in a better way. Frozen mango chunks are commonly found in the freezer section of most markets, but if you have extra fresh mangos on hand, you can peel, pit, chop and freeze them yourself!

MAKES 3 CUPS / SERVES 2

2 cups frozen mango chunks

2 cups unsweetened almond milk

½ teaspoon vanilla extract

⅛ teaspoon rhodiola powder

⅛ teaspoon schisandra powder

2 Medjool dates, pitted

1 tablespoon chia seeds

Liquid stevia, to taste (optional)

— Place all the ingredients, except the stevia, in a blender and process until the consistency is smooth. Taste the smoothie; depending on the sweetness and size of the fruits used, you may want to add a bit of liquid stevia to balance the flavor.

FOOD FOR THOUGHT: Mango

A mango may taste more like a dessert than a more obvious brain food (like dulse or broccoli), but don't be deceived by all that sweetness: the nutrients in mangos are hard at work to keep your brain in peak condition. Along with vitamin C, vitamin A, vitamin E, and vitamin K, the sweet fruit is also an excellent source of brain-essential B vitamins—particularly vitamin B_6—which help regulate neurotransmitter activity, balance mood, and maintain focus.

Calm

Vanilla-Lavender Latte

A mug of lavender tea on its own is probably one of the most relaxing drinks to curl up with, but in the form of a creamy latte it is exponentially more delicious. What's more, the floral essence of lavender is an ideal way to mask the flavor of calming nootropics like reishi and ashwagandha (which don't exactly have the best reputation for tasting great on their own). If you can't find pure lavender tea at the store, a lavender blend—such as lavender and chamomile—will absolutely do the trick. Any which way, this beautiful latte will help put you in a better frame of mind!

MAKES 3 CUPS / SERVES 2

3 lavender tea bags

3 tablespoons raw cashews

2 Medjool dates, pitted

3 cups boiling water

1 teaspoon reishi powder

½ teaspoon ashwagandha powder

½ teaspoon vanilla extract

— Place the tea bags, cashews, and dates in a heatproof container or a small saucepan, and pour the boiling water on top. Let the tea steep for 3–4 minutes, and then remove the tea bags. Pour the tea, along with the soaked nuts and dates, into a blender, and add the reishi, ashwagandha, and vanilla. Blend the mixture until it is smooth and creamy. Serve warm.

Perfect Matcha Latte

I realize it's more than a little pompous to call your own matcha latte recipe "perfect"— especially since the drink is ubiquitous and a favorite for so many people—so please allow me to explain. At my house, with two creative professionals under one roof, getting "a good flow on" is in extremely high demand. Consequently, matcha lattes are on almost constant rotation in the kitchen and are usually the first thing offered to anyone who comes through the door, too. So, out of necessity, we've standardized the process over the years—and this formula is the result. It's basically our family recipe, and we like to think it's pretty near . . . well . . . perfect!

MAKES 3 CUPS /
SERVES 2

2 cups unsweetened almond milk

1 cup water

1 teaspoon matcha powder

1 tablespoon MCT oil*

1/2 teaspoon vanilla extract

1/8 teaspoon almond extract (optional)

10 drops liquid stevia, or to taste

*If you don't have MCT oil, you can use regular coconut oil.

— Combine the almond milk and water in a saucepan and bring the liquid to a low simmer over medium heat. Pour the liquid into a blender and add all the remaining ingredients. Blend the mixture very briefly to combine (less than 10 seconds should do the trick), and serve warm.

Golden Goji Latte

Experience the invigorating effects of goji berries, turmeric, ginger, and black pepper in this warming latte—a lightly spiced beverage that doesn't just appear golden; it *is* golden, as far as your brain is concerned. This latte is memory-boosting, protects against inflammation and disease, and enhances cognitive functioning. For an extra layer of caramel-like flavor, you can use 1 tablespoon of coconut sugar instead of liquid stevia.

MAKES 2 CUPS / SERVES 2

2 cups unsweetened almond milk

3 tablespoons dried goji berries

¾ teaspoon ground turmeric

½ teaspoon ground ginger

⅛ teaspoon finely ground black pepper

½ teaspoon vanilla extract

1 tablespoon MCT oil*

8–10 drops liquid stevia, or to taste

*If you don't have MCT oil, you can use regular coconut oil instead.

— Place all the ingredients, except the stevia, into a small saucepan and bring the mixture to a gentle simmer. Once the mixture is hot, pour it into a blender and process until it is smooth and frothy. Blend in 8–10 drops of liquid stevia, or sweeten to taste, and serve warm.

Happy Chocolate Latte

What's better than hot chocolate? Happy hot chocolate! Cacao and ashwagandha make a phenomenal nootropic pair for boosting mood. During stressful times, a daily serving of this comforting latte can help keep spirits high and anxiety low—and if it's warm out, you can even enjoy it as a cool, refreshing, and delicious chocolate "milk."

MAKES 2 CUPS /
SERVES 2

1 cup coconut water

1 cup water

1 tablespoon roasted almond butter

2 Medjool dates, pitted

1 tablespoon cacao powder

½ teaspoon ashwagandha powder

— Place all the ingredients in a blender and process until the mixture is very smooth. Pour the mixture into a saucepan and place it over low heat, until the latte is warm. Serve immediately.

Focus

Spiced Chai Latte

Who needs coffee when you have an exciting, slightly spicy latte that can awaken both your taste buds and your mind. You can always reduce the black pepper and ginger a bit if you want to bring down the heat, but they do add flavor (and help digestion, too).

MAKES 2 CUPS / SERVES 2

2 cups unsweetened almond milk

2 Medjool dates, pitted

2 teaspoons lion's mane powder

¼ scant teaspoon schisandra powder

½ teaspoon ground cinnamon

½ teaspoon ground ginger

⅛ teaspoon ground cardamom

¼ teaspoon finely ground black pepper

Liquid stevia, to taste (optional)

— Place all the ingredients in a blender and process until the mixture is smooth. Pour the mixture into a saucepan and place it over low heat, until it comes to a light simmer. Give the warm latte a stir before serving, and enjoy it immediately. Sweeten with additional stevia, only if needed.

 Fig & Walnut Bites

My love affair with figgy treats began with my grandmother's special holiday cookies: Round, ravioli-shaped pastries that revealed a secret pocket of sweet fig-raisin paste with the first bite. For me, those cookes were *all* about that fruity paste. These bites play off that fig-cookie flavor, minus all the sugar, of course, and include a couple ingredients that Grandma definitely didn't add, like reishi powder. In fact, every ingredient in this mix—from the almonds to the goji berries to the figs—has functional benefits to promote relaxation.

MAKES 24 BITES / SERVES 8

1 cup raw almonds

½ cup raw walnuts

¾ cup (packed) dried figs*

⅓ cup dried goji berries

1½ tablespoons reishi powder

1 teaspoon vanilla extract

1 teaspoon ground cinnamon

¼ teaspoon anise seeds (optional)

¼ teaspoon sea salt

*You can use any kind of dried fig in this recipe. Black Mission or white Turkish figs work very well.

1. Place the almonds and walnuts in a food processor and pulse the ingredients briefly to reduce them to the size of large gravel. Add all the remaining ingredients to the food processor and process the mixture into a crumbly "dough," while leaving a little bit of texture from the almonds and walnuts. Check the consistency: The dough should stick together very easily when pressed between two fingers. (Depending on the natural moisture of the figs, you may need to adjust the consistency of the dough: If it is too dry, blend in a little water, 1 teaspoon at a time, until the dough is malleable.)

2. Line a flat surface with plastic wrap. Place the dough on top of the wrap and shape it into a compact rectangle, about 1 inch thick. Wrap the plastic tightly around the rectangle and flatten it into an even layer with a rolling pin or with your hands. Remove the plastic wrap and cut the dough into 24 "bites" with a chef's knife or a pastry cutter.

3. The bites can be stored in an airtight container at room temperature for up to 1 week, or in the refrigerator for several weeks.

FOOD FOR THOUGHT: Figs

Rich in many essential minerals, figs are a particularly good source of potassium—just three little figs can offer even more potassium than a banana! Potassium is a vital nutrient for nerve cell transmission as well as all-around brain functioning.

Lemon Hemp Bites

Calling all lemon lovers! These irresistibly zesty bites will awaken your senses without over-stimulating them. They make an ideal snack at any time of the day or night to help get your creative juices flowing.

**MAKES 24 BITES /
SERVES 8**

1 cup raw almonds

¾ cup (packed)
Medjool dates, pitted
(about 12)

2 teaspoons
schisandra powder

½ teaspoon rhodiola
powder

2 teaspoons fresh
lemon zest

1 tablespoon fresh
lemon juice

¼ teaspoon sea salt

¼ cup unsweetened
shredded coconut

¼ cup hemp seeds

1. Place the almonds, dates, schisandra, rhodiola, lemon zest, lemon juice, and salt in a food processor. Process the mixture into a crumbly "dough," while leaving a little bit of texture from the nuts. Add the shredded coconut and hemp seeds, and process briefly to combine, keeping the coconut and hemp seeds mostly intact for texture. Check the consistency: The dough should stick together very easily when pressed between two fingers. (Depending on the natural moisture of the dates, you may need to adjust the consistency of the dough: If it is too dry, add in a little water, 1 teaspoon at a time, until the dough is malleable.)

2. Line a flat surface with plastic wrap. Place the dough on top of the wrap and shape it into a compact rectangle, about 1 inch thick. Wrap the plastic tightly around the rectangle and flatten it into an even layer with a rolling pin or your hands. Remove the plastic wrap and cut the dough into 24 "bites" with a chef's knife or a pastry cutter.

3. The bites can be stored in an airtight container at room temperature for up to 1 week, or in the refrigerator for several weeks.

Spiced Coconut Bites

From a flavor standpoint, these treats are like a chewy version of a turmeric latte with a slight berry-like twist, while their highly protective ingredients, including lion's mane and walnuts, make them the epitome of "smart snacking."

MAKES 24 BITES / SERVES 8

1 cup unsweetened shredded coconut

½ cup (packed) Medjool dates, pitted (about 8)

1 teaspoon ground turmeric

½ teaspoon ground ginger

¼ teaspoon sea salt

¼ teaspoon ground black pepper

2 tablespoons lion's mane powder

¾ cup raw walnuts

¼ cup hemp seeds

3 tablespoons unsweetened dried blueberries or dried currants

1. Place the coconut, dates, turmeric, ginger, salt, pepper, and lion's mane in a food processor. Process the mixture into a crumbly "dough." Add the walnuts and hemp seeds and process briefly, leaving plenty of texture. Add the dried blueberries or currants and process briefly, keeping the dried fruits largely intact. Check the consistency: The dough should stick together easily when pressed between two fingers. (Depending on the natural moisture of the dates, you may need to adjust the consistency: If the dough is too dry, blend in a little water, 1 teaspoon at a time, until the dough is malleable.)

2. Line a flat surface with plastic wrap. Place the dough on top of the wrap and shape it into a compact rectangle, about 1 inch thick. Wrap the plastic tightly around the rectangle and flatten it into an even layer with a rolling pin or your hands. Remove the plastic wrap and cut the dough into 24 "bites" with a chef's knife or a pastry cutter.

3. The bites can be stored in an airtight container at room temperature for up to 1 week, or in the refrigerator for several weeks.

   VARIATION: If you happen to have a superfood berry powder (or blend) on hand for making smoothies and other recipes (like acai berry powder or maqui berry powder), you can add up to 2 tablespoons to the food processor, along with the other ingredients in this recipe, for additional memory-boosting antioxidants.

Matcha Mint Bites

Keep your mind focused and improve your activities with these minty, matcha-boosted chocolate snacks. They take just a few minutes to prepare, which makes it easy to whip up a batch on days when you're doing lots of deskwork, studying, or planning.

MAKES 24 BITES / SERVES 8

1 cup raw cashews

¾ cup (packed) Medjool dates (about 12)

1 tablespoon lion's mane powder

1½ teaspoons matcha powder

½ teaspoon vanilla extract

½ teaspoon mint extract

¼ teaspoon sea salt

¼ cup unsweetened shredded coconut

2 tablespoons cacao nibs

1. Place the cashews, dates, lion's mane, matcha, vanilla, mint, and salt in a food processor. Process the mixture into a crumbly "dough." Add the coconut and cacao nibs, and process briefly, keeping them mostly intact for texture. Check the consistency: The dough should stick together very easily when pressed between two fingers. (Depending on the natural moisture of the dates, you may need to adjust the consistency: If the dough is too dry, add a little water, 1 teaspoon at a time, until the dough is malleable.)

2. Line a flat surface with plastic wrap. Place the dough on top of the wrap and shape it into a compact rectangle, about 1 inch thick. Wrap the plastic tightly around the rectangle and flatten it into an even layer with a rolling pin or your hands. Remove the plastic wrap and cut the dough into 24 "bites" with a chef's knife or a pastry cutter.

3. The bites can be stored in an airtight container at room temperature for up to 1 week, or in the refrigerator for several weeks.

Chocolate Goji Bites

These treat-like bites are a symphony of feel-good foods, featuring cacao, goji berries, rhodiola, and omega 3–packed pecans and chia. With all those great ingredients playing beautifully together while boasting a chocolate brownie–like flavor, what's not to love?

**MAKES 24 BITES /
SERVES 8**

1 cup raw pecans

½ cup (packed) Medjool dates, pitted (about 8)

⅓ cup dried goji berries

1 tablespoon chia seeds

3 tablespoons cacao powder

¼ teaspoon rhodiola powder

¼ teaspoon sea salt

1 teaspoon vanilla extract

1. Place all the ingredients in a food processor. Process the mixture into a crumbly "dough," leaving little bits of the nuts and goji berries for texture. Check the consistency: The dough should stick together very easily when pressed between two fingers. (Depending on the natural moisture of the dates, you may need to adjust the consistency: If the dough is too dry, add a little water, 1 teaspoon at a time, until the dough is malleable.)

2. Line a flat surface with plastic wrap. Place the dough on top of the wrap and shape it into a compact rectangle, about 1 inch thick. Wrap the plastic tightly around the rectangle and flatten it into an even layer with a rolling pin or your hands. Remove the plastic wrap and cut the dough into 24 "bites" with a chef's knife or pastry cutter.

3. These bites can be stored in an airtight container at room temperature for up to 1 week, or in the refrigerator for several weeks.

FOOD FOR THOUGHT: Chia —————————————

Like a tiny treasure chest, chia seeds are filled to the brim with brain-friendly micronutrients. Loaded with important minerals (like magnesium and calcium), packed with gut-friendly and glucose-stabilizing fiber, and stocked with all nine essential amino acids, chia seeds are an ideal food for everyday brain priming. Additionally, they are saturated with ALA omega 3 fats: The anti-inflammatory, building-block nutrients your brain craves.

RECIPES BY MEAL

BREAKFAST

MAINS

SOUPS

STARTERS & SIDES

SNACKS

SWEETS

BEVERAGES

7-DAY SMART PLANTS CHALLENGE

From neurotransmitters to nootropic-boosted smoothies, we've covered a lot of ground in these pages. But the transformation doesn't need to stop here.

To guide you on your next steps and help you put your cognition-boosting concepts into action, I've created a bonus set of free extra resources for you. Our **7-day Smart Plants Challenge** is a fun, brain-friendly, follow-up series delivered directly to your inbox, offering you a useful kit full of ways to ensure smart plants become part of your everyday lifestyle. Each day of the challenge you'll receive valuable tools, including:

- SMART PLANTS DAILY CHECKLIST: We've condensed the important dietary lessons from this book into a simple, one-sheet checklist you can use for everyday brain optimization.

- SMART PLANTS GROCERY GUIDE: Need some help with your weekly grocery shopping? Use our easy, printable shopping list to ensure you always remember to pick up the most helpful brain-friendly foods.

- MIND METER QUIZ: Not sure what your specific cognitive goals are? Identify the areas you can look to improve through our personality quiz, and discover what nootropics may be best for you.

Get all seven email challenges at: **www.Luminberry.com/bonus**.

RESOURCES GUIDE

COURSES

If you loved *Smart Plants*, you may be interested in some of our Luminberry online cooking courses:

Brain-Boosting Breakfasts

Want to start the day the brain-boosting way? In this course Julie will teach you about the performance-enhancing foods that are best suited for morning hours, and why they work. Then put your skills to use as you follow along in the Luminberry kitchen to make three delicious breakfast recipes.

Learn more: www.luminberry.com/courses

Low-Sugar Superfood Smoothies

Do you love smoothies but want to follow a low-sugar lifestyle? In this course Julie will share the secrets to making smoothies packed with the nutrition and flavor you crave, without the sugar. Master your skills as you follow along in the Luminberry kitchen to make three revitalizing smoothie recipes.

Learn more: www.luminberry.com/courses

PRODUCTS

Many of these products can be purchased at your local natural food store or easily ordered online from retailers like Thrive Market, iHerb, Vitacost, or Amazon.

Nootropic Ingredients (Powder/Dried)

Ashwagandha Powder
myojio.com

Fresh Berries
driscolls.com

Lion's Mane Powder
ommushrooms.com

Cacao Powder, Cacao Nibs
navitasorganics.com

Goji Berries
navitasorganics.com

Matcha Powder (culinary grade)
navitasorganics.com

Reishi Powder
ommushrooms.com

Schisandra Berry Powder
moutainroseherbs.com

Rhodiola (3% rosavins)
microingredients.com

Turmeric Powder
navitasorganics.com

Supplements (Capsules/Tinctures)

Algae Omega Supplement
  (DHA & EPA)
nordicnaturals.com
  (choose algae variety)
vegetology.com
  (Opti3 Omega-3 EPA
& DHA)

Artichoke Extract
herbpharm.com

Astaxanthin
nutrex-hawaii.com

Bacopa Monnieri Capsules
himalayausa.com

CBD Oil
lazarusnaturals.com

Curcumin
thorne.com ("Meriva-SF")

Gotu Kola
herbpharm.com

Holy Basil
gaiaherbs.com

Panax Ginseng
dragonherbs.com

St. John's Wort
gaiaherbs.com

Pantry Favorites

Algae Cooking Oil
thrivealgae.com

Amaranth
bobsredmill.com

Arrowroot Flour
bobsredmill.com

Beans (pressure-cooked)
edenfoods.com

Chia Seeds & Powder
navitasorganics.com

Dulse (pieces and flakes)
seaveg.com

Farro
bobsredmill.com

Flaked Salt
maldonsalt.com

Freekeh
bobsredmill.com

Garbanzo Bean Flour
bobsredmill.com

Hemp Seeds
navitasorganics.com

MCT Oil
vivanaturals.com

Miso Paste
great-eastern-sun.com

Monk Fruit Sugar Substitute
lakanto.com

Nondairy Yogurt
sodeliciousdairyfree.com

Stevia, Liquid
omicaorganics.com

Sunflower Lecithin
microingredients.com

Za'atar (spice blend)
spicely.com

MORE WELLNESS EDUCATION

Julie Morris's Cookbooks
Superfood Kitchen
Superfood Juices
Superfood Smoothies
Superfood Snacks
Superfood Soups

Julie Morris's Superfood Cooking Courses
luminberry.com

Neurofeedback Training & QEEG
  ("Brain Mapping")
peakbraininstitute.com

Recommended Reading

Further research from Dr. Paula Bickford:
researchgate.net/profile/Paula_Bickford

The Blue Zones: 9 Lessons for Living Longer from the People Who've Lived the Longest, 2nd ed. by Dan Buettner

How Not to Die: Discover the Foods Scientifically Proven to Prevent and Reverse Disease by Michael Greger, MD, FACLM with Gene Stone

Plant-Based Nutrition, 2nd ed. by Julieanna Hever, MS, RD, CPT, and Raymond J. Cronise

Diet for the MIND: The Latest Science on What to Eat to Prevent Alzheimer's and Cognitive Decline—From the Creator of the MIND Diet by Dr. Martha Clare Morris

Alzheimer's Disease: What If There Was a Cure? The Story of Ketones by Mary T. Newport, MD

Coconut: The Complete Guide to the World's Most Versatile Superfood by Stephanie Pedersen

Further research from Dr. Barbara Shukitt-Hale:
researchgate.net/profile/Barbara_Shukitt-Hale

GLOSSARY

acetylcholine: a neurotransmitter that triggers increased focus, enhanced calmness, and decreased symptoms of anxiety; also helps the brain process information.

adaptogens: a special class of foods that support the endocrine system (the collection of glands that produce and regulate hormones, metabolism, sleep, and mood, among other functions) and the immune system in a natural way; help the body adapt to stress and restore the body's natural state of balance.

alpha linolenic acid (ALA): an omega-3 fatty acid that bolsters cardiovascular health and curbs inflammation.

amino acids: the building blocks of protein; an organic compound.

amygdala: the part of the brain (an element of the limbic system) responsible for controlling emotional response.

anandamide: a fatty acid neurotransmitter that's been called "the bliss molecule."

antibodies: proteins made by the immune system to fight foreign molecules.

antinutrients: compounds in foods that can interfere with the absorption of good nutrients and minerals.

antioxidants: oxidation-fighting micronutrients that can counter the destructive activity of free radicals, as well as help to offset the premature aging of cells.

autoimmune disorder: a destructive condition where a person's immune system attacks its own tissue.

autonomic nervous system: a structure that regulates the involuntary functions of the body's internal organs, including the heart, stomach, and intestines; also controls some muscle function.

axons: branchlike structures on one end of a neuron responsible for taking information away from the cell body.

Ayurveda: a system of natural therapy developed in India more than 2,000 years ago, that is now practiced throughout the world.

bioavailability: the proportion of a substance that, once entered into the body's circulation, is effectively used for biological activity.

blood-brain barrier: a "wall" made up of a semipermeable layer of cells between the bloodstream and neurons that blocks out some substances and lets other materials through; helps to maintain a constant and stable environment for the brain.

Blue Zones: a term coined by Dan Buettner that refers to the five areas in the world that boast the longest-living populations (on average).

brain-derived neurotrophic factor (BDNF): a substance that can protect your brain cells, promote healthy new neuron growth, and enhance memory.

dendrites: branchlike structures on one end of a neuron responsible for bringing information into the cell body.

docosahexaenoic acid (DHA): an omega-3 fatty acid that is a primary structural component of the brain.

dopamine: a neurotransmitter that governs moods and behavior plus motivation and drive.

down-regulate: to induce a reduction in the level of gene expression through genetic means.

eicosapentaenoic acid (EPA): an omega-3 fatty acid with anti-inflammatory properties.

endorphins: the "feel-good" chemicals the brain manufactures that can override pain and put you in a better mood.

epinephrine (also known as noradrenaline): an excitatory neurotransmitter and a stress hormone; plays a role in quick decision-making in times of extreme stress.

excitotoxicity: a condition where neurons are damaged and killed by overactive excitatory neurotransmitter activity.

flavonoids (also called bioflavonoids): a subgroup of polyphenol antioxidants that have shown great promise in improving memory, learning, decision-making, and reasoning.

free radicals: malignant cells that are the result of an unpaired "free" electron, which makes cells highly reactive and prone to disease.

GABA (gamma-aminobutyric acid): an inhibitory neurotransmitter that reduces stress, induces calm, and promotes sleep.

glutamate: an excitatory neurotransmitter that figures prominently in learning and memory.

glycemic index: a relative ranking of carbohydrates in foods and how they affect blood glucose levels.

gray matter: brain tissue that is richest in cellular bodies and synapses.

heavy metals: metals with a high density that are toxic or poisonous at low concentrations.

high smoke point: a characteristic of some cooking oils, meaning they don't easily oxidize from heat and can withstand higher temperatures while cooking.

hippocampus: a part of the brain (an element of the limbic system) responsible for learning and memory.

inflammation: part of the body's immune response to heal and repair damaged tissue and defend against foreign invaders, like bacteria and viruses; inflammation can be harmful if it becomes chronic.

ketones: a class of organic compounds produced by the body as an alternative fuel source once glucose is not readily available.

lectins: carbohydrate-binding proteins.

lipids: fatty acids, including natural oils, waxes, and steroids.

medium-chain triglycerides (MCTs): saturated fatty acids with 6–12 carbon atoms; an easily digestible source of fat-based energy.

microbiome: an ecosystem of microorganisms (bacteria, fungi, viruses, and more) that live in and on the body.

micronutrients: dietary components needed in small quantities by the body (including vitamins, minerals, antioxidants, and phytochemicals) that are important and often essential for wellness.

monounsaturated fats: beneficial fatty acids that are good for heart health and brain health; are anti-inflammatory; and help maintain neurotransmitter activity.

myelin sheath: the protective covering around nerve cells.

neural adenosine triphosphate (ATP): a central metabolite that serves as the main source of energy for most cellular processes.

neurofeedback: a type of biofeedback where brainwave activity is monitored through real-time digital tracking and regulated or reorganized through sound or visual signals to improve brain function.

neurons: nerve cells.

neuroprotective: referring to actions or nutrients that tend to protect nerve cells from damage or degeneration.

neurotoxin: a substance that destroys nerve tissue.

neurotransmitters: a group of brain chemicals that act as a catalyst for all kinds of mental and physical tasks.

nootropics: cognition-enhancing substances that can improve the way you think, feel, and function.

norepinephrine (also known as noradrenaline): an excitatory neurotransmitter released by the brain and a stress hormone; figures in mood, motivation, focus, and attention.

nutrient density: the ratio of micronutrients per calorie in food.

omega-3 fatty acids (also called omega 3s): essential polyunsaturated fats that are a crucial component of cell membranes throughout the body and an integral component of the brain.

parasympathetic nervous system: part of the autonomic nervous system; regulates the body's "rest and digest" responses.

phytochemicals: beneficial plant-based chemicals.

phytonutrients: naturally-occuring plant-based nutrients.

polyphenol antioxidants (also known as polyphenols): micronutrients that supply a highly protective shield for the brain, keeping neurons in peak condition by preventing inflammation and oxidation and even improving the way neurons communicate and grow.

polyunsaturated fat: a type of good dietary fat that includes omega fatty acids and is often found in seeds and grains.

prebiotics: the "food" that probiotics need to develop, grow, and flourish.

prefrontal cortex (frontal lobe): the part of the brain that determines what you pay attention to and how you respond to it.

probiotics: the "good" bacteria in the gastrointestinal tract.

programmed cell death (also known as apoptosis): the death of cells, which occurs as a controlled part of a biological process.

quantitative electroencephalogram (QEEG): a type of "brain mapping" test that analyzes the electrical activity of the brain to measure and display patterns for diagnostic information.

saturated fat: a type of dietary fat that is most often solid at room temperature.

serotonin: an inhibitory neurotransmitter that figures prominently in mood and emotion.

synapse: the small gap that separates neurons across which information flows from one cell to another.

theanine: a "calming amino acid" that counteracts anxiety and promotes relaxation.

theobromine: a phytochemical touted for its ability to increase attention span.

trans fats (also known as partially hydrogenated vegetable oils): dietary fats that are extremely harmful to cognitive function.

tryptophan: a major essential amino acid that is the precursor to serotonin.

tyrosine: an amino acid that is the precursor of three major neurotransmitters: norepinephrine, epinephrine, and dopamine.

up-regulate: the process of increasing the response to a stimulus.

vagus nerve: the long, acetylcholine-activating nerve that runs from the brain stem to the abdomen and acts a conduit between the brain and the gut.

vegan: a fully plant-based eating regimen.

METRIC CONVERSION CHARTS

NONLIQUID INGREDIENTS (Weights of common ingredients in grams)

INGREDIENT	1 CUP	3/4 CUP	2/3 CUP	1/2 CUP	1/3 CUP	1/4 CUP	2 TBSP
Chia	163 g	122 g	108 g	81 g	54 g	41 g	20 g
Chopped fruits and vegetables	150 g	110 g	100 g	75 g	50 g	40 g	20 g
Coconut oil	216 g	162 g	144 g	108g	72 g	54 g	27 g
Dates, chopped	151 g	117 g	100 g	75 g	50 g	39 g	19 g
Goji berries	111 g	83 g	74 g	55 g	37 g	28 g	14 g
Nuts, chopped	150 g	110 g	100 g	75 g	50 g	40 g	20 g
Nuts, ground	120 g	90 g	80 g	60 g	40 g	30 g	15 g
Sea salt, crystals	269 g	202 g	179 g	135 g	90 g	67 g	34 g

Note: Nonliquid ingredients specified in American recipes by volume (if more than about 2 tablespoons or 1 fluid ounce) can be converted to weight with the table above. If you need to convert an ingredient that isn't in this table, the safest thing to do is to measure it with a traditional measuring cup and then weigh the results with a metric scale. In a pinch, you can use the volume and weight conversion tables below.

VOLUME CONVERSIONS (Used for liquids)

CUSTOMARY QUANTITY	METRIC EQUIVALENT
1 teaspoon	5 mL
1 tablespoon or 1/2 fluid ounce	15 mL
1 fluid ounce or 1/8 cup	30 mL
1/4 cup or 2 fluid ounces	60 mL
1/3 cup	80 mL
1/2 cup or 4 fluid ounces	120 mL
2/3 cup	160 mL
1 cup or 8 fluid ounces or 1/2 pint	250 mL
1 1/2 cups or 12 fluid ounces	350 mL
2 cups or 1 pint or 16 fluid ounces	475 mL
3 cups or 1 1/2 pints	700 mL
4 cups or 2 pints or 1 quart	950 mL
4 quarts or 1 gallon	3.8 L

Note: In cases where higher precision is not justified, these conversions can be rounded off as follows:

1 cup = 250 mL
1 pint = 500 mL
1 quart = 1 L
1 gallon = 4 L

WEIGHT CONVERSIONS

CUSTOMARY QUANTITY	METRIC EQUIVALENT
1 ounce	28 g
4 ounces or 1/4 pound	113 g
1/3 pound	150 g
8 ounces or 1/2 pound	230 g
2/3 pound	300 g
12 ounces or 3/4 pound	340 g
1 pound or 16 ounces	450 g
2 pounds	900 g

Note: Ounces referred to in this table are not the same as fluid ounces.

NOTES

Chapter 1: SHIFT HAPPENS

3 **In an article published in *Stanford Engineering*:** Tom Abate and Amy Adams, "Stanford Scientists Create Circuit Board Modeled on the Human Brain," *Stanford Engineering*, April 24, 2014, https://engineering.stanford.edu/magazine/article /stanford-scientists-create-circuit-board-modeled-human-brain.

9 **Studies show that some volitional breathing exercises:** Bruno Bordoni et al, "The Influence of Breathing on the Central Nervous System," *Cureus Journal of Medical Science*, June 10, 2018, https://www.ncbi.nlm.nih.gov/pmc/articles /PMC6070065/.

Andrea Zaccaro et al, "How Breath-Control Can Change Your Life: A Systematic Review on Psycho-Physiological Correlates of Slow Breathing," *Frontiers in Human Neuroscience*, September 7, 2018, https://www.ncbi.nlm.nih .gov/pmc/articles/PMC6137615/.

11 **recent studies have shown that up to 95 percent:** Michael Camilleri, "Serotonin in the Gastrointestinal Tract," *Current Opinion in Endocrinology, Diabetes, and Obesity*, February 1, 2010, https://www.ncbi.nlm.nih.gov/pmc/articles /PMC2694720/.

11 **The American Psychiatric Association estimates that one in fifteen people suffer from depression:** "What is Depression?" *American Psychiatric Association,* January 2017, https://www.psychiatry.org/patients-families/depression /what-is-depression.

12 **effects on overall cognitive function are well studied:** Oscar Arias-Carrión et al, "Dopaminergic reward System: A Short Integrative Review," *International Archives of Medicine*, October 6, 2010, https://www.ncbi.nlm.nih.gov/pmc/articles/ PMC2958859/.

19 **A 2013 study:** Lawrence A. David et al, "Diet Rapidly and Reproducibly Alters the Human Gut Microbiome," *Nature International Journal of Science*, December 11, 2013, https://www.ncbi.nlm.nih.gov/pmc/articles/PMC3957428/.

Chapter 2: WHY PLANTS?

21 **recent studies have reversed the generally accepted position:** Mura Boldrini et al, "Human Hippocampal Neurogenesis Persists throughout Aging," *Cell Stem Cell*, April 5, 2018, https://www.cell.com/cell-stem-cell/fulltext/ S1934-5909(18)30121-8.

23 **a 2005 study found that a group of medical students:** Bogdan Draganski et al, "Temporal and Spatial Dynamics of Brain Structure Changes during Extensive Learning," *Journal of Neuroscience*, June 7, 2006, http://www.jneurosci.org /content/26/23/6314.

Chapter 3: FUELING YOUR BRAIN

29 **In a 2012 Harvard study exploring fat's effect on the brain:** Harvard Medical School, "Protect Your Brain with 'Good' Fat," *Harvard Health Publishing*, September 2012, https://www.health.harvard.edu/mind-and-mood/protect-your-brain -with-good-fat.

30 **In a 2015 podcast interview:** Martha Morris, "The MIND Diet with Dr. Martha Morris," interview by Jesse Lawler, *Smart Drug Smarts*, September 22, 2017, https://smartdrugsmarts.com/episodes/199-mind-diet/.

32 **Human trials have shown that:** "Essential Fatty Acids," *Linus Pauling Institute*, https://lpi.oregonstate.edu/mic/other-nutrients/essential-fatty-acids.

Holger Gerster, "Can Adults Adequately Convert Alpha-Linolenic Acid (18:3n-3) to Eicosapentaenoic Acid (20:5n-3) and Docosahexaenoic Acid (22:6n-3)?" *International Journal for Vitamins and Nutrition Research*, 1998, https://www.ncbi.nlm.nih.gov/pubmed/9637947.

32 **A 2013 study published by the National Cancer Institute:** Theodore M. Brasky et al, "Plasma Phospholipid Fatty Acids and Prostate Cancer Risk in the SELECT Trial," *Journal of the National Cancer Institute*, August 7, 2013, https://www.ncbi.nlm.nih.gov/pubmed/23843441.

32 **A 2017 report published in *Scientific Reports*:** Ali Karami et al, "Microplastics in Eviscerated Flesh and Excised Organs of Dried Fish," *Scientific Reports*, July 14, 2017, https://www.nature.com/articles/s41598-017-05828-6.

33 **A team of scientists from Malaysia and France discovered:** See above reference.

34 **studies indicate they may be very helpful in your quest for a better-functioning brain:** Alexandre Courchesne-Loyer et al, "Stimulation of Mild, Sustained Ketonemia by Medium-Chain Triacylglycerols in Healthy Humans: Estimated Potential Contribution to Brain Energy Metabolism," *Nutrition*, April 2013, https://www.sciencedirect.com/science/article/pii/S0899900712003656.

Etienne Croteau et al, "Ketogenic Medium Chain Triglycerides Increase Brain Energy Metabolism in Alzheimer's Disease," *Journal of Alzheimer's Disease*, 2018, https://www.ncbi.nlm.nih.gov/pubmed/29914035.

34 **research warns of the negative ramifications of consuming excess saturated fat:** Meghan Jardine, "Seven Reasons to Keep Saturated Fat Off Your Plate," *Physicians Committee for Responsible Medicine*, November 5, 2018, https://www.pcrm.org/news/blog/seven-reasons-keep-saturated-fat-your-plate.

37 **one study on fasting reporting an increase of neuron growth:** Silvia Manzanero et al, "Intermittent Fasting Attenuates Increases in Neurogenesis after Ischemia and Reperfusion and Improves Recovery," *Journal of Cerebral Blood Flow & Metabolism*, May 2014, https://www.ncbi.nlm.nih.gov/pmc/articles/PMC4013772/.

38 **In 2012, a comprehensive meta-analysis of dietary restriction:** Shinichi Nakagawa et al, "Comparative and Meta-analytic Insights into Life Extension Via Dietary Restriction," *Aging Cell*, June 11, 2012, https://www.ncbi.nlm.nih.gov/pubmed/22268691.

38 **In 2013, another scientific report in *Biochemical Journal*:** Jordan Gallinetti et al, "Amino Acid Sensing in Dietary-Restriction-Mediated Longevity: Roles of Signal-Transducing Kinases GCN2 and TOR," *Biochemical Journal*, January 2013, https://www.ncbi.nlm.nih.gov/pmc/articles/PMC3695616/.

38 **some research has shown that there is a connection between a diet that is low in leucine:** See above reference.

Xuemin Wang and Christopher G. Proud, "Nutrient Control of TORC1, a Cell-cycle Regulator," *Trends in Cell Biology*, June 2009, https://www.ncbi.nlm.nih.gov/pubmed/19419870.

39 **some research has indicated that consuming some tyrosine via diet:** Bryant J. Jongkees et al, "Effect of Tyrosine Supplementation on Clinical and Healthy Populations under Stress or Cognitive Demands—A Review," *Journal of Psychiatric Research,* November 2015, https://www.ncbi.nlm.nih.gov/pubmed/26424423.

Harris R. Lieberman, "Tyrosine and Stress: Human and Animal Studies," *Food Components to Enhance Performance: An Evaluation of Potential Performance-Enhancing Food Components for Operational Rations*, 1994, https://www.ncbi.nlm.nih.gov/books/NBK209061/.

40 **In an *On the Brain* article, published by Harvard Medical School:** Scott Edwards, "Sugar and the Brain," *On the Brain*, 2019, https://neuro.hms.harvard.edu/harvard-mahoney-neuroscience-institute/brain-newsletter/and-brain-series/sugar-and-brain.

41 **Research suggests that overconsumption of sugar:** Margaret L. Westwater et al, "Sugar Addiction: The State of the Science." *European Journal of Nutrition*, 2016, https://www.ncbi.nlm.nih.gov/pmc/articles/PMC5174153/.

Chapter 4: THE POWER OF MICRONUTRIENTS

52 **In 2010, the results of a game-changing, two-year-long study:** A. David Smith et al, "Homocysteine-Lowering by B Vitamins Slows the Rate of Accelerated Brain Atrophy in Mild Cognitive Impairment: A Randomized Controlled Trial," *PloS One*, September 8, 2010, https://www.ncbi.nlm.nih.gov/pmc/articles/PMC2935890/.

52 **in 2015, a second two-year-long study took place in Oxford:** David Smith et al, "Beneficial Interactions Between B Vitamins and Omega-3 Fatty Acids in the Prevention of Brain Atrophy and of Cognitive Decline in Early Stage Alzheimer's Disease," *The FASEB Journal*, April 1, 2016, https://www.fasebj.org/doi/abs/10.1096/fasebj.30.1 _supplement.407.6.

59 **In a 2013 study, researchers at UCLA Geffen School of Medicine:** Kirsten Tillisch et al, "Consumption of Fermented Milk Product with Probiotic Modulates Brain Activity," *Gastroenterology*, June 2013, https://www.ncbi.nlm.nih.gov /pubmed/23474283.

Case Adams, "Probiotics Change Brain Activity, Emotional Response," *Reset.Me*, April 1, 2016, http:// snip.ly/63wpf#http://reset.me/study/probiotics-change-brain-activity-emotional-response/.

61 **Researchers have focused on a few antioxidants that are known to be particularly effective:** Georgina E. Crichton et al, "Dietary Antioxidants, Cognitive Function and Dementia—A Systematic Review," *Plant Foods for Human Nutrition*, September 2013, https://www.ncbi.nlm.nih.gov/pubmed/23881465.

Chapter 5: STACKING YOUR DIET TO SHARPEN YOUR MIND

70 **a 2018 follow-up of a 23-year study:** Séverine Sabiares et al, "Alcohol Consumption and Risk of Dementia: 23 Year Follow-up of Whitehall II Cohort Study," *BMJ*, August 1, 2018, https://www.bmj.com/content/362/bmj.k2927.

73 **some research indicates that specific varieties of lectins may have a future:** Jhon Alberto Ochoa-Alvarez et al, "Plant Lectin Can Target Receptors Containing Sialic Acid, Exemplified by Podoplanin, to Inhibit Transformed Cell Growth and Migration," *PLoS One*, 2012, https://www.ncbi.nlm.nih.gov/pubmed/22844530.

Bo Liu et al, "Plant Lectins: Potential Antineoplastic Drugs from Bench to Clinic," *Cancer Letters,* January 1, 2010, https://www.ncbi.nlm.nih.gov/pubmed/19487073.

73 **one recent study found that eating certain types of pigmented potatoes:** Kerrie L. Kaspar et al, "Pigmented Potato Consumption Alters Oxidative Stress and Inflammatory Damage in Men," *The Journal of Nutrition*, January 2011, https://www.ncbi.nlm.nih.gov/pubmed/21106930.

73 **Most do not seem to pose significant danger to humans in clinical trials:** Jeremy M. Berg et al, ed., *Biochemistry*, 5th edition (New York: W H Freeman; 2002), Section 11.4, "Lectins Are Specific Carbohydrate-Binding Proteins," https://www.ncbi.nlm.nih.gov/books/NBK22545/.

David L. J. Freed, "Do Dietary Lectins Cause Disease? The Evidence Is Suggestive—and Raises Interesting Possibilities for Treatment," *BMJ*, April 17 1999, https://www.ncbi.nlm.nih.gov/pmc/articles/PMC1115436/.

Ramona L. Rea et al, "Lectins in Foods and their Relation to Starch Digestibility," *Nutrition Research*, 1985, https:// www.sciencedirect.com/science/article/pii/S0271531785801056.

Chapter 6: THE WORLD OF NOOTROPICS

81 **In a 2017 survey:** Arran Frood, "Use of 'smart drugs' on the rise," *Nature*, July 15, 2018, https://www.nature.com/articles /d41586-018-05599-8.

82 **the subjects of many short-term studies:** G. G. Neznamov and E. S. Teleshova, "Comparative Studies of Noopept and Piracetam in the Treatment of Patients with Mild Cognitive Disorders in Organic Brain Diseases of Vascular and Traumatic Origin," *Neuroscience and Behavioral Physiology*, March 2009, https://www.ncbi.nlm.nih.gov /pubmed/19234797.

89 **Studies have shown cacao's nutrients:** Lee Berk et al, "Dark chocolate (70% Cacao) Effects Human Gene Expression: Cacao Regulates Cellular Immune Response, Neural Signaling, and Sensory Perception," *The FASEB Journal*, April 20, 2018, https://www.fasebj.org/doi/10.1096/fasebj.2018.32.1_supplement.755.1.

Lee Berk et al, "Dark Chocolate (70% Organic Cacao) Increases Acute and Chronic EEG Power Spectral Density (μV2) Response of Gamma Frequency (25–40 Hz) for Brain Health: Enhancement of Neuroplasticity, Neural Synchrony, Cognitive Processing, Learning, Memory, Recall, and Mindfulness Meditation," *The FASEB Journal*, April 20, 2018, https://www.fasebj.org/doi/10.1096/fasebj.2018.32.1_supplement.878.10.

Astrid Nehlig, "The Neuroprotective Effects of Cocoa Flavanol and its Influence on Cognitive Performance," *British Journal of Clinical Pharmacology*, March 2013, https://www.ncbi.nlm.nih.gov/pmc/articles/PMC3575938/.

89 **One delicious-sounding study showed that simply eating chocolate:** Valentina Socci et al, "Enhancing Human Cognition with Cocoa Flavonoids," *Fronteirs in Nutrition*, May 16, 2017, https://www.frontiersin.org/articles/10.3389/fnut.2017.00019/full.

89 **it's been documented that countries with the highest chocolate consumption:** Franz H. Messerli, "Chocolate Consumption, Cognitive Function, and Nobel Laureates," *The New England Journal Of Medicine*, October 18, 2012, https://www.nejm.org/doi/full/10.1056/NEJMon1211064.

92 **Scientists have also found that theanine promotes alpha brain-wave patterns:** Kanari Kobayashi et al, "Effects of L-Theanine on the Release of Alpha-Brain Waves in Human Volunteers," *Journal of the Agricultural Chemical Society of Japan* 1998, https://www.researchgate.net/publication/273220751_Effects_of_L-Theanine_on_the_Release_of_ALPHA-Brain_Waves_in_Human_Volunteers.

92 **being the most studied for its relaxation benefits and compatibility with caffeine:** David J. White et al, "Anti-Stress, Behavioural and Magnetoencephalography Effects of an l-Theanine-Based Nutrient Drink: A Randomised, Double-Blind, Placebo-Controlled, Crossover Trial," *Nutrients*, January 19, 2016, https://www.ncbi.nlm.nih.gov/pmc/articles/PMC4728665/.

F. L. Dodd et al, "A Double-Blind, Placebo-Controlled Study Evaluating the Effects of Caffeine and L-Theanine Both Alone and in Combination on Cerebral Blood Flow, Cognition and Mood," *Psychopharmacology*, 2015, https://www.ncbi.nlm.nih.gov/pmc/articles/PMC4480845/.

93 **matcha (and regular green tea as well) has been linked:** Silvia A. Mandel et al, "Simultaneous Manipulation of Multiple Brain Targets by Green Tea Catechins: A Potential Neuroprotective Strategy for Alzheimer and Parkinson Diseases," *CNS Neuroscience and Therapeutics,* Winter 2008, https://www.ncbi.nlm.nih.gov/pubmed/19040558.

Juan C. Jurado-Coronel et al, "Implication of Green Tea as a Possible Therapeutic Approach for Parkinson Disease," *CNS & Neurological Disorders Drug Targets*, 2016, https://www.ncbi.nlm.nih.gov/pubmed/26831259.

96 **A 2010 Japanese study tested the effectiveness of lion's mane:** Mayumi Nagano et al, "Reduction of Depression and Anxiety by 4 Weeks *Hericium erinaceus* Intake," *Biomedical Research*, August 2010, https://www.ncbi.nlm.nih.gov/pubmed/20834180.

100 **participants in a study where goji berry juice was consumed for 14 days:** Harunobu Amagase and Dwight M. Nance, "A Randomized, Double-blind, Placebo-controlled, Clinical Study of the General Effects of a Standardized Lycium barbarum (Goji) Juice, GoChi," *Journal of Alternative and Complimentary Medicine*, May 2008, https://www.ncbi.nlm.nih.gov/pubmed/18447631.

100 **in preliminary animal studies:** Jiang Cheng et al, "An Evidence-Based Update on the Pharmacological Activities and Possible Molecular Targets of Lycium barbarum Polysaccharides," *Drug Design, Development and Therapy*, December 17, 2014, https://www.ncbi.nlm.nih.gov/pubmed/25552899.

102 **Scientists have found that once they are digested, anthocyanins:** The Peninsula College of Medicine and Dentistry, "Getting Forgetful? Then Blueberries May Hold The Key," *ScienceDaily*, April 12, 2008, www.sciencedaily.com/releases/2008/04/080410115405.htm.

103 **in one of Dr. Shukitt-Hale's studies:** Robert Krikorian et al, "Blueberry Supplementation Improves Memory in Older Adults," *Journal of Agricultural and Food Chemistry*, January 4, 2010, https://www.ncbi.nlm.nih.gov/pmc/articles /PMC2850944/.

103 **A study showed that children aged seven to ten:** Adrian R. Whyte et al, "Cognitive Effects Following Acute Wild Blueberry Supplementation in 7- to 10-Year-Old Children," *European Journal of Nutrition,* September 2016, https:// www.ncbi.nlm.nih.gov/pubmed/26437830.

107 **In preliminary studies, for example, ashwagandha has shown to be:** Dnyanraj Choudhary et al, "Body Weight Management in Adults Under Chronic Stress Through Treatment with Ashwagandha Root Extract: A Double-Blind, Randomized, Placebo-Controlled Trial," *Journal of Evidence-Based Complementary & Alternative Medicine*, April 6, 2016, https://www.ncbi.nlm.nih.gov/pmc/articles/PMC5871210/.

108 **Studies have shown that ashwagandha can dramatically improve:** Kartik Chandrasekhar et al, "A Prospective, Randomized Double-Blind, Placebo-Controlled Study of Safety and Efficacy of a High-Concentration Full-Spectrum Extract of Ashwagandha Root in Reducing Stress and Anxiety in Adults," *Indian Journal of Psychological Medicine*, July–September 2012, https://www.ncbi.nlm.nih.gov/pmc/articles/PMC3573577/.

108 **one study reported a 68.1 percent improvement in social interaction:** See above reference.

108 **Other studies have focused on ashwagandha's potential impact on Huntington's disease:** Puneet Kumar and Anil Kumar, "Possible Neuroprotective Effect of Withania somnifera Root Extract Against 3-Nitropropionic Acid-Induced Behavioral, Biochemical, and Mitochondrial Dysfunction in an Animal Model of Huntington's Disease," *Journal of Medicinal Food*, June 2009, https://www.ncbi.nlm.nih.gov/pubmed/19627208.

108 **preliminary animal-based tests indicate:** Dnyanraj Choudhary et al, "Efficacy and Safety of Ashwagandha (Withania somnifera (L.) Dunal) Root Extract in Improving Memory and Cognitive Functions," *Journal of Dietary Supplements*, November 2, 2017, https://www.ncbi.nlm.nih.gov/pubmed/28471731.

108 **some research has indicated that ashwagandha can affect neurogenesis:** Arpita Konar et al, "Protective Role of Ashwagandha Leaf Extract and Its Component Withanone on Scopolamine-Induced Changes in the Brain and Brain-Derived Cells," *PloS One*, November 2011, https://www.ncbi.nlm.nih.gov/pmc/articles/PMC3214041/.

Narendra Singh et al, "An Overview on Ashwagandha: A Rasayana (Rejuvenator) of Ayurveda," *African Journal of Traditional, Complementary, and Traditional Medicine*, July 3, 2011, https://www.ncbi.nlm.nih.gov/pmc/articles /PMC3252722/.

109 **Studies have also shown its potential benefits in the treatment of rheumatoid arthritis:** Gajendra Kumar et al, "Efficacy & Safety Evaluation of Ayurvedic Treatment (Ashwagandha Powder & Sidh Makardhwaj) in Rheumatoid Arthritis Patients: a Pilot Prospective Study," *The Indian Journal of Medicinal Research*, January 2015, https://www.ncbi .nlm.nih.gov/pubmed/25857501.

110 **evidenced by numerous studies and clinical trials that are currently underway:** Shrikant Mishra and Kalpana Palanivelu, "The Effect of Curcumin (Turmeric) on Alzheimer's Disease: An Overview," *Annals of Indian Academy of Neurology*, January–March 2008, https://www.ncbi.nlm.nih.gov/pmc/articles/PMC2781139/.

Dalia Al-Karawi et al, "The Role of Curcumin Administration in Patients with Major Depressive Disorder: Mini Meta-Analysis of Clinical Trials," *Phytotherapy Research*, February 2016, https://www.ncbi.nlm.nih.gov /pubmed/26610378.

Aiguo Wu et al, "Curcumin Boosts DHA in the Brain: Implications for the Prevention of Anxiety Disorders," *Biochimica et Biophysica Acta*, May 2015, https://www.ncbi.nlm.nih.gov/pubmed/25550171.

111 **In a 2018 study, consumption of high amounts of curcumin:** Gary W. Small et al, "Memory and Brain Amyloid and Tau Effects of a Bioavailable Form of Curcumin in Non-Demented Adults: A Double-Blind, Placebo-Controlled 18-Month Trial," *The American Journal of Geriatric Psychiatry*, March 2018, https://www.sciencedirect.com/science /article/pii/S1064748117305110?via%3Dihub.

111 **Researchers are now investigating whether this effect:** P. Hemachandra Reddy et al, "Protective Effects of Indian Spice Curcumin Against Amyloid Beta in Alzheimer's Disease," *Journal of Alzheimer's Disease*, Feb 2, 2018, https://www.ncbi.nlm.nih.gov/pmc/articles/PMC5796761/.

112 **In-vitro and animal studies suggest that turmeric:** Miguel López-Lázaro, "Anticancer and Carcinogenic Properties of Curcumin: Considerations for its Clinical Development as a Cancer Chemopreventive and Chemotherapeutic Agent," *Molecular Nutrition & Food Research*, June 2008, https://www.ncbi.nlm.nih.gov/pubmed/18496811.

113 **several animal studies showing that it helps reduce anxiety:** Fang Huang et al, "Sedative and Hypnotic Activities of the Ethanol Fraction from Fructus Schisandrae in Mice and Rats," *Journal of Ethnopharmacology*, April 4, 2007, https://www.ncbi.nlm.nih.gov/pubmed/17127021.

Wai-Wei Chen et al, "Pharmacological Studies on the Anxiolytic Effect of Standardized Schisandra lignans Extract on Restraint-Stressed Mice," *Phytomedicine*, October 15, 2011, https://www.ncbi.nlm.nih.gov/pubmed/21757327.

Alexander Panossian and Georg Wikman, "Pharmacology of Schisandra chinensis Bail: An Overview of Russian Research and Uses in Medicine," *Journal of Ethnopharmacology*, July 23, 2008, https://www.ncbi.nlm.nih.gov/pubmed/18515024.

113 **Animal studies have shown that the active component of schisandra berries:** Nobuaki Egashira et al, "Schizandrin Reverses Memory Impairment in Rats," *Phytotherapy Research*, January 2008, https://www.ncbi.nlm.nih.gov/pubmed/17705144.

Vijayasree V. Giridharan et al, "Prevention of Scopolamine-Induced Memory Deficits by Schisandrin B, an Antioxidant Lignan from Schisandra chinensis in Mice," *Free Radical Research*, August, 2011, https://www.ncbi.nlm.nih.gov/pubmed/21615274.

113 **A recent double blind, placebo-controlled, randomized (albeit small) human study:** Gayane Aslanyan et al, "Double-Blind, Placebo-Controlled, Randomised Study of Single Dose Effects of ADAPT-232 on Cognitive Functions," *Phytomedicine*, June 2010, https://www.ncbi.nlm.nih.gov/pubmed/20374974.

114 **According to a 2010 article in the medical journal *Phytomedicine*:** See above reference.

115 **research is underway to test the effectiveness:** Adriana Nowak et al, "Potential of *Schisandra chinensis* (Turcz.) Baill. in Human Health and Nutrition: A Review of Current Knowledge and Therapeutic Perspectives," *Nutrients*, February 4, 2019, https://www.mdpi.com/2072-6643/11/2/333/pdf.

Chapter 7: MIND-ENHANCING SUPPLEMENTS

119 **the tremendous number of papers published on bacopa:** Sebastian Aguiar and Thomas Borowski, "Neuropharmacological Review of the Nootropic Herb *Bacopa monnieri*," *Rejuvenation Research*, August 2013, https://www.ncbi.nlm.nih.gov/pmc/articles/PMC3746283/.

Carlo Calabrese et al, "Effects of a Standardized *Bacopa monnieri* Extract on Cognitive Performance, Anxiety, and Depression in the Elderly: A Randomized, Double-Blind, Placebo-Controlled Trial," *Journal of Alternative and Complementary Medicine*, July 2008, https://www.ncbi.nlm.nih.gov/pmc/articles/PMC3153866/.

BIBLIOGRAPHY

Chapter 1: SHIFT HAPPENS

Abate, Tom, and Amy Adams. "Stanford Scientists Create Circuit Board Modeled on the Human Brain." *Stanford Engineering.* April 24, 2014. https://engineering.stanford.edu/magazine/article/stanford-scientists-create-circuit-board-modeled -human-brain.

American Psychiatric Association. "What Is Depression?" Last modified January 2017. https://www.psychiatry.org/patients -families/depression/what-is-depression.

Arias-Carrión, Oscar, Maria Stamelou, Eric Murillo-Rodriguez, Manuel Menéndez-González, and Ernst Pöppel. "Dopaminergic Reward System: A Short Integrative Review." *International Archives of Medicine* 3, no. 24. October 6, 2010. https://www. ncbi.nlm.nih.gov/pmc/articles/PMC2958859/.

Boahen, Kwabena. "Making a Computer That Works Like the Brain." YouTube video, 17:48. Posted July 30, 2018. https:// www.youtube.com/watch?v=nyLYQYHGbvI.

Bordoni, Bruno, Shahin Purgol, Annalisa Bizzarri, Maddalena Modica, and Bruno Morabito. "The Influence of Breathing on the Central Nervous System." *Cureus Journal of Medical Science* 10, no. 6: e2724. June 10, 2018. https://www.ncbi.nlm. nih.gov/pmc/articles/PMC6070065/.

Brand, Evan, NTP, CPT. *The Everything Guide to Nootropics: Boost Your Brain Function with Smart Drugs and Memory Supplements.* Avon, Massachusetts: Adams Media, 2016.

Brown, Jessica. "Is Social Media Bad for You? The Evidence and the Unknowns." *BBC Future.* January 5, 2018. http://www.bbc .com/future/story/20180104-is-social-media-bad-for-you-the-evidence-and-the-unknowns.

Camilleri, Michael. "Serotonin in the Gastrointestinal Tract," *Current Opinion in Endocrinology, Diabetes, and Obesity.* February 1, 2010. https://www.ncbi.nlm.nih.gov/pmc/articles/PMC2694720/.

David, Lawrence A., Corinne F. Maurice, Rachel N. Carmody, David B. Gootenberg, Julie E. Button, Benjamin E. Wolfe, Alisha V. Ling, et al. "Diet Rapidly and Reproducibly Alters the Human Gut Microbiome." *Nature International Journal of Science* 505 (January 23–24): 559–563. https://www.ncbi.nlm.nih.gov/pmc/articles/PMC3957428/.

Godman, Heidi. "Regular Exercise Changes the Brain to Improve Memory, Thinking Skills." *Harvard Health Blog.* April 9, 2014. https://www.health.harvard.edu/blog/regular-exercise-changes-brain-improve-memory-thinking -skills-201404097110.

Harris, Raymond C., and Ming-Zhi Zhang. "Dopamine, the Kidney, and Hypertension." *Curr Hypertense Reports* 14, no. 2 (April 2012): 138–143. https://www.ncbi.nlm.nih.gov/pmc/articles/PMC3742329/.

Lee, James. *Better Living through Neurochemistry.* CreateSpace Independent Publishing Platform, 2014.

Levine, Hallie. "The Link between Your Gut Health and Autoimmune Diseases." *Yahoo Lifestyle.* March 21, 2018. https:// www.yahoo.com/lifestyle/link-gut-health-autoimmune-disorders-120024072.html.

Medrano, Kastalia. "Where Do You Go When You Die? The Increasing Signs That Human Consciousness Remains after Death." *Newsweek.* February 10, 2018. https://www.newsweek.com/where-do-you-go-when-you-die-increasing-signs -human-consciousness-after-death-800443.

Naegele, Janice R. "Controversial Brain Study Has Scientists Rethinking Neuron Research." *The Conversation*. March 14, 2018. http://theconversation.com/controversial-brain-study-has-scientists-rethinking-neuron-research-93183.

Pozhitkov, Alex E., Rafik Neme, Tomislav Domazet-Loso, Brian G. Leroux, Shivani Soni, Diethard Tautz, and Peter A. Noble. "Tracing the Dynamics of Gene Transcripts of Organismal Death." *Open Biology* 7, no. 1 (January 2017). https://doi.org/10.1098/rsob.160267.

Swaminathan, Nikhil. "Why Does the Brain Need So Much Power?" *Scientific American*. April 29, 2008. https://www.scientificamerican.com/article/why-does-the-brain-need-s/.

Zaccaro, Andrea, Andrea Piarulli, Marco Laurino, Erika Garbella, Danilo Menicucci, Bruno Neri, and Angelo Gemignani. "How Breath-Control Can Change Your Life: A Systematic Review on Psycho-Physiological Correlates of Slow Breathing." *Frontiers in Human Neuroscience,* 12 (September 7, 2018): 353. https://www.ncbi.nlm.nih.gov/pmc/articles/PMC6137615/.

Chapter 2: WHY PLANTS?

Bergland, Christopher. "How Do Neuroplasticity and Neurogenesis Rewire Your Brain?" *Psychology Today*. February 6, 2017. https://www.psychologytoday.com/us/blog/the-athletes-way/201702/how-do-neuroplasticity-and-neurogenesis-rewire-your-brain.

Boldrini, Mura, Camille A. Fulmore, Alexandria N. Tartt, Laika R. Simeon, Ina Pavlova, Verica Poposka, Gorazd B. Rosoklija, et al. "Human Hippocampal Neurogenesis Persists throughout Aging." *Cell Stem Cell* 22, no. 4 (April 5, 2018). https://www.cell.com/cell-stem-cell/fulltext/S1934-5909(18)30121-8.

Buchanan, Leigh. "The 4 Brain Superpowers You Need to Be a Successful Leader, According to Neuroscience." *Inc.* February 21, 2018. https://www.inc.com/leigh-buchanan/4-brain-superpowers-you-need-to-be-a-successful-leader.html?cid=mustread1.

Draganski, Bogdan, Christian Gaser, Gerd Kempermann, H. Georg Kuhn, Jürgen Winkler, Christian Büchel, and Arne May. "Temporal and Spatial Dynamics of Brain Structure Changes during Extensive Learning." *Journal of Neuroscience* 26, no. 23, (June 7, 2006): 6314–6317. http://www.jneurosci.org/content/26/23/6314.

Fangyi, Gu, Jiali Han, Francine Laden, An Pan, Neil E. Caporaso, Meir J. Stampfer, Ichiro Kawachi, et al. "Rotating Night Shift Work Can Be Hazardous to Your Health." *Science Daily*. January 5, 2015. https://www.sciencedaily.com/releases/2015/01/150105081757.htm.

Harvard Medical School. "Can You Grow New Brain Cells?" *Harvard Health Publishing*. September 2016. https://www.health.harvard.edu/mind-and-mood/can-you-grow-new-brain-cells.

Joy, Scott. "Neuroplasticity Overview." *Neuroscience*. July 9, 2017. http://neuroscience.onair.cc/category/special-topics/neuroplasticity/.

Matthews, Melissa. "Do You Lose Brain Cells When You Age? Adults Make Neurons into Their 70s." *Newsweek*. April 5, 2018. https://www.newsweek.com/adults-can-make-new-brain-cells-even-their-70s-study-says-870649.

Ming, Guo-li, and Hongjun Song. "Adult Neurogenesis in the Mammalian Brain: Significant Answers and Significant Questions." *Neuron* 70, no. 4 (May 26, 2011): 687–702. https://www.ncbi.nlm.nih.gov/pmc/articles/PMC3106107/.

Song, Juan, Reid H. J. Olsen, Jiaqi Sun, Guo-li Ming, and Hongjun Song. "Neuronal Circuitry Mechanisms Regulating Adult Mammalian Neurogenesis." *Cold Spring Harbor Perspectives in Biology* 8, no. 8 (2016): a018937. https://www.ncbi.nlm.nih.gov/pmc/articles/PMC4968157/.

Williamson, A. M., and Anne-Marie Feyer. "Moderate Sleep Deprivation Produces Impairment in Cognitive and Motor Performance Equivalent to Legally Prescribed Levels of Alcohol Intoxication." *Occupational and Environmental Medicine* 57 (2000): 649–655. https://www.ncbi.nlm.nih.gov/pmc/articles/PMC1739867/pdf/v057p00649.pdf.

Chapter 3: FUELING YOUR BRAIN

Arterburn L. M., H. A. Oken, Hall E. Bailey, J. Hamersley, C. N. Kuratko, and J. P. Hoffman. "Algal-Oil Capsules and Cooked Salmon: Nutritionally Equivalent Sources of Docosahexaenoic Acid." *Journal of the American Dietetic Association* 108, no. 7 (July 2008): 1204–1209. https://www.ncbi.nlm.nih.gov/pubmed/18589030.

Brasky, T. M., A. K. Darke, X. Song, C. M. Tangen, P. J. Goodman, I. M. Thompson, F. L. Meyskens Jr., et al. "Plasma Phospholipid Fatty Acids and Prostate Cancer Risk in the SELECT Trial." *Journal of the National Cancer Institute* 105, no. 15 (August 7, 2013): 1132–1141. https://www.ncbi.nlm.nih.gov/pubmed/23843441.

Courchesne-Loyer, Alexandre, Mélanie Fortier, Jennifer Tremblay-Mercier, Raphaël Chouinard-Watkins, Maggie Roy, Scott Nugent, Christian-Alexandre Castellano, and Stephen C. Cunnane. "Stimulation of Mild, Sustained Ketonemia by Medium-Chain Triacylglycerols in Healthy Humans: Estimated Potential Contribution to Brain Energy Metabolism." *Nutrition* 29, no. 4 (April 2013): 635–340. https://www.sciencedirect.com/science/article/pii/S0899900712003656.

Croteau, Etienne, Christian-Alexandre Castellano, Marie Anne Richard, Mélanie Fortier, Scott Nugent, Martin Lepage, Simon Duchesne, et al. "Ketogenic Medium Chain Triglycerides Increase Brain Energy Metabolism in Alzheimer's Disease." *Journal of Alzheimer's Disease* 64, no. 2 (2018): 551–561. https://www.ncbi.nlm.nih.gov/pubmed/29914035.

DHA/EPA Omega-3 Institute. "Differentiation of ALA (Plant Sources) from DHA + EPA (Marine Sources) as Dietary Omega-3 Fatty Acids for Human Health." Accessed January 17, 2019. http://www.dhaomega3.org/Overview/Differentiation-of-ALA-plant-sources-from-DHA-+-EPA-marine-sources-as-Dietary-Omega-3-Fatty-Acids-for-Human-Health.

Ede, Georgia, MD. "Your Brain on Plants: Micronutrients and Mental Health." *Diagnosis: Diet*. http://www.diagnosisdiet.com/micronutrients-mental-health/.

Edwards, Scott. "Sugar and the Brain." *On the Brain: The Harvard Mahoney Neuroscience Institute Letter*. http://neuro.hms.harvard.edu/harvard-mahoney-neuroscience-institute/brain-newsletter/and-brain-series/sugar-and-brain.

Fuhrman, Joel. "DHA+EPA Purity." *Dr. Fuhrman*. Accessed January 17, 2019. https://www.drfuhrman.com/shop/products/52/dhaepa-purity.

Gallinetti Jordan, Eylul Harputlugil, and James R. Mitchell. "Amino Acid Sensing in Dietary-Restriction-Mediated Longevity: Roles of Signal-Transducing Kinases GCN2 and TOR." *Biochemical Journal* 449, no. 1 (January 2013): 1–10. https://www.ncbi.nlm.nih.gov/pmc/articles/PMC3695616/.

Gerster, Holger. "Can Adults Adequately Convert Alpha-Linolenic Acid (18:3n-3) to Eicosapentaenoic Acid (20:5n-3) and Docosahexaenoic Acid (22:6n-3)?" *International Journal for Vitamins and Nutrition Research* 68, no. 3 (1998): 159–73. https://www.ncbi.nlm.nih.gov/pubmed/9637947.

Greger, Michael, MD, FACLM. "Are Sugary Foods Addictive?" *Nutrition Facts*. November 18, 2013. https://nutritionfacts.org/video/are-sugary-foods-addictive/.

———. "How Much Added Sugar Is Too Much?" *Nutrition Facts*. July 19, 2016. https://nutritionfacts.org/2016/07/19/much-added-sugar-much/.

———. "What about Coconuts, Coconut Milk, & Coconut Oil MCTs?" *Nutrition Facts*. August 21, 2017. https://nutritionfacts.org/video/what-about-coconuts-coconut-milk-and-coconut-oil-mcts/.

Harvard Medical School. "Protect Your Brain with 'Good' Fat." *Harvard Health Publishing*. September 2012. https://www.health.harvard.edu/mind-and-mood/protect-your-brain-with-good-fat.

Heal with Food. "10 of the Best Sources of Alpha-Linolenic Acid (ALA)." Accessed January 17, 2019. https://www.healwithfood.org/foods-that-contain/alpha-linolenic-acid-best-sources.php.

Jardine, Meghan. "Seven Reasons to Keep Saturated Fat Off Your Plate." *Physicians Committee for Responsible Medicine*. November 5, 2018. https://www.pcrm.org/news/blog/seven-reasons-keep-saturated-fat-your-plate.

Johnston, Ian. "Plastic Microparticles Found in Flesh of Fish Eaten by Humans." *Independent*. July 26, 2017. https://www.independent.co.uk/environment/plastic-microparticles-fish-flesh-eaten-humans-food-chain-mackerel-anchovy-mullet-a7860726.html.

Jongkees, Bryant J., Bernhard Hommel, Simone Kühn, and Lorenza S. Colzato. "Effect of Tyrosine Supplementation on Clinical and Healthy Populations under Stress or Cognitive Demands—A Review." *Journal of Psychiatric Research* 70 (November 2015): 50–57. https://www.ncbi.nlm.nih.gov/pubmed/26424423.

Karami, Ali, Abolfazl Golieskardi, Yu Bin Ho, Vincent Larat, and Babak Salamatinia. "Microplastics in Eviscerated Flesh and Excised Organs of Dried Fish." *Scientific Reports* 7, no. 5473 (July 14, 2017). https://www.nature.com/articles/s41598-017-05828-6.

Kresser, Chris. "Why Vegetarians and Vegans Should Supplement with DHA." *Chris Kresser: Let's Take Back Your Health.* September 13, 2016. https://chriskresser.com/why-vegetarians-and-vegans-should-supplement-with-dha/.

Lieberman, Harris R. "Tyrosine and Stress: Human and Animal Studies." *Food Components to Enhance Performance: An Evaluation of Potential Performance-Enhancing Food Components for Operational Rations.* Washington (DC): National Academies Press, 1994. https://www.ncbi.nlm.nih.gov/books/NBK209061/.

Linus Pauling Institute, Oregon State University. "Micronutrients for Health." Accessed November 20, 2018. https://lpi.oregonstate.edu/publications/micronutrients-health.

Manzanero, Silvia, Joanna R. Erion, Tomislav Santro, Frederik J. Steyn, Chen Chen, Thiruma V. Arumugam, and Alexis M. Stranahan. "Intermittent Fasting Attenuates Increases in Neurogenesis after Ischemia and Reperfusion and Improves Recovery." *Journal of Cerebral Blood Flow & Metabolism* 34, no. 5 (May 2014): 897–905. https://www.ncbi.nlm.nih.gov/pmc/articles/PMC4013772/.

Mattson, M. P., W. Duan, and Z. Guo. "Meal Size and Frequency Affect Neuronal Plasticity and Vulnerability to Disease: Cellular and Molecular Mechanisms." *Journal of Neurochemistry* 84, no. 3 (February 2003): 417–431. https://www.ncbi.nlm.nih.gov/pubmed/12558961.

Mirzaei, Hamed, Rachel Raynes, and Valter D. Longo. "The Conserved Role for Protein Restriction During Aging and Disease." *Current Opinion in Clinical Nutrition & Metabolic Care* 19, no. 1 (2016): 74–79. https://www.ncbi.nlm.nih.gov/pmc/articles/PMC4807119/.

Moon, Maggie, MS, RD. *The MIND Diet: A Scientific Approach to Enhancing Brain Function and Helping Prevent Alzheimer's and Dementia.* Berkeley, California: Ulysses Press, 2016.

Morris, Martha. "The MIND Diet with Dr. Martha Morris." Interview by Jesse Lawler. *Smart Drug Smarts.* September 22, 2017. https://smartdrugsmarts.com/episodes/199-mind-diet/.

Nakagawa, Shinichi, Malgorzata Lagisz, Katie L. Hector, and Hamish G. Spencer. "Comparative and Meta-analytic Insights into Life Extension Via Dietary Restriction," *Aging Cell* 11, no. 3 (June 11, 2012): 401–409. https://www.ncbi.nlm.nih.gov/pubmed/22268691.

National Institutes of Health. "Omega-3 Fatty Acids: Fact Sheet for Health Professionals." Last modified November 21, 2018. https://ods.od.nih.gov/factsheets/Omega3FattyAcids-HealthProfessional/.

New Health Guide. "Convert Grams of Sugars into Teaspoons." Accessed January 16, 2019. https://www.newhealthguide.org/How-Many-Grams-Of-Sugar-In-A-Teaspoon.html.

Pedersen, Stephanie. *Coconut: The Complete Guide to the World's Most Versatile Superfood.* New York: Sterling, 2015.

Stoler, Diane Roberts, EdD. "Trans Fats: Bad for Your Brain." *Psychology Today.* June 25, 2015. https://www.psychologytoday.com/us/blog/the-resilient-brain/201506/trans-fats-bad-your-brain.

Tremblay, Sylvie, MSc. "Chia Seeds vs Flaxseeds." *SF Gate.* November 27, 2018. https://healthyeating.sfgate.com/chia-seeds-vs-flaxseeds-2070.html.

Wang, Xuemin, and Christopher G. Proud. "Nutrient Control of TORC1, a Cell-cycle Regulator." *Trends in Cell Biology* 19, no. 6 (June 2009): 260–267. https://www.ncbi.nlm.nih.gov/pubmed/19419870.

Westwater, Margaret L., Paul C. Fletcher, and Hisham Ziauddeen. "Sugar Addiction: The State of the Science." *European Journal of Nutrition* 55, suppl. 2 (2016): 55–69. https://www.ncbi.nlm.nih.gov/pmc/articles/PMC5174153/.

Wilson, Debra Rose, PhD, MSN, RN, IBCLC, AHN-BC, CHT. "What Are the Possible Benefits of MCT Oil?" *Medical News Today.* December 6, 2017. https://www.medicalnewstoday.com/articles/320251.php?sr.

Zerbe, Leah, MS, NASM-CPT, NASM-CES. "Is Coconut Oil Healthy? (The American Heart Association Doesn't Think So)." *Dr. Axe.* June 20, 2017. https://draxe.com/coconut-oil-healthy/.

Chapter 4: THE POWER OF MICRONUTRIENTS

Adams, Case. "Probiotics Change Brain Activity, Emotional Response." *Reset.Me*. April 1, 2016. http://snip.ly/63wpf.

Crichton, Georgina E., Janet Bryan, and Karen J. Murphy. "Dietary Antioxidants, Cognitive Function and Dementia—A Systematic Review." *Plant Foods for Human Nutrition* 68, no. 3 (September 2013): 279–292. https://www.ncbi.nlm.nih.gov/pubmed/23881465.

Davis, Brenda, RD. "Vegetarian's Challenge—Optimizing Essential Fatty Acid Status." *Today's Dietitian*. February 2010. https://www.todaysdietitian.com/newarchives/020810p22.shtml.

Hammond Jr., Billy R., L. Stephen Miller, Medina O. Bello, Cutter A. Lindbergh, Catherine Mewborn, and Lisa M. Reszni-Hammond. "Effects of Lutein/Zeaxanthin Supplementation on the Cognitive Function of Community Dwelling Older Adults: A Randomized, Double-Masked, Placebo-Controlled Trial." *Front Aging Neuroscience* 9, no. 254 (August 3, 2017). https://www.ncbi.nlm.nih.gov/pubmed/28824416.

Jäpelt, Rie B., and Jette Jakobsen. "Vitamin D in Plants: A Review of Occurrence, Analysis, and Biosynthesis." *Frontiers in Plant Science* 4, no. 136 (May 13, 2013). https://www.ncbi.nlm.nih.gov/pmc/articles/PMC3651966/.

Johnston, Lucy. "Supplements Can Halt Alzheimer's in Groundbreaking Dementia Prevention Treatment." *Express*. April 19, 2015. https://www.express.co.uk/life-style/health/385884/Supplements-halt-Alzheimer-s-groundbreaking-dementia-prevention-treatment.

Keegan, Raphael-John H., Lu Zhiren, Jaimee M. Bogusz, Jennifer E. Williams, and Michael F. Holick. "Photobiology of Vitamin D in Mushrooms and Its Bioavailability in Humans." *Dermato Endocrinology* 5, no. 1 (January 2013): 165–176. https://www.ncbi.nlm.nih.gov/pmc/articles/PMC3897585/.

Lieberman, Harris R. "Amino Acid and Protein Requirements: Cognitive Performance, Stress, and Brain Function." *The Role of Protein and Amino Acids in Sustaining and Enhancing Performance,* edited by Institute of Medicine (US) Committee on Military Nutrition Research, Chapter 14. Washington, DC: National Academies Press, 1999. https://www.ncbi.nlm.nih.gov/books/NBK224629/.

Mayo Clinic. "Thiamin." Last modified October 25, 2017. https://www.mayoclinic.org/drugs-supplements-thiamin/art-20366430.

Mead, M. Nathaniel. "Benefits of Sunlight: A Bright Spot for Human Health." *Environmental Health Perspectives* 116, no. 4 (April 2008): A160–A167. https://www.ncbi.nlm.nih.gov/pmc/articles/PMC2290997/.

Methodist Hospital, Houston. "B-Complex Vitamins May Help Slow Progression of Dementia." *Science Daily*. October 28, 2010. https://www.sciencedaily.com/releases/2010/10/101027155126.htm.

National Institutes of Health. "Riboflavin: Fact Sheet for Health Professionals." Last modified August 20, 2018. https://ods.od.nih.gov/factsheets/Riboflavin-HealthProfessional/.

———. "Biotin: Fact Sheet for Health Professionals." Last modified September 17, 2018. https://ods.od.nih.gov/factsheets/Biotin-HealthProfessional/.

———. "Pantothenic Acid: Fact Sheet for Health Professionals." Last modified September 17, 2018. https://ods.od.nih.gov/factsheets/PantothenicAcid-HealthProfessional/.

———. "Vitamin B6: Fact Sheet for Health Professionals." Last modified September 17, 2018. https://ods.od.nih.gov/factsheets/VitaminB6-HealthProfessional/.

Poly, C., J. M. Massaro, S. Seshadri, P. A. Wolf, E. Cho, E. Krall, P. F. Jacques, and R. Au. "The Relation of Dietary Choline to Cognitive Performance and White-Matter Hyperintensity in the Framingham Offspring Cohort." *American Journal of Clinical Nutrition* 94, no. 6 (December 2011): 1584–1591. https://www.ncbi.nlm.nih.gov/pubmed/22071706.

Smith, David, Helga Refsum, Abderrahim Oulhaj, Celeste A. de Jager, and Fredrik Jerneren. "Beneficial Interactions Between B Vitamins and Omega-3 Fatty Acids in the Prevention of Brain Atrophy and of Cognitive Decline in Early Stage Alzheimer's Disease." *The FASEB Journal* 30, suppl. 1 (April 1, 2016). https://www.fasebj.org/doi/abs/10.1096/fasebj.30.1_supplement.407.6.

Smith, A. David, Stephen M. Smith, Celeste A. de Jager, Philippa Whitbread, Carole Johnston, Grzegorz Agacinski, Abderrahim Oulhaj, Kevin M. Bradley, Robin Jacoby, and Helga Refsum. "Homocysteine-Lowering by B Vitamins Slows the Rate of Accelerated Brain Atrophy in Mild Cognitive Impairment: A Randomized Controlled Trial." *PloS One* 5, no. 9 (September 8, 2010): e12244. https://www.ncbi.nlm.nih.gov/pmc/articles/PMC2935890/.

Tillisch, Kirsten, Jennifer Labus, Lisa Kilpatrick, Zhiguo Jiang, Jean Stains, Bahar Ebrat, Denis Guyonnet, et al. "Consumption of Fermented Milk Product with Probiotic Modulates Brain Activity." *Gastroenterology* 144, no. 7 (June 2013): 1394–1401. https://www.ncbi.nlm.nih.gov/pubmed/23474283.

Walsh, William J. *Nutrient Power: Heal Your Biochemistry and Heal Your Brain.* New York: Skyhorse Publishing, 2014.

Chapter 5: SHAPING YOUR DIET TO SHARPEN YOUR MIND

Berg, J. M., J. L. Tymoczko, and L. Stryer. "Lectins Are Specific Carbohydrate-Binding Proteins." *Biochemistry*, 5th ed., Section 11.4. New York: W. H. Freeman, 2002.

Butler, Natalie, RD, LD. "7 Foods That Could Boost Your Serotonin: The Serotonin Diet." *Healthline*. August 29, 2018. https://www.healthline.com/health/healthy-sleep/foods-that-could-boost-your-serotonin.

Cleveland Clinic. "Why Beans, Packed with Vitamin B, Can Boost Your Brain Power." Last modified September 28, 2016. https://health.clevelandclinic.org/boost-your-brain-with-b-vitamins-and-beans/.

Crews, Fulton T. "Alcohol and Neurodegeneration." *CNS Drug Reviews* 5, no. 4 (1999): 379–394. https://onlinelibrary.wiley.com/doi/pdf/10.1111/j.1527-3458.1999.tb00112.x.

Freed, David L. J. "Do Dietary Lectins Cause Disease?" *BMJ* 318, no. 7190 (April 17, 1999): 1023–1024. https://www.ncbi.nlm.nih.gov/pmc/articles/PMC1115436/.

Grant, George, Linda J. More, Norma H. McKenzie, and Arpad Pusztai. "The Effect of Heating on the Haemagglutinating Activity and Nutritional Properties of Bean (Phaseolus Vulgaris) Seeds." *Journal of the Science of Food and Agriculture* 33, no. 12 (December 1982). https://onlinelibrary.wiley.com/doi/abs/10.1002/jsfa.2740331220.

Greger, Michael. "Nutrient-Blocking Effects of Dairy." *Nutrient Facts*. January 7, 2010. https://nutritionfacts.org/video/nutrient-blocking-effects-of-dairy/.

Harvard Medical School. "Boost Your Memory by Eating Right." *Harvard Health Publishing*. August 2012. https://www.health.harvard.edu/mind-and-mood/boost-your-memory-by-eating-right.

Healy, Melissa. "Kale and Other Leafy Vegetables May Make Your Brain Seem 11 Years Younger." *Los Angeles Times*. December 20, 2017. https://www.latimes.com/science/sciencenow/la-sci-sn-leafy-vegetables-brain-20171220-story.html?utm_medium=post&utm_campaign=outside-news&utm_source=facebook.

Jennings, Kerri-Ann, MS, RD. "11 Best Foods to Boost Your Brain and Memory." *Healthline*. May 9, 2017. https://www.healthline.com/nutrition/11-brain-foods#section2.

Kaspar, Kerrie L., Jean Soon Park, Charles R. Brown, Bridget D. Mathison, Duroy A. Navarre, and Boon P. Chew. "Pigmented Potato Consumption Alters Oxidative Stress and Inflammatory Damage in Men." *Journal of Nutrition* 141, no. 1 (January 1, 2011): 108–111. https://academic.oup.com/jn/article/141/1/108/4630555.

Lajolo, F., and M. Genovese. "Nutritional Significance of Lectins and Enzyme Inhibitors from Legumes." *Journal of Agricultural and Food Chemistry* 50, no. 22 (October 23, 2002): 6592–6598. https://www.ncbi.nlm.nih.gov/pubmed/12381157.

Levy, Jillian, CHHC. "Buckwheat Nutrition: Is This Gluten-Free 'Grain' Good for You?" *Dr. Axe*. January 8, 2019. https://draxe.com/buckwheat-nutrition/.

Liu, B., H. J. Bian, J. K. Bao. "Plant lectins: potential antineoplastic drugs from bench to clinic." *Cancer Letters* 287 (2010): 1–12. https://www.ncbi.nlm.nih.gov/pubmed/19487073.

Mandl, Elise, BSc, APD. "The 7 Worst Foods for Your Brain." *Healthline*. January 28, 2018. https://www.healthline.com/nutrition/worst-foods-for-your-brain.

Mercola, Joseph. "3 Ounces of This a Day May Be Harming Your Brain." *Dr. Dekel: Precision in Prevention.* July 4, 2011. http://www.drdekel.com/content/3-ounces-day-may-be-harming-your-brain.

Ochoa-Alvarez, J. A., H. Krishnan, Y. Shen, N. K. Acharya, M. Han, D. E. McNulty, H. Hasegawa, et al. "Plant lectin can target receptors containing sialic acid, exemplified by podoplanin, to inhibit transformed cell growth and migration." *PLoS One* 7 (2012): e41845. https://www.ncbi.nlm.nih.gov/pubmed/22844530.

Physicians Committee for Responsible Medicine. "Health Concerns about Dairy: Avoid the Dangers of Dairy with a Plant-Based Diet." Accessed January 18, 2019. https://www.pcrm.org/good-nutrition/nutrition-information/health-concerns-about-dairy.

Rea, Ramona L., Lilian U. Thompson, and David J. A. Jenkins. "Lectins in Foods and their Relation to Starch Digestibility." *Nutrition Research* 5, no. 9 (September 1985): 919–929. https://www.sciencedirect.com/science/article/pii/S0271531785801056.

Reddivari, Lavanya, Anna L. Hale, and J. Creighton Miller. "Determination of Phenolic Content, Composition and Their Contribution to Antioxidant Activity in Specialty Potato Selections." *American Journal of Potato Research* 84, no. 275 (August 2007). https://link.springer.com/article/10.1007%2FBF02986239.

Reynolds, E. H. "Folic Acid, Ageing, Depression, and Dementia." *BMJ* 324, no. 7352 (June 22, 2002): 1512–1515. https://www.ncbi.nlm.nih.gov/pmc/articles/PMC1123448/.

Sabia, Séverine, Aurore Fayosse, Julien Dumurgier, Aline Dugravot, Tasnime Akbaraly, Annie Britton, Mika Kivimäki, and Archana Singh-Manoux. "Alcohol Consumption and Risk of Dementia: 23 Year Follow-Up of Whitehall II Cohort Study." *BMJ* 362 (August 1, 2018): k2927. https://www.bmj.com/content/362/bmj.k2927.

Takeda, A. "Manganese Action in Brain Function." *Brain Research Brain Research Reviews* 41, no. 1 (January 2003): 79–87. https://www.ncbi.nlm.nih.gov/pubmed/12505649.

Tremblay, Sylvie. "Peas & Brain Chemicals." *SF Gate.* Accessed January 18, 2019. https://healthyeating.sfgate.com/peas-brain-chemicals-10549.html.

Ware, Megan, RDN, LD. "Everything You Need to Know about the Lectin-Free Diet." *Medical News Today.* October 3, 2017. https://www.medicalnewstoday.com/articles/319593.php.

Wu, Albert M., Yia-jen Jianga, P. Y. Hwang, and F-shiun Shen. "Characterization of the Okra Mucilage by Interaction with Gal, Ga1NAc and GlcNAc Specific Lectins." *Biochimica et Biophysica Acta (BBA)—General Subjects* 1243, no. 2 (February 23, 1995): 157–160. https://www.sciencedirect.com/science/article/pii/030441659400130P.

Yau, T. X. Dan, C. C. Ng, and T. B. Ng. "Lectins with Potential for Anti-Cancer Therapy." *Molecules* 20, no. 3 (February 26, 2015): 3791–3810. https://www.ncbi.nlm.nih.gov/pubmed/25730388.

Chapter 6: THE WORLD OF NOOTROPICS

Wu, Aiguo, Emily E. Noble, Ethika Tyagi, Zhe Ying, Yumei Zhuang, and Fernando Gomez-Pinilla. "Curcumin Boosts DHA in the Brain: Implications for the Prevention of Anxiety Disorders." *Biochimica et Biophysica Acta* 1852, no. 5 (May 2015): 951–691. https://www.ncbi.nlm.nih.gov/pubmed/25550171.

Al-Karawi, D., D. A. Al Mamoori, and Y. Tayyar. "The Role of Curcumin Administration in Patients with Major Depressive Disorder: Mini Meta-Analysis of Clinical Trials." *Phytotherapy Research* 30, no. 2 (February 2016): 175–183. https://www.ncbi.nlm.nih.gov/pubmed/26610378.

Amagase, Harunobu, and Dwight M. Nance. "A Randomized, Double-Blind, Placebo-Controlled, Clinical Study of the General Effects of a Standardized Lycium Barbarum (Goji) Juice, GoChi." *Journal of Alternative Complementary Medicine* 14, no. 4 (May 2008): 403–412. https://www.ncbi.nlm.nih.gov/pubmed/18447631.

Aslanyan, G., E. Amroyan, E. Gabrielyan, M. Nylander, G. Wikman, and A. Panossian. "Double-Blind, Placebo-Controlled, Randomised Study of Single Dose Effects of ADAPT-232 on Cognitive Functions." *Phytomedicine* 17, no. 7 (June 2010): 494–499. https://www.ncbi.nlm.nih.gov/pubmed/20374974.

Azam, Faizul, Abdualrahman M. Amer, Abdullah R. Abulifa, and Mustafa M. Elzwawi. "Ginger Cmponents as New Leads for the Design and Development of Novel Multi-Targeted Anti-Alzheimer's Drugs: A Computational Investigation." *Drug Design, Development and Therapy* 8 (2014): 2045–2059. https://www.ncbi.nlm.nih.gov/pmc/articles/PMC4211852/.

Becker, Anne. "Green Tea on the Brain." *Psychology Today*. June 10, 2003. https://www.psychologytoday.com/us/articles/200306/green-tea-the-brain.

Berk, Lee, Kristin Bruhjell, Warren Peters, Peter Bastian, Evertt Lohman, Gurinder Bains, Jesusa Arevalo, and Steve Cole. "Dark chocolate (70% Cacao) Effects Human Gene Expression: Cacao Regulates Cellular Immune Response, Neural Signaling, and Sensory Perception." *The FASEB Journal* 32, suppl. 1(April 20, 2018). https://www.fasebj.org/doi/10.1096/fasebj.2018.32.1_supplement.755.1.

Berk, Lee, Josh Miller, Kristin Bruhjell, Sayali Dhuri, Krisha Patel, Everett Lohman, Gurinder Bains, and Ryan Berk. "Dark Chocolate (70% Organic Cacao) Increases Acute and Chronic EEG Power Spectral Density (μV2) Response of Gamma Frequency (25–40 Hz) for Brain Health: Enhancement of Neuroplasticity, Neural Synchrony, Cognitive Processing, Learning, Memory, Recall, and Mindfulness Meditation." *The FASEB Journal* 32, suppl. 1 (April 20, 2018). https://www.fasebj.org/doi/10.1096/fasebj.2018.32.1_supplement.878.10.

Bode, Ann M., and Zigang Dong. "The Amazing and Mighty Ginger." In I. F. F. Benzie and S. Galor, eds., *Herbal Medicine: Biomolecular and Clinical Aspects*, 2nd ed., Chapter 7. Boca Raton, Florida: CRC Press/Taylor & Francis, 2011. https://www.ncbi.nlm.nih.gov/books/NBK92775/.

Bush, Bradley, ND, and Tori Hudson, ND. "The Role of Cortisol in Sleep." *Natural Medicine Journal* 2, no. 6 (June 2010). https://www.naturalmedicinejournal.com/journal/2010-06/role-cortisol-sleep.

Butt, M. S., I. Pasha, M. T. Sultan, M. A. Randhawa, F. Saeed, and W. Ahmed. "Black Pepper and Health Claims: A Comprehensive Treatise." *Critical Reviews in Food Science and Nutrition* 53, no. 9 (2013): 875–886. https://www.ncbi.nlm.nih.gov/pubmed/23768180.

Devore, Elizabeth E., ScD; Jae Hee Kang, ScD; Monique M. B. Breteler, MD, PhD; and Francine Grodstein, ScD. "Dietary Intake of Berries and Flavonoids in Relation to Cognitive Decline." *Annals of Neurology* 72, no. 1 (2012): 135–143. https://www.ncbi.nlm.nih.gov/pmc/articles/PMC3582325/.

Frood, Arran. "Use of 'Smart Drugs' on the Rise." *Scientific American*. July 6, 2018. https://www.scientificamerican.com/article/use-of-ldquo-smart-drugs-rdquo-on-the-rise/.

Chandrasekhar, Kartik, Jyoti Kapoor, and Sridhar Anishetty. "A Prospective, Randomized Double-Blind, Placebo-Controlled Study of Safety and Efficacy of a High-Concentration Full-Spectrum Extract of Ashwagandha Root in Reducing Stress and Anxiety in Adults." *Indian Journal of Psychological Medicine* 34, no. 3 (July–September, 2012): 255–262. https://www.ncbi.nlm.nih.gov/pmc/articles/PMC3573577/.

Chen, Weiwei, Xiang Cheng, Jinzhong Chen, Xin Yi, Dekang Nie, Xiaohui Sun, and Jianbing Qin. "Lycium Barbarum Polysaccharides Prevent Memory and Neurogenesis Impairments in Scopolamine-Treated Rats." *PLoS ONE* 9, no. 2 (February 5, 2014): e88076. https://doi.org/10.1371/journal.pone.0088076.

Chen, Wai-Wei, Rong-Rong He, Yi-Fang Li, Shan-Bing Li, Bun Tsoi, and Hiroshi Kurihara. "Pharmacological Studies on the Anxiolytic Effect of Standardized Schisandra Lignans Extract on Restraint-Stressed Mice." *Phytomedicine* 18, no. 13 (October 15, 2011): 1144–1147. https://www.ncbi.nlm.nih.gov/pubmed/21757327.

Cheng, J., Z. W. Zhou, H. P. Sheng, J. He, X. W. Fan, Z. X. He, T. Sun, et al. "An Evidence-Based Update on the Pharmacological Activities and Possible Molecular Targets of Lycium Barbarum Polysaccharides." *Drug Design, Development and Therapy* 9 (December 17, 2014): 33–78. https://www.ncbi.nlm.nih.gov/pubmed/25552899.

Chiu, P. Y., and K. M. Ko. "Time-Dependent Enhancement in Mitochondrial Glutathione Status and ATP Generation Capacity by Schisandrin B Treatment Decreases the Susceptibility of Rat Hearts to Ischemia-Reperfusion Injury." *Biofactors* 19, nos. 1–2 (2003): 43–51. https://www.ncbi.nlm.nih.gov/pubmed/14757976.

Choudhary, Dnyanraj, Sauvik Bhattacharyya, and Kedar Joshi. "Body Weight Management in Adults Under Chronic Stress Through Treatment with Ashwagandha Root Extract: A Double-Blind, Randomized, Placebo-Controlled Trial." *Journal of Evidence-Based Complementary & Alternative Medicine* 22, no. 1 (April 6, 2016): 96–106. https://www.ncbi.nlm.nih.gov/pmc/articles/PMC5871210/.

Choudhary, Dnyanraj, Sauvik Bhattacharyya, and Sekhar Bose. "Efficacy and Safety of Ashwagandha (Withania somnifera (L.) Dunal) Root Extract in Improving Memory and Cognitive Functions." *Journal of Dietary Supplements* 14, no. 6 (November 2, 2017): 599–612. https://www.ncbi.nlm.nih.gov/pubmed/28471731.

Cortés-Rojas, Diego Francisco, Claudia Regina Fernandes de Souza, and Wanderley Pereira Oliveira. "Clove (Syzygium Aromaticum): A Precious Spice." *Asian Pacific Journal of Tropical Biomedicine* 4, no. 2 (February 2014): 90–96. https://www.ncbi.nlm.nih.gov/pmc/articles/PMC3819475/.

Dodd, F. L., D. O. Kennedy, L. M. Riby, and C. F. Haskell-Ramsay. "A Double-Blind, Placebo-Controlled Study Evaluating the Effects of Caffeine and L-Theanine Both Alone and in Combination on Cerebral Blood Flow, Cognition and Mood." *Psychopharmacology*, 232, no. 14 (2015): 2563–2576. https://www.ncbi.nlm.nih.gov/pmc/articles/PMC4480845/.

Egashira, N., K. Kurauchi, K. Iwasaki, K. Mishima, K. Orito, R. Oishi, and M. Fujiwara. "Schizandrin Reverses Memory Impairment in Rats." *Phytotherapy Research* 22, no. 1 (January 2008): 49–52. https://www.ncbi.nlm.nih.gov/pubmed/17705144.

Enyeart, Judith A., Haiyan Liu, and John J. Enyeart. "Curcumin Inhibits ACTH- and Angiotensin II-Stimulated Cortisol Secretion and Cav3.2 Current." *Journal of Natural Products* 72, no. 8 (August 2009): 1533–1537. https://www.ncbi.nlm.nih.gov/pmc/articles/PMC2853174/.

Field, D. T., C. M. Williams, and L. T. Butler. "Consumption of Cocoa Flavanols Results in an Acute Improvement in Visual and Cognitive Functions." *Physiology & Behavior* 103, nos. 3–4 (June 1, 2011): 255–260. https://www.ncbi.nlm.nih.gov/pubmed/21324330.

Filiptsova, O. V., L. V. Gazzavi-Rogozina, I. A. Timoshyna, O. I. Naboka, Ye. V. Dyomina, and A. V. Ochkur. "The Essential Oil of Rosemary and Its Effect on the Human Image and Numerical Short-Term Memory." *Egyptian Journal of Basic and Applied Sciences* 4, no. 2 (June 2017): 107–111. https://www.sciencedirect.com/science/article/pii/S2314808X16301890.

Frood, Arran. "Use of 'smart drugs' on the rise." *Nature*. July 15, 2018. https://www.nature.com/articles/d41586-018-05599-8.

Gao, J., C. Chen, Y. Liu, Y. Li, Z. Long, H. Wang, Y. Zhang, J. Sui, Y. Wu, L. Liu, and C. Yang. "Lycium Barbarum Polysaccharide Improves Traumatic Cognition Via Reversing Imbalance of Apoptosis/Regeneration in Hippocampal Neurons after Stress." *Life Sciences* 15, no. 121 (January 15, 2015): 124–134. https://www.ncbi.nlm.nih.gov/pubmed/25497708.

Giridharan, V. V., R. A. Thandavarayan, S. Sato, K. M. Ko, and T. Konishi. "Prevention of Scopolamine-Induced Memory Deficits by Schisandrin B, an Antioxidant Lignan from Schisandra Chinensis in Mice." *Free Radical Research* 45, no. 8 (August 2011): 950–958. https://www.ncbi.nlm.nih.gov/pubmed/21615274.

Glionna, John M. "Seeking an Edge, These Brain Hackers Mix Up Risky Chemical Cocktails for Breakfast." *PBS News Hour*. February 19, 2016. https://www.pbs.org/newshour/science/nootropics-brain-enhancement.

Hawks, John. "How Has the Human Brain Evolved?" *Scientific American*. Accessed January 18, 2019. https://www.scientificamerican.com/article/how-has-human-brain-evolved/.

He, X., X. Wang, J. Fang, Y. Chang, N. Ning, H. Guo, L. Huang, X. Huang, Z. Zhao. "Structures, Biological Activities, and Industrial Applications of the Polysaccharides from Hericium Erinaceus (Lion's Mane) Mushroom: A Review." *International Journal of Biological Macromolecules* 97 (April 2017): 228–237. https://www.ncbi.nlm.nih.gov/pubmed/28087447.

Ho, Yuen-Shan, Man-Shan Yu, Cora Sau-Wan Lai, Kwok-Fai So, Wai-Hung Yuen, Wai-Hung Yuen, and Raymond Chuen-Chung Chang. "Characterizing the Neuroprotective Effects of Alkaline Extract of Lycium Barbarum on β-Amyloid Peptide Neurotoxicity." *Brain Research* 1158 (July 16, 2007): 123–134. https://www.sciencedirect.com/science/article/pii/S0006899307010220.

Huang, Fang, Yating Ziong, Lihua Xu, Shiping Ma, and Changgui Dou. "Sedative and Hypnotic Activities of the Ethanol Fraction from Fructus Schisandrae in Mice and Rats." *Journal of Ethnopharmacology* 110, no. 3 (April 4, 2007): 471–475. https://www.ncbi.nlm.nih.gov/pubmed/17127021.

Jintanaporn, Wattanathorn, Pennapa Chonpathompikunlertb, Supaporn Muchimapuraa, Aroonsri Pripremc, and Orathai Tankamnerdthai. "Piperine, the Potential Functional Food for Mood and Cognitive Disorders." *Food and Chemical Toxicology* 46, no. 9 (September 2008): 3106–3110. https://www.researchgate.net/publication/51413766_Piperine_the_potential_functional_food_for_mood_and_cognitive_disorders.

Johnson, S. A., A. Figueroa, N. Navaei, A. Wong, R. Kalfon, L. T. Ormsbee, R. G. Feresin, et al. "Daily Blueberry Consumption Improves Blood Pressure and Arterial Stiffness in Postmenopausal Women with Pre- and Stage 1-Hypertension: A Randomized, Double-Blind, Placebo-Controlled Clinical Trial." *Journal of the Academy of Nutrition and Dietetics* 115, no. 3 (March 2015): 369–377. https://www.ncbi .nlm.nih.gov/pubmed/25578927.

Joseph, J. A., B. Shukitt-Hale, N. A. Denisova, D. Bielinski, A. Martin, J. J. McEwen, and P. C. Bickford. "Reversal of Age-Related Declines in the Neuronal Signal Transduction, Cognitive, and Motor Behavioral Deficits with Blueberry, Spinach, or Strawberry Dietary Supplementation." *Journal of Neuroscience* 19, no. 18 (September 1999): 8114–8121. https://www.ncbi.nlm.nih.gov/pubmed/10479711.

Jurado-Coronel, Juan C., Marco Ávila-Rodriguez, Valentina Echeverria, Oscar Alejandro Hidalgo, Janneth Gonzalez, Gjumrakch Aliev, and George E. Barreto. "Implication of Green Tea as a Possible Therapeutic Approach for Parkinson Disease." *CNS & Neurological Disorders Drug Targets* 15, no. 3 (2016): 292–300. https://www.ncbi.nlm.nih.gov /pubmed/26831259.

Khasnavis, S., and K. Pahan. "Cinnamon Treatment Upregulates Neuroprotective Proteins Parkin and DJ-1 and Protects Dopaminergic Neurons in a Mouse Model of Parkinson's Disease." *Journal of NeuroImmune Pharmacology* 9, no. 4 (September 9, 2014): 569–581. https://www.ncbi.nlm.nih.gov/pubmed/24946862.

Kobayashi, Kanari, Yukiko Nagato, Nobuyuki Aoi, Lekh Raj Juneja, Mujo Kim, Takehiko Yamamoto, and Sukeo Sugimoto. "Effects of L-Theanine on the Release of Alpha-Brain Waves in Human Volunteers." *Journal of the Agricultural Chemical Society of Japan* 72, no. 2 (1998). https://www.researchgate.net/publication/273220751_Effects_of_L-Theanine_on_the _Release_of_ALPHA-Brain_Waves_in_Human_Volunteers.

Konar, Arpita, Navjot Shah, Rumani Singh, Nishant Saxena, Sunil C. Kaul, Renu Wadhwa, and Mahendra K. Thakur. "Protective Role of Ashwagandha Leaf Extract and Its Component Withanone on Scopolamine-Induced Changes in the Brain and Brain-Derived Cells." *PloS One* 6, no. 11 (November 2011). https://www.ncbi.nlm.nih.gov/pmc/articles /PMC3214041/.

Kong, J. M., L. S. Chia, N. K. Goh, T. F. Chia, and R. Brouillard. "Analysis and Biological Activities of Anthocyanins." *Phytochemistry* 64, no. 5 (November 2003): 923–933. https://www.ncbi.nlm.nih.gov/pubmed/14561507.

Koulivand, Peir Hossein, Maryam Khaleghi Ghadiri, and Ali Gorji. "Lavender and the Nervous System." *Evidence-Based Complementary and Alternative Medicine* 2013 (2013): 681304. https://www.ncbi.nlm.nih.gov/pmc/articles /PMC3612440/.

Krikorian, Robert, Marcelle D. Shidler, Tiffany A. Nash, Wilhelmina Kalt, Melinda R. Vinqvist-Tymchuk, Barbara Shukitt-Hale, and James A. Joseph. "Blueberry Supplementation Improves Memory in Older Adults." *Journal of Agricultural and Food Chemistry* 58, no. 7 (April 14, 2010): 3996–4000. https://www.ncbi.nlm.nih.gov/pmc/articles/PMC2850944/.

Kumar, Gajendra, Amita Srivastava, Surinder Kumar Sharma, T. Divakara Rao, and Yogendra Kumar Gupta. "Efficacy & Safety Evaluation of Ayurvedic Treatment (Ashwagandha Powder & Sidh Makardhwaj) in Rheumatoid Arthritis Patients: a Pilot Prospective Study." *The Indian Journal of Medicinal Research* 141, no. 1 (January 2015): 100–106. https://www .ncbi.nlm.nih.gov/pubmed/25857501.

Kumar, Puneet, and Anil Kumar. "Possible Neuroprotective Effect of Withania somnifera Root Extract Against 3-Nitropropionic Acid-Induced Behavioral, Biochemical, and Mitochondrial Dysfunction in an Animal Model of Huntington's Disease." *Journal of Medicinal Food* 12, no. 3 (June 2009): 591–600. https://www.ncbi.nlm.nih.gov /pubmed/19627208.

Kuo, Hsing-Chun, Chien-Chang Lu, Chien-Heng Shen, Shui-Yi Tung, Meng Chiao Hsieh, Ko-Chao Lee, Li-Ya Lee, et al. "Hericium Erinaceus Mycelium and Its Isolated Erinacine: A Protection from MPTP-Induced Neurotoxicity through the ER Stress, Triggering an Apoptosis Cascade. *Journal of Translational Medicine* 14 (2016): 78. https://www.ncbi.nlm.nih.gov/ pmc/articles/PMC4797317/.

Lam, P. Y., and K. M. Ko. "Schisandrin B as a Hormetic Agent for Preventing Age-Related Neurodegenerative Diseases." *Oxidative Medicine and Cellular Longevity* (2012): 250825. https://www.ncbi.nlm.nih.gov/pubmed/22666518.

Liu, Y., D. Zhang, Y. Wu, D. Wang, Y. Wei, J. Wu., and B. Ji. "Stability and Absorption of Anthocyanins from Blueberries Subjected to a Simulated Digestion Process." *International Journal of Food Sciences and Nutrition* 65, no. 4 (June 2014): 440–448. https://www.ncbi.nlm.nih.gov/pubmed/24393027.

López-Lázaro, Miguel, "Anticancer and Carcinogenic Properties of Curcumin: Considerations for its Clinical Development as a Cancer Chemopreventive and Chemotherapeutic Agent." *Molecular Nutrition & Food Research* 52, suppl. 1(June 2008): 103–127. https://www.ncbi.nlm.nih.gov/pubmed/18496811.

Mancini, E., C. Beglinger, J. Drewe, D. Zanchi, U. E. Lang, and S. Borgwardt. "Green Tea Effects on Cognition, Mood and Human Brain Function: A Systematic Review." *Phytomedicine* 34 (October 15, 2017): 26–37. https://www.ncbi.nlm.nih.gov/pubmed/28899506.

Mandel, Silvia A., Tamar Amit, Orly Weinreb, Lydia Reznichenko, and Moussa B. H. Youdim. "Simultaneous Manipulation of Multiple Brain Targets by Green Tea Catechins: A Potential Neuroprotective Strategy for Alzheimer and Parkinson Diseases." *CNS Neuroscience and Therapeutics* 14, no. 4 (Winter 2008): 352–365. https://www.ncbi.nlm.nih.gov/pubmed/19040558.

Matthew, B. C., and R. S. Biju. "Neuroprotective Effects of Garlic: A Review." *Libyan Journal of Medical Sciences* 3, no. 1 (2008): 23–33. https://www.ncbi.nlm.nih.gov/pmc/articles/PMC3074326/.

Meamarbashi, Abbas. "Instant Effects of Peppermint Essential Oil on the Physiological Parameters and Exercise Performance." *Avicenna Journal of Phytomedicine* 4, no. 1 (January–February 2014): 72–78. https://www.ncbi.nlm.nih.gov/pmc/articles/PMC4103722/.

Memorial Sloan Kettering Cancer Center. "Reishi Mushroom." Last modified June 5, 2018. https://www.mskcc.org/cancer-care/integrative-medicine/herbs/reishi-mushroom.

Messerli, Franz H., MD. "Chocolate Consumption, Cognitive Function, and Nobel Laureates." *New England Journal of Medicine* 367 (2012): 1562–1564. https://www.nejm.org/doi/full/10.1056/NEJMon1211064.

Min, H. Y., E. J. Park, J. Y. Hong, Y. J. Kang, S. J. Kim, H. J. Chung, E. R. Woo, et al. "Antiproliferative Effects of Dibenzocyclooctadiene Lignans Isolated from Schisandra Chinensis in Human Cancer Cells." *Bioorganic & Medicinal Chemistry Letters* 18, no. 2 (January 15, 2008): 523–526. https://www.ncbi.nlm.nih.gov/pubmed/18063366.

Mishra, Shrikant, and Kalpana Palanivelu. "The Effect of Curcumin (Turmeric) on Alzheimer's Disease: An Overview." *Annals of Indian Academy of Neurology* 11, no. 1 (Jan–Mar 2008): 13–19. https://www.ncbi.nlm.nih.gov/pmc/articles/PMC2781139/.

Moss M., S. Hewitt, L. Moss, and K. Wesnes. "Modulation of Cognitive Performance and Mood by Aromas of Peppermint and Ylang-Ylang." *International Journal of Neuroscience* 118, no. 1 (January 2008): 59–77. https://www.ncbi.nlm.nih.gov/pubmed/18041606.

Nagano, Mayumi, Kuniyoshi Shimizu, Ryuichiro Kondo, Chickako Hayashi, Daigo Sato, Katsuyuki Kitagawa, and Koichiro Ohnuki. "Reduction of Depression and Anxiety by 4 Weeks *Hericium Erinaceus* Intake." *Biomedical Research* 31, no. 4 (August 2010): 231–237. https://www.ncbi.nlm.nih.gov/pubmed/20834180.

National Center for Complementary and Integrative Health. "Study Shows Chamomile Capsules Ease Anxiety Symptoms." Last modified October 21, 2015. https://nccih.nih.gov/research/results/spotlight/040310.htm.

Nehlig, Astrid. "The Neuroprotective Effects of Cocoa Flavanol and its Influence on Cognitive Performance." *British Journal of Clinical Pharmacology* 75, no. 3 (March 2013): 716–727. https://www.ncbi.nlm.nih.gov/pmc/articles/PMC3575938/.

Neznamov, G. G., and E. S. Teleshova. "Comparative Studies of Noopept and Piracetam in the Treatment of Patients with Mild Cognitive Disorders in Organic Brain Diseases of Vascular and Traumatic Origin." *Neuroscience and Behavioral Physiology* (March 2009). https://www.ncbi.nlm.nih.gov/pubmed/19234797.

Nobre, A. C., A. Rao, and G. N. Owen. "L-Theanine, a Natural Constituent in Tea, and Its Effect on Mental State." *Asia Pacific Journal of Clinical Nutrition* 17, suppl. 1 (2008): 167–168. https://www.ncbi.nlm.nih.gov/pubmed/18296328.

Nowak, Adriana, Małgorzata Zakłos-Szyda, Janusz Błasiak, Agnieszka Nowak, Zhuo Zhang, and Bolin Zhang. "Potential of *Schisandra chinensis* (Turcz.) Baill. in Human Health and Nutrition: A Review of Current Knowledge and Therapeutic Perspectives." *Nutrients* 11, no. 2 (February 4, 2019). https://doi.org/10.3390/nu11020333.

Oken, Barry S. "Effects of Sage on Memory and Mental Performance in Alzheimer's Disease Patients." *US National Library of Medicine*. Last modified October 29, 2014. https://clinicaltrials.gov/ct2/show/NCT00110552.

Panossian, Alexander, and Georg Wikman. "Pharmacology of Schisandra chinensis Bail: An Overview of Russian Research and Uses in Medicine." *Journal of Ethnopharmacology* 118, no. 2 (July 23, 2008): 183–212. https://www.ncbi.nlm.nih.gov/pubmed/18515024.

Pase, M. P., A. B. Scholey, A. Pipingas, M. Kras, K. Nolidin, A. Gibbs, K. Wesnes, et al. "Cocoa Polyphenols Enhance Positive Mood States But Not Cognitive Performance: A Randomized, Placebo-Controlled Trial." *Journal of Psychopharmacology* 27, no. 5 (May 2013): 451–458. https://www.ncbi.nlm.nih.gov/pubmed/23364814.

The Peninsula College of Medicine and Dentistry. "Getting Forgetful? Then Blueberries May Hold the Key." *ScienceDaily*. April 12, 2008. www.sciencedaily.com/releases/2008/04/080410115405.htm.

Peterson, D. W., R. C. George, F. Scaramozzino, N. E. LaPointe, R. A. Anderson, D. J. Graves, and J. Lew. "Cinnamon Extract Inhibits Tau Aggregation Associated with Alzheimer's Disease in Vitro." *Journal of Alzheimer's Disease* 17, no. 3 (2009): 585–597. https://www.ncbi.nlm.nih.gov/pubmed/19433898.

Pu, H. J., Y. F. Cao, R. R. He, Z. L. Zhao, J. H. Song, B. Jiang, T. Huang, S. H. Tang, J. M. Lu, and H. Kurihara. "Correlation between Antistress and Hepatoprotective Effects of Schisandra Lignans Was Related with Its Antioxidative Actions in Liver Cells." *Evidence-Based Complementary and Alternative Medicine* (2012): 161062. https://www.ncbi.nlm.nih.gov/pubmed/22792122.

Reddy, P. Hemachandra, Maria Manczak, Xiangling Yin, Mary Catherine Grady, Andrew Mitchell, Sahil Tonk, Chandra Sekhar Kuruva, et al. "Protective Effects of Indian Spice Curcumin Against Amyloid Beta in Alzheimer's Disease." *Journal of Alzheimer's Disease* 61, no. 3 (February 2, 2018): 843–866. https://www.ncbi.nlm.nih.gov/pmc/articles/PMC5796761/.

Saenghong, Naritsara, Jintanaporn Wattanathorn, Supaporn Muchimapura, Terdthai Tongun, Nawanant Piyavhatkul, Chuleratana Banchonglikitkul, and Tanwarat Kajsongkram. "Zingiber Officinale Improves Cognitive Function of the Middle-Aged Healthy Women." *Evidence-Based Complementary and Alternative Medicine* (2012): 383062. https://www.ncbi.nlm.nih.gov/pmc/articles/PMC3253463/.

Sanodiya, B. S., G. S. Thakur, R. K. Baghel, G. B. Prasad, and P. S. Bisen. "Ganoderma Lucidum: A Potent Pharmacological Macrofungus." *Current Pharmaceutical Biotechnology* 10, no. 8 (December 2009): 717–742. https://www.ncbi.nlm.nih.gov/pubmed/19939212.

Sathyapalan, Thozhukat, Stephen Beckett, Alan S. Rigby, Duane D. Mellor, and Stephen L. Atkin. "High Cocoa Polyphenol Rich Chocolate May Reduce the Burden of the Symptoms in Chronic Fatigue Syndrome." *Journal of Nutrition* 9 (2010): 55. https://www.ncbi.nlm.nih.gov/pmc/articles/PMC3001690/.

Scholey, Andrew, Amy Gibbs, Chris Neale, Naomi Perry, Anastasia Ossoukhova, Vanessa Bilog, Marni Kras, Claudia Scholz, Mathias Sass, and Sybille Buchwald-Werner. "Anti-Stress Effects of Lemon Balm-Containing Foods." *Nutrients* 6, no. 11 (November 2014): 4805–4821. https://www.ncbi.nlm.nih.gov/pmc/articles/PMC4245564/.

Scholey, Andrew, and Lauren Owen. "Effects of Chocolate on Cognitive Function and Mood: A Systematic Review." *Nutrition Reviews* 71, no. 10 (October 2013): 655–681. https://onlinelibrary.wiley.com/doi/abs/10.1111/nure.12065.

Shoeb, Ahsan, Mukta Chowta, Gokul Pallempati, Amritha Rai, and Ashish Singh. "Evaluation of Antidepressant Activity of Vanillin in Mice." *Indian Journal of Pharmacology* 45, no. 2 (March–April 2013): 141–144. https://www.ncbi.nlm.nih.gov/pmc/articles/PMC3660925/.

Singh, Narendra, Mohit Bhalla, Prashanti de Jager, and Marilena Gilca. "An Overview on Ashwagandha: A Rasayana (Rejuvenator) of Ayurveda." *African Journal of Traditional, Complementary, and Traditional Medicine* 8, suppl. 5 (July 3, 2011): 208–213. https://www.ncbi.nlm.nih.gov/pmc/articles/PMC3252722/.

Small, Gary W., Prabha Siddarth, Zhaoping Li, Karen J. Miller, Linda Ercoli, Natacha D. Emerson, Jacqueline Martinez, et al. "Memory and Brain Amyloid and Tau Effects of a Bioavailable Form of Curcumin in Non-Demented Adults: A Double-Blind, Placebo-Controlled 18-Month Trial." *The American Journal of Geriatric Psychiatry* 26, no. 3 (March 2018): 266–277. https://www.sciencedirect.com/science/article/pii/S1064748117305110?via%3Dihub.

Socci, Valentina, Daniela Tempesta, Giovambattista Desideri, Luigi De Gennaro, and Michele Ferrara. "Enhancing Human Cognition with Cocoa Flavonoids." *Frontiers in Nutrition* (May 16, 2017). https://www.frontiersin.org/articles/10.3389/fnut.2017.00019/full.

Sorond, F. A., S. Hurwitz, D. H. Salat, D. N. Greve, and N. D. Fisher. "Neurovascular Coupling, Cerebral White Matter Integrity, and Response to Cocoa in Older People." *Neurology* 81, no. 10 (September 3, 2013): 904–909. https://www.ncbi.nlm.nih.gov/pubmed/23925758.

Sowndhararajan, Kandhasamy, and Songmun Kim. "Influence of Fragrances on Human Psychophysiological Activity: With Special Reference to Human Electroencephalographic Response." *Scientia Pharmaceutica* 84, no. 4 (2016): 724–752. https://www.ncbi.nlm.nih.gov/pmc/articles/PMC5198031/.

Srivastava, Janmejai K., Eswar Shankar, and Sanjay Gupta. "Chamomile: A Herbal Medicine of the Past with Bright Future." *Molecular Medicine Reports* 3, no. 6 (2010): 895–901.

Stringer, Christopher. "Why Have Our Brains Started to Shrink?" *Scientific American*. Accessed January 18, 2019. https://www.scientificamerican.com/article/why-have-our-brains-started-to-shrink/.

Sun L. J., G. H. Wang, B. Wu, J. Wang, Q. Wang, L. P. Hu, J. Q. Shao, et al. "Effects of Schisandra on the Function of the Pituitary-Adrenal Cortex, Gonadal Axis and Carbohydrate Metabolism in Rats Undergoing Experimental Chronic Psychological Stress, Navigation and Strenuous Exercise." *National Journal of Andrology* 15, no. 2 (February 2009): 126–129. https://www.ncbi.nlm.nih.gov/pubmed/19323371.

Takeda, A. "Manganese Action in Brain Function." *Brain Research Reviews* 41, no. 1 (2003): 79–87. https://www.ncbi.nlm.nih.gov/pubmed/12505649.

Tsuda, Takanori. "Recent Progress in Anti-Obesity and Anti-Diabetes Effect of Berries." *Antioxidants (Basel)* 5, no. 2 (2016): 13. https://www.ncbi.nlm.nih.gov/pmc/articles/PMC4931534/.

University of Edinburgh. "Eating Licorice in Pregnancy May Affect a Child's IQ and Behavior." *Science Daily*. October 7, 2009. https://www.sciencedaily.com/releases/2009/10/091006093349.htm.

University Health News Staff. "Chocolate Benefits for Your Brain: Memory and Mood Improvement." *University Health News Daily*. October 30, 2018. https://universityhealthnews.com/daily/memory/2-chocolate-benefits-for-your-brain-improves-memory-and-mood/.

University of Newcastle upon Tyne. "Sage Improves Memory, Study Shows." *Science Daily*. September 1, 2003. https://www.sciencedaily.com/releases/2003/09/030901091846.htm.

University of South Carolina. "Liquorice Root May Protect Brain Cells." *Medical Press*. November 12, 2010. https://medicalxpress.com/news/2010-11-liquorice-root-brain-cells.html.

VA Research Currents. "Cinnamon May Be Fragrant Medicine for the Brain." *US Department of Veterans Affairs*. July 21, 2016. https://www.research.va.gov/currents/0716-6.cfm.

Wallace, Taylor C., and Victor L. Fulgoni III. "Assessment of Total Choline Intakes in the United States." *Science Daily*. May 3, 2016. https://www.sciencedaily.com/releases/2016/05/160503131652.htm.

White, David J., Suzanne de Klerk, William Woods, Shakuntla Gondalia, Chris Noonan, and Andrew B. Scholey. "Anti-Stress, Behavioural and Magnetoencephalography Effects of an l-Theanine-Based Nutrient Drink: A Randomised, Double-Blind, Placebo-Controlled, Crossover Trial." *Nutrients* 8 no. 1 (January 19, 2016). https://www.ncbi.nlm.nih.gov/pmc/articles/PMC4728665/.

Whiteman, Honor. "Turmeric Compound Could Boost Memory and Mood." *Medical News Today.* January 25, 2018. https://www.medicalnewstoday.com/articles/320732.php.

Whyte, Adrian R., Graham Schafer, and Claire M. Williams. "Cognitive Effects Following Acute Wild Blueberry Supplementation in 7- to 10-Year-Old Children." *European Journal of Nutrition* 55, no. 6 (September 2016): 2151–2162. https://www.ncbi.nlm.nih.gov/pubmed/26437830.

Winston, David. *Adaptogens: Herbs for Strength, Stamina, and Stress Relief.* Rochester, Vermont: Healing Arts Press, 2007.

World Health Organization. *WHO Monographs on Selected Medicinal Plants,* vol. 3. Ottawa, Ontario: World Health Organization, 2001. http://apps.who.int/medicinedocs/documents/s14213e/s14213e.pdf.

Wu, A., E. E. Noble, E. Tyagi, Z. Ying, Y. Zhuang, and F. Gomez-Pinilla. "Curcumin Boosts DHA in the Brain: Implications for the Prevention of Anxiety Disorders." *Biochimica et Biophysica Acta* 1852, no. 5 (May 2015): 951–961. https://www.ncbi.nlm.nih.gov/pubmed/25550171.

Yang, D., S. Y. Li, C. M. Yeung, R. C. Chang, K. F. So, D. Wong, and A. C. Lo. "Lycium Barbarum Extracts Protect the Brain from Blood-Brain Barrier Disruption and Cerebral Edema in Experimental Stroke." *PLOS One* 7, no. 3 (2012): e33596. https://www.ncbi.nlm.nih.gov/pubmed/22438957.

Zhang, Jian, Oxana P. Lazarenko, Michael L. Blackburn, Thomas M. Badger, Martin J. J. Ronis, and Jin-Ran Chen. "Blueberry Consumption Prevents Loss of Collagen in Bone Matrix and Inhibits Senescence Pathways in Osteoblastic Cells." *Journal of the American Aging Association* 35, no. 3 (June 2013): 807–820. https://www.ncbi.nlm.nih.gov/pmc/articles/PMC3636388/.

Zhang, Junrong, Shengshu An, Wenji Hu, Meiyu Teng, Xue Wang, Yidi Qu, Yang Liu, Ye Yuan, and Di Wang. "The Neuroprotective Properties of Hericium erinaceus in Glutamate-Damaged Differentiated PC12 Cells and an Alzheimer's Disease Mouse Model." *International Journal of Molecular Sciences* 17, no. 11 (2016): 1810. https://www.ncbi.nlm.nih.gov/pmc/articles/PMC5133811/.

Zhao, H., Q. Zhang, L. Zhao, X. Huang, J. Wang, and X. Kang. "Spore Powder of Ganoderma lucidum Improves Cancer-Related Fatigue in Breast Cancer Patients Undergoing Endocrine Therapy: A Pilot Clinical Trial." *Evidence-Based Complementary and Alternative Medicine* (2012): 809614. https://www.ncbi.nlm.nih.gov/pubmed/22203880.

Chapter 7: MIND-ENHANCING SUPPLEMENTS

Aguiar, Sebastian, and Thomas Borowski. "Neuropharmacological Review of the Nootropic Herb *Bacopa monnieri.*" *Rejuvenation Research* 16, no. 4 (August 2013): 313–326. https://www.ncbi.nlm.nih.gov/pmc/articles/PMC3746283/.

Calabrese, Carlo, William L. Gregory, Michael Leo, Dale Kraemer, Kerry Bone, and Barry Oken. "Effects of a Standardized *Bacopa monnieri* Extract on Cognitive Performance, Anxiety, and Depression in the Elderly: A Randomized, Double-Blind, Placebo-Controlled Trial." *Journal of Alternative and Complementary Medicine* 14, no. 6 (July 2008): 707–713. https://www.ncbi.nlm.nih.gov/pmc/articles/PMC3153866/.

ACKNOWLEDGMENTS

This book is lovingly dedicated to my mom.

A brain is only as good as the sum of its many parts, and to be quite frank, a book about the brain is really not much different! That's why I am so deeply grateful for all the time, talent, thought, trust, and support that was brought to the *Smart Plants* table over the many years of its development.

I'd like to extend my heartfelt thanks to:

Oliver Barth, my immeasurably special partner in life and all things creative, for whom I am so grateful every day. Thank you, firstly, for animating the recipes in this book so beautifully through your exquisite food photography. And thank you for supporting me day in and day out and making sure the fire of big ideas is always well fueled.

The deeply inspiring scientific, medical, and health experts interviewed for this book, thank you (and thank you and thank you) for your contributions and for lending your valuable time to share your wisdom: Meg Adelman, Paula Bickford, Samantha Brody, Sandra Carter, Ray Cronise, Steve Farrar, Julieanna Hever, Andrew Hill, Alex Jamora, Arthur Mullin, Mary Newport, Stephanie Pedersen, and Barbara Shukitt-Hale.

My Navitas Organics family, thank you for your superfood support all these years and for ensuring that I'm always in a bountiful position to share the superfood and nootropic love with others.

The wonderful team at OM Mushrooms, thank you for making sure my test kitchen stayed well stocked with nootropic mushrooms for recipe-making and for patiently answering all my pesky questions. Also thank you to the team at Lakanto for supporting my low-sugar culinary endeavors.

Alyssa Ochs, a sincere thank-you for all your organizational help.

Marilyn Allen, for the unwavering support every step of the way; without you this book would not have been a book at all. You're the best agent-and-then-some I could have ever wished for. Thank you for making dreams come true.

The great team at Sterling Publishing—I am so appreciative to have created this meaningful book with you. Thank you to Theresa Thompson for your steadfast support of this project from the beginning and for bringing it to light, to Betsy Beier for opening the doors of opportunity, and to Edward Ash-Milby at Barnes & Noble for giving this book life in the real world. To Maha Khalil and Sandra Ballabio, thank you for tirelessly sowing the message everywhere imaginable, and to Toula Ballas, for circling it around the globe. To Jo Obarowski, Elizabeth Mihaltse Lindy, and David Ter-Avanesyan, thank you for bringing so much creativity (and patience!) to the look and feel of the cover design. Thank you to Samara Hardy for your brilliant illustrations and to Shannon Plunkett for ensuring every page inside is a beautiful one. Renee Yewdaev, thank you for all your behind-the-curtain organizational magic and for keeping this book on the right path, one step at a time. And Jennifer Williams: Thank you for the laughs, enthusiasm, wisdom, and, unquestionably, your generous amounts of hard work. I don't know how I got so lucky to have you as my editor, but through the years I'm even more grateful to also call you a dear friend.

And finally, my family, near and far, thank you for your ongoing encouragement despite the miles between us all. And a standing ovation to my mom, for enduring my billions of book-related tests and ideas, big and small, and for consistently providing the most constructive (and surprisingly unbiased) feedback I could ask for. You'll always be my most trusted teacher.

Also special thanks to Fritz for always "protecting" the kitchen floor from wayward food scraps so very dutifully.

INDEX

ABOUT THE AUTHOR

New York Times best-selling author Julie Morris is a natural food chef, writer, culinary consultant, and pioneering advocate of superfoods and a plant-rich diet for optimal health. Based in the greater Los Angeles area, Julie has traveled the United States and abroad to share her cutting-edge nutritional expertise and connects with a worldwide audience through her online superfood cooking school, Luminberry.

She is the author of five books with Sterling, which together have been translated into nine languages: *Superfood Kitchen*, *Superfood Smoothies*, *Superfood Juices*, *Superfood Snacks*, and *Superfood Soups*. Her in-depth knowledge of superfoods has been cited by diverse publications such as the *Wall Street Journal*, *GQ*, and *Women's Health* magazine, as well as featured in numerous culinary magazines and blogs. And she has led numerous courses, talks, and classes, all dedicated to making a vibrantly healthy lifestyle both easy to achieve and delicious to follow. Julie lives with her husband, Oliver Barth, and their German Shepherd, Fritz, both of whom are addicted to kale.

To learn more about Julie, visit JulieMorris.net and Luminberry.com; Instagram: @superfoodjules; Facebook: @superfoodcuisine; or Twitter: @greenjules.

About the Photographer

Oliver Barth is a Berlin-born food photographer and cofounder of Luminberry.com. He currently lives and works out of the beautiful coastal city of Ventura, in southern California.

Also available by Julie Morris

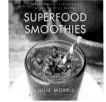
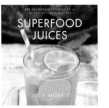
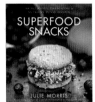
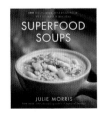